Using qualitative research to hear the voice of children and young people: The work of British educational psychologists

Edited by
Julia Hardy
and Charmian Hobbs

BPS Division of Educational
and Child Psychology

British Library Cataloguing-in-Publication Data

A catalogue record for this book is available from the British Library.

ISBN 978-1-85433-745-0

Printed and published by
The British Psychological Society
St Andrews House
48 Princess Road East
Leicester LE1 7DR
www.bps.org.uk

Contents

About the Contributors

Matt Baker is an Educational Psychologist at Plymouth Community Psychology Service. Contact: confoundingvariable@hotmail.com

Tom Billington is Professor of Educational and Child Psychology and Director of the Centre Critical Psychology and Education at the University of Sheffield.

Fiona Brown is Principal Educational Psychologist, Midlothian Council Educational Psychology Service. Contact: Fiona.brown@midlothian.gov.uk

Claire Cox works as an educational psychologist and can be contacted at Claire.a.cox@hotmail.co.uk

Abigail Croydon is a Research Officer at the Centre for Research in Autism and Education (CRAE: http://crae.ioe.ac.uk) at UCL Institute of Education, University College London.

Dr Mark Fox was Programme Director for the Professional Doctorate in Educational and Child Psychology at the University of East London. He previously worked at the Tavistock Clinic and at Scope. Contact: m.d.fox@uel.ac.uk

Dan Goodley is Professor of Disability Studies and Education at the University of Sheffield. Recent publications include *Dis/ability studies* (Routledge, 2014).

Irvine Gersch is Emeritus Professor at the University of East London and has published widely in the field of listening to children and young people.

Scot Greathead is a Consultant Speech and Language Therapist and has worked within the National Health Service, Local Education Authorities and in independent practice. He has had a career long interest in designing integrated health and education services.

Dr Emma Harding is the Principal Educational Psychologist at Bury LA Educational Psychology Service and is also an Academic and Professional Tutor on the Doctorate in Educational and Child Psychology course at the University of Manchester. Contact: e.harding@bury.gov.uk

Rachel Hayton works as a Chartered Educational Psychologist with Dumfries and Galloway Council. Current research foci include mindfulness, positive approaches to behaviour management and reflective dialogue with school leaders. Contact: Rachel.hayton@dumgal.gov.uk

Dr Julia Hardy works as an Associate Educational Psychologist for Achieving for Children and for other organisations, through Psychological Services GB, with interests in consultation, qualitative research, deafness, CBT and leadership skills.

Vivian Hill, is the Programme Director for the Doctorate in Educational, Child and Adolescent Psychology at University College London's Institute of Education. Her research interests include: the medicalisation of childhood behaviours, the educational and psycho-social development of children and young people with autism, and the rights of children, in particular the rights of children who live within the care system.

Charmian Hobbs works with the professional training programme for educational psychologists at Newcastle University and as an independent practitioner drawing on narrative therapy.

Imogen Howarth works as an Educational Psychologist for Suffolk Psychology and Therapy Services, and holds a specialist post working with the Youth Offending Service.

Martin Hughes is Principal Educational Psychologist in Sheffield City Council's Educational Psychology Service and a course co-director on the initial doctoral training programme for people training to become educational psychologists at Sheffield University. Contact: m.j.hughes@sheffield.ac.uk

Lorcan Kenny is a PhD student based at the Centre for Research in Autism and Education (CRAE) at UCL Institute of Education, University College London.

Dr Anna Lipscomb is an Educational Psychologist currently working for the London Borough of Tower Hamlets. Contact: anna.lipscomb@gmail.com

Karen Majors is Assistant Programme Director on the UCL Institute of Education, Doctorate in Professional Educational, Child and Adolescent Psychology and a Senior Educational Psychologist for Barking and Dagenham Community Educational Psychology Service. Contact: k.majors@ioe.ac.uk.

Dr Sandra Meehan works as an Educational Psychologist at Stockton on Tees Council. Contact: sandra.meehan@stockton.gov.uk.

Liz Pellicano is Professor of Autism Education and Director of the Centre for Research in Autism and Education (CRAE: http://crae.ioe.ac.uk) at UCL Institute of Education, University College London. She is committed to understanding the distinctive opportunities and challenges faced by autistic children, young people and adults and tracing their impact on everyday life.

Sarah Philp is Principal Educational Psychologist, Midlothian Council Educational Psychology Service. Contact: sphilp@osiriseducational.co.uk

Dr Anita Potton is a researcher at the University of East London.

Jane Reichardt is an Educational Psychologist working in the London Borough of Barnet.

Sue Roffey is an Associate Professor (Adjunct) at Western Sydney University and an international consultant on school and student wellbeing.

Anita Soni is an academic and professional tutor to the Applied Educational and Child Psychology Doctorate Programme at the University of Birmingham and an independent early years trainer and consultant

Dr Charlie Tellis-James is an Educational Psychologist who, having trained at the University of East London, now works for Achieving for Children in the London Borough of Richmond upon Thames.

Dr Fiona Weidberg is an Educational Psychologist working for Somerset Educational Psychology Service. She completed her doctoral research with the University of Bristol. Contact: fiona.weidberg@googlemail.com

Antony Williams is Lecturer in Educational and Child Psychology at the University of Sheffield where he is Academic Director of the professional training programme in Educational and Child Psychology.

Rhiannon Yates is a final year doctorate student and Trainee Educational Psychologist at the Institute of Education, University College London.

Introduction

Julia Hardy & Charmian Hobbs

Fundamental to the work of educational psychologists (EPs) is the effort to gain the views of children and young people in order to inform interventions, both educational and therapeutic, an effort which is fundamental to the participatory process. This book produced by the Division of Educational and Child Psychology (DECP) sets out to explore the ways in which this role can be supported by drawing on qualitative methodologies. The book does not purport to be a comprehensive guide to qualitative methodologies which EPs could potentially use to elicit the voice of children and young people. There are a plethora of recently published articles detailing distinct qualitative methodologies in this area, such as Warham (2012), and influential textbooks (e.g. Smith et al., 1995; Smith 2008, and Willig, 2013). What the book does aim to do is to provide a historical and current background to the role of an EP as an advocate for children, a counter-argument to the prevailing emphasis on quantitative understandings and approaches to working with children, and an exploration of how this impacts on our construction of children and childhood. Yardley (2000) acknowledges the pluralistic ethos which is central to non-realist philosophical traditions underpinning qualitative research. We need to acknowledge that our knowledge and experience does not represent an objective view of an external reality but is 'profoundly shaped by our subjective and cultural perspective, and by our conversations and activities' (Yardley, 1997). This book then provides the reader with a rich resource of qualitative research which has illuminated the lived experience of many children and young people, whose lives can be accessed only by listening to their own voices.

In the first chapter, Billington and Williams consider the growth of qualitative approaches within psychology and educational psychology as researchers have come to acknowledge the importance of language in the construction of the social world. Majors and Hardy, in Chapter 2, introduce two qualitative methodologies, interpretative phenomenological analysis (IPA) and grounded theory (GT), as illustrative of a number of qualitative approaches that focus on highlighting the voice of young people. Methodologies employed by EPs are many and varied and are further illustrated later in the book, particularly in Chapter 8. In Chapter 3, Gersch et al. demonstrate from a historical perspective the value educational psychology has placed on recognising the voice of the child. Williams and Goodley, in Chapter 4, chart the increasing awareness within the profession of educational psychology of the influence that it has had and continues to have, in both the problematisation of children and in enabling the celebration of difference. They emphasise that language has the potential to both help and harm, depending on the particularities of the context. In chapters 5 and 6, Hill et al. and Philp and Brown highlight how educational psychologists seek to develop and enhance the co-production of knowledge with children and young people; Hill et al. through using participatory research with young people in residential settings and Philp and Brown in engaging with young people to support them in actively planning for their futures. Roffey, in Chapter 7, considers the link between voice and wellbeing, in particular for those young people with least access to influence, and outlines work which focuses on developing young people as agents of change.

Chapter 8 provides a rich set of examples of the use of research methodologies that are sensitive to ways in which talk can shape the sense children and young people make of the reality of their lives. The examples were chosen as they highlight the voices of children and young people who are often marginalised in the wider social world. Research has been undertaken as a part of both initial training doctoral programmes and ongoing professional practice, providing us with the opportunity to engage in the lived experience of children and young people. So we hear the voices of young people who have extended absence from school (Baker), of Separated Refugee Young People (Cox), the experience of young people who live in a rural community (Hayton), those who self-harm (Reichardt), those who are excluded (Tellis-James and Fox), those who are the children of prisoners (Weidberg), those who have a visual impairment (Meehan), those who have complex difficulties (Harding), and those who are very young (Soni), while Hughes illustrates how the Q sort methodology, with its mixed-methods approach, can consider young people's voices within everyday EP practice.

Chapters 9 and 10 ask us to consider the future. Howarth draws our attention to the digital world and the opportunities this provides for the use of technologies in eliciting voice. In Chapter 10, Hardy and Hobbs invite a consideration of the participation of children and young people in everyday life and in particular in the development and delivery of educational psychology services.

This short book does not seek to cover all the qualitative approaches that are available to us as educational psychologists, or to consider the breadth of work that educational psychologists are undertaking to access the voice of children and young people. We are sure that there is work that has been undertaken or that is being undertaken that could be added to this volume. We accessed work of which we were aware as a way of illustrating the potential of using qualitative approaches in our work.

We hope that you will be encouraged to develop your own professional practice in working with children and young people by drawing on qualitative methodologies that allow their voices to be heard.

References

Smith, J.A. (Ed.) (2008). *Qualitative psychology* (2nd edn). London: Sage.

Smith, J.A., Harré, R. and van Langenhove, L. (1995). *Rethinking methods in psychology*. London: Sage.

Warham, K. (2012) Engaging with young people through narrative co-construction: Beyond categorisation. *Educational and Child Psychology, 29*(2), 77–85.

Willig, C. (2013). *Introducing qualitative research in psychology* (3rd edn.). Maidenhead: Open University Press.

Yardley, L. (1997). Introducing material-discursive approaches to health and illness. In L. Yardley (Ed.) *Material discourses of health and illness*. London: Routledge.

Yardley, L. (2000). Dilemmas in qualitative health research. *Psychology and Health, 15*(2), 215–228.

Chapter 1 The national and international growth in qualitative research within the field of educational psychology

Tom Billington & Antony Williams

The emergence of qualitative approaches in psychology

The growth of qualitative research in psychology has been significant, if not exponential, during the last thirty to forty years. There have been textbooks (for example, Banister et al., 2011; Parker, 2015; Willig and Stainton-Rogers, 2008), new journals (*Qualitative Research in Psychology*) and even initiatives in two of the world's two largest psychology organisations: the Qualitative Methods in Psychology Section of the British Psychological Society, and the American Psychological Association's Society for Qualitative Inquiry in Psychology. This growth and influence has many roots and in this opening chapter our intention is not to provide a detailed literature review of specific research papers (for a helpful earlier account see Miller et al., 2008) but to reflect on the historical, institutional and intellectual foundations for qualitative approaches, which we argue are currently creating a renaissance in the field of educational psychology theory and practice.

Education and psychology: Institutional and conceptual origins

While both education and psychology share much older classical roots, it was compulsory school attendance which provided the catalyst for the creation of compulsory state-controlled education systems (for example in the US in 1852, Britain in 1870 and France in 1892). While not all young people were, of course, to receive the same kind of education, instruction of the majority of children (eventually of the same age), herded together in clusters of rooms, was generally considered to be the most effective way of transferring knowledge (i.e. from the head of a teacher or the words on a page) into the head of the child.

Whatever the difference in pedagogies, from Comenius (1592–1670) and Rousseau (1712–1778) onwards educational and psychological approaches to human development and learning have often been found in the same place: for example, Pestalozzi (1746–1827), Herbart (1776–1841), and Frobel (1782–1852) were just three early educationists who utilised psychological ideas. Institutionalised forms of education and psychology were born almost as monozygotic twins, sharing not only a cultural and political context but also ideas about learning and development in schools. This was because schools were to provide a location, a material space or even a laboratory for the study of human development, and became a site in which the category 'child' could be constructed and regulated.

Following the creation of mass schooling systems, the ideas and works of John

Dewey (1859–1952) – a philosopher, psychologist and by instinct a social reformer – provided a model for liberal, progressive education (1897). Dewey took a particular kind of psychology into the classroom, one which emphasised the importance of individual experience but which was concerned also with moral and social issues. Dewey sought to place a democratic agenda at the heart of educational practices, one which emphasised not only the importance of community but also the experiences of individual child learners (1916). Such themes have continued to encourage many educational psychologists, whether researchers or practitioners.

Dewey's mentor William James (1842–1910) had presided over the early history of the emerging institutional forms (both psychology and education). Like Wilhelm Wundt (1832–1920) James created a scientific laboratory (the first in the US, in 1875). James also taught many of the first generation of American psychologists and educationalists, including Dewey, G.S. Hall (1844–1924, the first President of the American Psychological Association), and Edward Thorndike (1874–1949) who was one of the first and most influential educational psychologists in the US.

James (1890) provided a seminal exposition of key concepts which were to underpin the development of much psychological research during the 20th century, for example, those in relation to behaviour and cognition. However, most psychologists (both then and perhaps even now) were enticed to leave behind the liberal and what we might know now as the progressive potentials of psychology and education to develop particular theories or practices which accorded better with the more functional needs of government. The consequence of this choice was that the core activities associated with our discipline became focused on measurement. The creation and application of multiple technological devices, emboldened by the newly devised statistical models, would become the bedrock for educational psychologists throughout the 20th century. In the process these devices were to create and circulate particular ideas and discourses about children, their learning and development, mostly with measurement in mind. Any ways of thinking or talking about children (i.e. discourses) which were not so easily subject to quantification were diverted away from what we call mainstream psychology, for example, to philosophy, sociology, phenomenology and, of course, psychoanalysis.

Alfred Binet (1857–1911) famously assisted the French government in dealing with young people in Parisian schools who did not seem well suited to the new mass schooling system. Rather than investigating the structure of the schools themselves, however, or the nature of what was being taught and how, the gaze of the authorities invariably fell upon the children themselves. Following the adoption of the experimental method as the preferred kind of research activity to be conducted, it was the individual child who became the object of those practices which invariably involved measurement of some kind. Increasingly, psychological research and practice tended to avoid theoretical issues and hence had little intellectual purchase on more complex analyses – for example, those which might consider whether the models of the 'human' circulated in psychology were either discovering or creating the objects of their inquiry. Theory and philosophy were to be more or less excluded from the emerging discipline of educational psychology and, for both researchers and practitioners, certain culturally and politically specific ideas about the 'human' came to dominate. In particular, those discourses that accorded with a Cartesian model of mind (Parker, 2015; Ryle, 1948) assumed prominence, for instance the belief that as humans we are essentially individual and isolated and can be explained by a particular understanding of the 'cognitive' to the exclusion of other aspects.

However, in the early 20th century doubts persisted for many psychologists about the nature of the discipline's epistemological landscape. It should be noted, for example, that Binet – like his mentor Charcot, with whom he spent seven formative years – maintained a moderate stance on the heredity–environment problem, recognising that both had an impact upon development. Indeed Binet remained suspicious throughout his career about the usefulness of the concept of 'intelligence' with which he is always associated (for further detail see Williams & Goodley, Chapter 4).

Following James's early work, the development of psychology and education in the US involved a number of key individuals such as Cattell, Hall and Thorndike, and by about 1920 the experimental method and the practices of measurement could claim victory. The debates within psychology had for a time been fiercely contested, as highlighted by the Clark lectures of 1909, which at Hall's invitation were given by Freud. A number of distinguished figures, including James, Hall, Titchener, Stern, Mayer and Boas, attended these lectures, which were hosted by the departments of psychology, pedagogy and school hygiene at Clark University and which were designed to address Hall's view that education had become 'the chief problem of the world, its one holy cause' (Hall, quoted in Prochnik, 2006, p.99). It is from this time that psychology put some distance between the philosophical and theoretical elements and strengthened its ties with government, proving its usefulness by organising its activities around only those specific ideas which could be operationalised through measurement. Educational psychology failed to see that in these moments of our early history, scientific curiosity was sacrificed for the soothing re-assurances of the merely technological.

During the early years of the 20th century psychology and education, in their institutional forms, thus came to reflect the 'modern', a project in which psychological science managed simultaneously, somehow, both to individualise and homogenise all human functioning. Freud's seemingly rather pessimistic view of human nature was at odds with the missionary zeal that was the hallmark of the new institutions; the Freudian unconscious, 'an imagined cesspool' (Mayer, in Zaretsky, 2004, p.83), was rejected in favour of a psychology which focused only on the experimental method and which, as an arm of government, became antagonistic to theory. Even Wundt, considered by many to be the founder of 'scientific' psychology, had warned against separating psychology from philosophy and opposed the 'creation of a separate discipline of psychology' (Winter, 1999, p.162).

The dominant figure in British educational psychology, from the date of his first appointment in 1913, was to be Cyril Burt. Burt will always be associated with the allegedly fraudulent use of his experimental data (Hearnshaw, 1979; Mackintosh, 2013) but there are intriguing personal connections which facilitated the transformation of what were arguably Burt's personal prejudices into public policy (Chitty, 2007). Burt also contributed to the seminal report The Use of Psychological Tests in Education (Board of Education, 1924) and encouraged the development in England of a particular kind of educational psychology which drew on the positivist model being formulated in the US. Despite the reservations of the principal author of this influential report (W.H. Hadow), approaches to educational psychology re-search and practice in England for the rest of the century were to be dominated by the same assumptions about the nature of psychological knowledge that were embedded in Burt's work and which, we argue, were characterised by the following:

- a reductionist and scientifically inadequate understanding of human intelligence;
- a concentration on heritability as the single most important variable in human learning and development (virtually to the exclusion of all others); and
- an intrinsically eugenicist approach, which generated and circulated what we can now see as racist, sexist and ableist theories of human being (after Billington et al., forthcoming).

There were many distinguished and international contributors to the Hadow report, one of whom was to provide a very different reference point for educational psychology research and practice. Susan Isaacs (1885–1948) went from being a governess to a trainee teacher and was eventually awarded a scholarship at the Psychological Laboratory in Newnham College, Cambridge. She trained as a psychoanalyst, became a member of the British Psychoanalytic Society in 1921 and was between 1924 and 1927 the Head of Malting House School (see Williams and Goodley, Chapter 4, for further discussion of her early contribution). Isaacs's work kept alive something of James's intellectual creativity and curiosity (James, 1902) and agreed with Dewey's commitment to progressive and emancipatory forms of education (Dewey, 1938). Her approach also shed light on concerns both old and new about an educational psychology research and practice which fails to acknowledge epistemological complexity and uncertainty, and also fails to engage with any questions relating to experience, emotion or indeed consciousness.

We have failed to see that Freud's structural model of human psychology outlines a conceptual framework of mind as formed through social relations, which are inherently bound up in our intimate relations, ideas which we now think of as psychodynamics. Anna Freud, Melanie Klein (a close colleague of Isaacs) and others such as Winnicott and Bion have continued to influence contemporary discourse in the wider social world, for example through concepts such as 'defence mechanisms', 'transference' or 'projection', each of which has been inserted forcefully into western cultural discourse, though only by stealth into educational psychology. However, it is still possible to detect the influence of psychodynamics in educational and psychological practices today. For example, attachment theory and the use of terms such as attunement and containment, despite their flaws and lack of precision, continue to remind us that there are ways of thinking about human learning and development that cannot be easily explored or explained solely by quantification.

Qualitative research in psychology

While James, Dewey and Isaacs kept alive in psychology questions relating to the nature of human experience, it was Dilthey (1833–1911) who had previously articulated important methodological distinctions between the human and natural sciences. These were to be further developed in critiques of empiricism and the scientific method itself (for example, Feyerabend, 1975; Kuhn, 1962; Latour, 1979). Unfortunately, theories and questions that related on the one hand to the nature of human experience and on the other to the nature of scientific knowledge itself were largely jettisoned by what came to be known as mainstream psychology, finding homes in other domains of research and practice including philosophy, sociology, psychoanalysis and phenomenology. However, such theories and questions, having first been displaced to other disciplines, have recently begun to re-enter psychology and indeed educational psychology, contributing as crucial resources not only to progressive approaches in learning and development but also to the surge of interest in qualitative and theoretical approaches in psychological research and practice which have prompted this book (for example, Billington, 1996; Corcoran, 2012; Martin et al., in press).

It has been argued elsewhere that 20th century mainstream psychology (and thus by implication educational psychology) became focused on methodology rather than theory (Parker, 2014). The effect of this was to prevent us from understanding our own performativity, not least the ways in which our language use has been constructing and circulating ideas about understandings of the human which are either implicit or assumed in our research and practice, for example, in discourses dominated by concepts of (dis-)ability, gender, race and sexuality. Perhaps the single most important intellectual concern across the social sciences, and indeed the humanities, during the last one hundred years or so has related to the nature, status and reliability of language. From Wittgenstein onwards (1922), researchers (and practitioners) have increasingly been unable to ignore questions relating to the function of language, and not least its 'meaning'. It is this 'turn to language' which has laid the foundations on which qualitative research in psychology and, most recently, qualitative research in educational psychology, have been built.

Since William James attempted to delineate the field of a positivistic psychology (1890) there have been several educational psychologists alert to the dangers of neglecting questions and theories about the nature of persons. For example Dewey (1916), Vygotsky (1978) and Bruner (1986), each in their own way, envisaged a psychology of the person which was impossible to contain within discourses of isolated individuals. Dewey knew of the importance of social environments for human mind and behaviour, and Vygotsky also focused on explanations more obviously rooted in the social world, while Bruner developed accounts according to a humanist tradition. Deweyan ideas about school and social reform, and neo-Vygotskian ideas about learning and language have since shaped many contemporary professional understandings and practices concerning the nature of children and childhood. Brunerian narrative approaches have also supported the work of increasing numbers of psychologists and social scientists who aspired to less disabling forms of research and practice (White and Epston, 1990, Berliner, 1992), while other theorists and qualitative researchers have been developing analyses which are similarly sensitive to the dynamic, intrinsically social possibilities within human beings and their situations (Daniels et al., 2009; Gergen, 1994; Tolman, 1994).

In 1974 Bruner joined with Martin Richards and colleagues to produce The Integration of the Child into the Social World, which, along with Reconstructing Social Psychology (Armistead, 1974) and Margaret Donaldson's (1978) Piagetian critique, Children's Minds, articulated the fundamentally social nature of human development. In the UK the emergence of these publications, together with a growing interest in the recently translated works of Vygotsky, led to critical stirrings within

UK educational psychology, most clearly articulated by Reconstructing Educational Psychology (Gillham, 1978). Changing the Subject (Henriques et al., 1984) and Children of Social Worlds (Bruner, 1986) reflected the growing interest in and understanding of the fundamental importance of the social world when contemplating children, childhood and the kind of gaze we bring to bear on them. What began to emerge, for example in Changing the Subject, was an interdisciplinary conversation in which psychologists and others in the social sciences began to question the nature of the human subject that positivistic psychology had been assuming to be 'unitary' (isolated and unproblematic) and 'rational' (explained by cognitivist assumptions concerning human reason).

The mid-1980s was also a time when we began to hear the term 'psy-complex' (Ingleby, 1974; Rose, 1985), which was informed by Foucault's introduction of the genealogical method and had been coined as a critique of the influence and extent of psychological knowledge. Critical thinkers drew upon strands of psychology, psychoanalysis, linguistics and semiotics to examine the influence of language: Potter and Wetherell's (1987) Discourse and Social Psychology signalled an increasing appreciation of the power and influence of language in structuring what we accept as reality (see also Foucault, 1970; Parker, 1992). Potter and Wetherell (1987) couched their critique of psychological theory in methodological terms, emphasising the failure of dominant psychological methods (for example the rating scales that underlie attitude theory) to take account of the variability of human thought and action and their weakness in encouraging a spurious model of thinking as uniform, rational and classifiable into equal-interval categories. Hollway (1989) developed a version of this critique to import a psychoanalytic gender analysis, so that subjectivity, complexity and contradiction, long associated in institutional practices with the devalued and supposedly inferior [sic] thinking of women, was seen as not only inevitable but also vital features for a more adequate understanding of psychological life. Such works, together with those of Harré (1979), Shotter (1993), Gergen (2009), Danziger (1990), Gilligan (1982, 1989), Walkerdine et al. (2001) and Billig (2008), provided vital theoretical resources and thus also the impetus for the expansion of qualitative research in psychology.

As the qualitative movement has continued to grow in breadth and depth, so differences and specialisms have begun to emerge, and there are now a host of innovative qualitative approaches undergoing constant refinement. The ever-increasing sophistication of specific techniques, especially in the analysis of language, can be found in various kinds of discourse analysis (Parker, 2013, 2015; Potter, 1996), deconstructionist accounts (Burman, 2008, 2015), social constructionism (Burr, 1995; Corcoran, 2014; Gergen, 1985), feminist research (Butler, 1990; Wilkinson and Kitzinger, 1996), conversation analysis (Antaki, 2015), narrative approaches (Reissman, 1993) and other, often dialogically inclined texts (Bakhtin, 1984).

Many such discussions share principles or theoretical starting points and, at least implicitly, challenge and critique 'reductionist' or positivist approaches in a manner which has significant epistemological and ontological consequences, not least in questions of knowledge and truth: for example, psychology and educational psychology have become accustomed to accepting positivist assumptions about the status and reliability of knowledge as somehow 'out there', as something which the researcher can 'discover' and which can then be presented as 'findings'.

Psychologists engaged in qualitative research have often concluded that this is a problematic or even unsustainable position to take in their research, and argue that such a position should be open to critique. Those of us initially lured by the promise of finding psychological certainties in our research and practice under the guise of probabilities obtained via the experimental method ('discoveries') have struggled to understand the ways in which language seemed implicated in our work in ways which have been little understood. The work of many social scientists cited above has encouraged the development of qualitative approaches to research as a means of exploring the role and function of language in psychology, influenced variously by neo-Vygotskyan, post-structuralist or dialogically focused accounts. One particular aspect of the 'turn to language' has been the development of a critical psychology which is more robust in its analysis of psychology as part of the apparatus of government (Holzkamp, 2013; Rose, 1990).

The future of educational psychology: Qualitative research as science

The intense theoretical debates generated by the critical social and psychological scientists of the last fifty years have provided means by which educational psychologists can not only develop qualitative research but also critique our own discipline, sometimes with the aim of developing a research and practice agenda which could aspire to be emancipatory. This endeavour, based on social science critique, has enabled researchers and practitioners to challenge the premises upon which much positivist practice and research in psychology and education had previously been conducted (Billington, 2000; Martin, 2004; Prilleltensky, 1994). For example it has been possible to articulate:

- the ways in which the (mis)use of able-ist, gendered and racialised explanations continues to misrepresent and undermine the potentialities of human subjects;
- the belief that the aetiology of human functioning is a complete reversal from that popularly circulated as human organisms our development is defined and constrained by the 'conditions' (James, 1890) of our environment, and we are always a priori 'relational beings' (Gergen, 2009); and
- the fact that psychology's tendency to individualise invites a reduction of the complexities of being-in-the-world to simplistic psychological categories supposedly existing in isolated individuals (after Billington et al., forthcoming).

It has been argued that many of the ideas and practices circulated specifically within educational psychology bear a resemblance to science only insofar as they use numbers, statistics and mathematical formulae (Billington, 1996). Those powerful critiques of the nature of scientific knowledge cited earlier (Feyerabend, Kuhn, Latour) undermine the claims of educational psychology as science, especially since in our efforts to attain the status accorded to the natural sciences we have created non-human methodologies which are unable to capture the phenomena of persons under investigation (Sugarman, 2014). It is argued here that psychologists, including educational psychologists, have undertaken research and practice which too often:

- prioritises methodology over the phenomena to be studied (Costa & Shimp, 2011);
- adopts methods ill-suited to recognise the phenomena under scrutiny, i.e. the human (Goodley, 2014); and

- investigates and reinvestigates versions of persons it has itself constructed (Hacking, 1995).

In the UK, some practitioners during the 1990s thought that we were 'giving away' our psychology, as more and more of the population adopted psychological language to describe themselves and those around them, including their children. As new forms of social communication and social networking emerged the notion of the 'psy-complex' could be seen to have been prophetic, as it recognised the way in which psychological discourse increasingly became the given way in which people understood themselves and each other. Given the cultural changes of the last twenty years (see de Vos, 2012 for a discussion on 'psychologisation') we argue that the rise of qualitative research in educational psychology, with its emphasis on both personal and theoretical reflexivity, is timely and welcome. More specifically, and perhaps ironically, we argue that qualitative research can lead to better science through the vitality of the questions it formulates (Hacking, 2002; Harré, 2004; Packer, 2011).

Such critical approaches to psychology have been offering highly distinctive and theoretically rigorous epistemologies which have begun to generate potentially emancipatory applications of qualitative research. For example, Erica Burman's (2008, first published 1994) use of deconstruction as a tool for critiquing development narratives, together with her exploration of a feminist agenda, strengthened analyses of the potentially debilitating nature of certain theoretical preferences and practices in child care and education. Isaac Prilleltensky emphasised critical approaches and the possibility of community solutions (Fox et al., 2009; Nelson & Prilleltensky, 2005), and Ben Bradley employed critiques of the assumptions of psychological knowledge and developed alternatives in respect of professional training (2005).

There are increasing numbers of psychologists working across education globally whose qualitative research engages with theory and the critique of practice, including Newman and Holzman (1993), Bird (1999), Sloan (2000), Gallagher (2003), Leadbetter et al. (2005), Kincheloe (2006, 2008), Goodman (2010), Mercieca (2011), Martin and McLellan (2013), Vassallo (2013), Williams (2013), Corcoran (2014), Billington (2006, 2014), Sugarman (2014), Todd (2014) and Hughes (2014).

It is now twenty years since discourse analysis appeared in *Educational Psychology in Practice* (Billington, 1995; subsequently, Bozic & Leadbetter, 1999; Pomerantz, 2010; Lewis, 2011). Discourse analysis continues to be used to good effect in educational psychology research to examine how a range of phenomena, from the aspirations of Muslim girls (Hewitt, 2015) to the professional identity of educational psychologists (Waters, 2014), are shaped by dominant discourses that are part of a sociocultural history often far from benign. However, there are now not only many forms of discourse analysis but many other highly specialised qualitative research techniques providing the theoretical foundations on which an alternative vision for the future of our discipline could be created; not least, for example, those by which we examine how the actual ways of talking about phenomena shape both our understanding and our professional responses. Certain other techniques or approaches also have their roots elsewhere outside mainstream psychology: for example, phenomenology has been persistent in its examination of human experience (after Husserl; for example, Heidegger, Merleau-Ponty, Sartre). Its contemporary derivative, interpretative phenomenological analysis (IPA), articulates a double hermeneutic process involved in making sense of a person's account of their experience (Hefferon & Gil-Rodriguez, 2011; Smith et al., 2009). IPA reflects also the more recent 'affective turn' in psychology which takes an interest not only in what is being said but also in the experiencing subject, as well as in the phenomenology of the encounter. Narrative research, a further growing strand of qualitative research within educational psychology (Billington & Todd, 2012; Hobbs et al., 2012; Winslade, 2012), utilises (to varying degrees) post-structuralist and person-centred, humanist approaches. In all these approaches there is an emphasis on recognising the concept and importance of 'voice' and the relational complexities which ensue, especially when acknowledging the presence and impact of the researcher and the reflexivity this entails.

There is insufficient space in this short book to explore the wealth of ideas and practices evidenced in the above strands. However, for all those educational psychologists eager to engage with the richness of human experience, oft-neglected since James, or who wish to develop the emancipatory forms of psychological and educational research and practice envisioned by Dewey, qualitative forms of research provide invaluable resources upon which to base our future work. We recognise, in particular, a potential for the future of our discipline in actively seeking to:

- identify and make transparent the epistemological, ontological and methodological assumptions which populate the landscape of educational psychology;
- reveal the kinds of human subject constituted and restricted through these discursive knowledges, and which shape educational psychology research and practice; and
- identify ideas, practices and support mechanisms which enable children and young people to successfully resist and move beyond regimes of knowledge-making found to be oppressive, enabling them to navigate more successfully their (educational) lives.

References

Antaki, C. (2015). Conversation analysis, applied. In K. Tracy, (Ed.) *The International Encyclopedia of Language and Social Interaction*. London: Wiley-Blackwell.

Armistead, N. (1974). *Reconstructing social psychology*. Harmondsworth: Penguin Education.

Bakhtin, M.M. (1984). *The problems of Dostoevsky's poetics*. C. Emerson (Ed.). Manchester: University of Manchester Press.

Banister, P., Bunn, G., Burman, E., et al. (2011). *Qualitative methods in psychology: A research guide* (2nd edn.). Buckingham: Open University Press.

Berliner, D.C. (1992). Telling the stories of educational psychology. *Educational Psychologist, 27,* 143–152.

Billig, M. (2008). *The hidden roots of critical psychology: Understanding the impact of Locke, Shaftesbury and Reid*. London: Sage.

Billington, T. (1995). Discourse analysis: Acknowledging interpretation in everyday practice. *Educational Psychology in Practice, 11*(3), 36–45.

Billington, T. (1996). Pathologising children: Psychology in education and acts of government. In E. Burman et al., *Psychology discourse practice: From regulation to resistance*. London: Taylor and Francis.

Billington, T. (2000). *Separating, losing and excluding children: Narratives of difference*. London: RoutledgeFalmer.

Billington, T. (2006). Working with autistic children and young people: Sense, experience and the challenges for services, policies and practices. *Disability & Society, 21*(1), 1–14.

Billington, T. and Todd, L. (Eds.) (2012). Narrative: Approaches in research and professional practice. *Educational and Child Psychology, 29*(2), 5–9.

Billington, T. and Williams, A. (2015). Education and psychology: Change at last? In I. Parker (Ed.), *Handbook of critical psychology*. London: Routledge.

Billington, T., Williams, T., Goodley, D. and Corcoran, T. (forthcoming). Editorial. In T. Williams, T. Billington, D. Goodley and T. Corcoran (Eds.). *Critical educational psychology*. Oxford: Wiley/Blackwell.

Bird, L. (1999). Towards a more critical educational psychology. *Annual Review of Critical Psychology, 1*(1), 21–33.

Board of Education (1924). *Report of the consultative committee on psychological tests of educable capacity.* London: HMSO.

Bozic. N. and Leadbetter, J. (1999). Teacher assessments: how EPs respond to them in routine meetings. *Educational Psychology in Practice, 14*(4), 264–272.

Bradley, B.S. (2005). *Psychology and experience.* Cambridge: Cambridge University Press.

Bruner, J.S. (1986). *Actual minds, possible worlds.* Cambridge, MA: Harvard University Press.

Bruner, J.S. (1991). The narrative construction of reality. *Critical Inquiry, 18*(1), 1–21.

Burman, E. (2008). *Deconstructing developmental psychology* (2nd edn.). Hove: Routledge.

Burman, E. (2015). The turn to deconstruction. In I. Parker (Ed.) *Handbook of critical psychology.* London: Routledge.

Burr, V. (1995). *An introduction to social constructionism.* London: Routledge.

Burt, C. (1913). The inheritance of mental characters. *The Eugenics Review, 4,* 168–200.

Butler, J. (1990). *Gender trouble: Feminism and the subversion of identity.* New York, London: Routledge

Chitty, C. (2007). *Eugenics, race and intelligence in education.* London: Continuum.

Corcoran, T.D. (2012). Second nature. *British Journal of Social Psychology, 48*(2), 375–388.

Corcoran, T.D. (Ed.) (2014). *Psychology in education: Critical theory-practice.* Rotterdam: Sense Publishers.

Costa, R.E. and Shimp, C.P. (2011). Methods course and texts in psychology: 'Textbook science' and 'tourist brochures'. *Journal of Theoretical and Philosophical Psychology, 31*(1), 25–43.

Daniels, H., Edwards, A., Engestrom, Y. and Ludvigsen, S. (Eds.) (2009) *Activity theory in practice: Promoting learning across boundaries and agencies.* London: Routledge.

Danziger, K. (1990). *Constructing the subject: Historical origins of psychological research.* New York: Cambridge University Press.

De Vos, J. (2012). *Psychologisation in times of globalisation.* London: Routledge

Dewey, J. (1897). My pedagogic creed. *The School Journal, LIV*(3), 77–80.

Dewey, J. (1916). *Democracy and education: An introduction to the philosophy of education.* New York: The Macmillan Company.

Dewey, J. (1938). *Experience and education.* New York: Macmillan.

Donaldson, M. (1978). *Children's minds.* London: Fontana/Croom Helm

Feyerabend, P. (1975). *Against method.* London: Verso.

Freud, S., & Breuer, J. (1895). *Studies on hysteria.* London: Hogarth.

Foucault, M. (1970). *The order of things: An archaeology of the human sciences.* London: Tavistock Publications.

Foucault, M. (1988). *Technologies of the self: A seminar with Michel Foucault.* Amherst: University of Massachusetts Press.

Fox, D, Prilleltensky, I., Austin, S. (Eds.) (2009). *Critical psychology: An introduction.* London: Sage.

Gallagher, S. (2003). *Educational psychology: Disrupting the dominant discourse.* New York: Peter Lang.

Gergen, K.J. (1985).The social constructionist movement in modern psychology. *American Psychologist, 40*(3), 266–275.

Gergen, K.J. (1994). *Towards a transformation in social knowledge* (2nd edn.). London: Sage. (Original work published 1982).

Gergen, K.J. (2009). *Relational being.* New York: Oxford University Press

Gillham, B. (Ed.) (1978). *Reconstructing educational psychology.* London: Croom Helm.

Gilligan, C. (1982). *In a different voice.* Harvard, MA: Harvard University Press.

Gilligan, C. (1989). *Mapping the moral domain: A contribution of women's thinking to psychological theory and education.* Harvard, MA: Harvard University Press.

Goodley, D. (2014). *Dis/ability studies: Theorising disablism and ableism.* London: Routledge.

Goodman, G.S. (2010). *Educational psychology reader: The art and science of how people learn.* New York: Peter Lang.

Hacking, I. (1995). The looping effect of human kinds. In D. Sperber and A.J. Premack (Eds.) *Causal cognition* (pp.351–383). Oxford: Oxford University Press.

Hacking, I. (2002). *Historical ontology*. Cambridge, MA: Harvard University Press.

Harré, R. (1979). *Social being: A theory for social psychology*. Oxford: Blackwell.

Harré, R. (2004). Staking our claim for qualitative psychology as science. *Qualitative Research in Psychology. 1*(1), 3–14.

Hearnshaw, L. (1979). *Cyril Burt – Psychologist*. London: Hodder and Stoughton.

Heferon, K. and Gil-Rodriguez, E. (2011). Methods: Interpretative phenomenological analysis. *The Psychologist, 24*, 756–759.

Henriques, J., Hollway, W., Urwin, C., et al. (1989). *Changing the subject: Psychology, social regulation and subjectivity*. London: Methuen.

Hewett, R. (2015). 'Their whole community might be watching them': Teacher and pupil constructions of Muslim girls' aspirations and the role of their families and the community. *Educational and Child Psychology, 32*(2), 68–78.

Hobbs, C., Durkin, R., Ellison, G., et al. (2012). The professional practice of educational psychologists: Developing narrative approaches. *Educational and Child Psychology, 29*(2), 41–52.

Hollway, W. (1989). *Subjectivity and method in psychology*. London: Sage Publications.

Holzkamp, K. (2013). Basic concepts of critical psychology. In E. Schraube and U. Osterkamp (Eds.) *Psychology from the standpoint of the subject: Selected writings of Klaus Holzkamp*. Basingstoke: Palgrave Macmillan.

Hughes, M. (2014). What might adults learn from working with young researchers? In J. Westwood, C. Larkins, D. Moxon, et al. *Participation, citizenship and intergenerational relations in children and young people's lives: Children and adults in conversation*. London: Palgrave Macmillan.

Ingleby, D. (1974). The job psychologists do. In N. Armistead (Ed.) *Reconstructing social psychology*. Harmondsworth: Penguin.

James, W. (1890). *Principles of psychology. Vols. 1 & 2*. Mineola, NY: Dover Publications.

James, W. (1902). *The varieties of religious experience*. New York: Modern Library.

Kincheloe, J.L. (2006). A critical politics of knowledge: Analyzing the role of educational psychology in educational policy. *Policy Futures in Education, 4*(3), 220–235.

Kincheloe, J.L. (2008). *Critical pedagogy primer*. New York: Peter Lang.

Kuhn, T. (1962). *The structure of scientific revolutions*. Chicago: University of Chicago Press.

Latour, B. (1979). *Laboratory life: The social construction of scientific facts*. Los Angeles: Sage.

Leadbetter, J., Daniels, H.R.J., Stringer, P. (Eds.) (2005). Editorial – Sociocultural psychology and activity theory: New paradigms to inform the practice of educational psychology. *Educational and Child Psychology, 22*, 1.

Lewis, V. (2011). 'Institutional talk' in the discourse between the educational psychologist and a parent: A single case study employing mixed research methods. *Educational and Child Psychology, 27*(3), 195–212.

Mackintosh, N.J. (2013) The Burt affair: 40 years on. *Educational and Child Psychology, 30*(3), 13–32

Martin, J. (2004). The educational inadequacy of concepts of self in educational psychology. *Interchange, 35*(2), 185–208.

Martin, J. and McLellan, A-M. (2013). *The education of selves: How psychology transformed students*. New York: Oxford University Press

Martin, J., Sugarman, J. and Slaney, K. (Eds.) (in press). *The Wiley handbook of theoretical and philosophical psychology*. Oxford, UK: Wiley

Mercieca, D. (2011). *Beyond conventional boundaries: Uncertainty in research and practice with children*. Rotterdam: Sense Publishers.

Miller, A., Billington, T., Lewis, V. and De Souza, L. Educational psychology. In C. Willig and W. Stainton-Rogers (Eds.). *The Sage handbook of qualitative research*. London: Sage.

Nelson, G. and Prilleltensky, I. (Eds.) (2005). *Community psychology: In pursuit of liberation and well-being*. Basingstoke: Palgrave MacMillan

Newman, F. and Holzman, L. (1993). *Lev Vygotsky: Revolutionary scientist*. London: Routledge.

Packer, M. (2011). *The science of qualitative research*. Cambridge, MA: Cambridge University Press.

Parker, I. (1992). *Discourse dynamics: Critical analysis for individual and social psychology*. London: Routledge.

Parker, I. (1997). 'Discourse analysis and psycho-analysis', *British Journal of Social Psychology, 36,* 479–495.

Parker, I. (1999). Critical psychology: Critical links. Annual Review of Critical Psychology, 1, 155–167.

Parker, I. (2005). *Qualitative psychology: Introducing radical research.* London: Routledge

Parker, I. (2013). Discourse analysis: dimensions of critique in psychology. *Qualitative Research in Psychology, 10*(3), 223–239.

Parker, I. (2014). *Psychology after discourse analysis: Concepts, methods, critique.* London: Routledge.

Parker, I. (Ed.) (2015). *Handbook of critical psychology.* London: Routledge.

Pomerantz, K. (2008). Analysing and interpreting spoken discourse: Educational psychologists as reflexive practitioners. *Educational and Child Psychology, 25*(1), 5–16.

Potter, J. (1996). *Representing reality: Discourse, rhetoric and social construction.* London: Sage

Potter, J., & Wetherell, M. (1987). *Discourse and social psychology: Beyond attitudes and behaviour.* London: Sage.

Prilleltensky, I. (1994). *The morals and politics of psychology: Psychological discourse and the status quo.* Albany, New York: State University of New York Press.

Prochnik, G. (2006). *Putnam Camp: Sigmund Freud, James Jackson Putnam, and the purpose of American psychology.* NY: Other Press.

Riessman, C.K. (1993). *Narrative analysis.* London: Sage.

Rogers, C. (1951). *Client-centered therapy: Its current practice, implications and theory.* London: Constable.

Rose, N. (1990). *Governing the soul: The shaping of the private self.* London: Taylor & Francis/Routledge.

Ryle, G. (1948). *The concept of mind.* Chicago: University of Chicago Press.

Shotter, J. (1993). *The cultural politics of everyday life: Social constructionism, rhetoric and knowing of the third kind.* Milton Keynes: Open University Press.

Sloan, T. (Ed.) (2000). *Critical psychology: Voices for change.* London: Palgrave.

Smith, J.A., Flowers, P. & Larkin, M. (2009). *Interpretative phenomenological analysis: Theory, method and research.* London: Sage.

Sugarman, J. (2014). Neo-Foucaultian approaches to critical inquiry in the psychology of education. In T. Corcoran (Ed.) *Psychology in education: Critical theory~practice.* Rotterdam: Sense Publishers.

Todd, L. (2014). Critical dialogue, critical methodology: Bridging the research gap to young people's participation in evaluating children's services. In G. Porter, J. Townsend and K. Hampshire (Eds.) *Children and young people as knowledge producers* (pp.187–200). London: Routledge.

Tolman, C. (1994). *Psychology, society and subjectivity: An introduction to German critical psychology.* London: Routledge.

Vassallo, S. (2013). *Self-regulated learning: An application of critical educational psychology.* New York: Peter Lang.

Vygotsky, L. (1978). *Mind in society.* Cambridge, MA: Harvard University Press

Walkerdine, V., Lucey, H. and Melody, J. (2001). *Growing up girl: Psycho-social explorations of gender and class.* Basingstoke: Palgrave.

Waters, H.T. (2014). *How are educational psychologists' professional identities shaped by the available discourses?* Unpublished doctoral thesis, University of Sheffield.

White, M. and Epston, D. (1990). *Narrative means to therapeutic ends.* New York: Norton.

Williams, A. (2013). Critical educational psychology: Fostering emancipatory potential within the therapeutic project. *Power and Education, 5*(3), 304–317.

Willig, C. and Stainton-Rogers, W. (Eds.) (2008). *The Sage handbook of qualitative research in psychology.* London: Sage.

Winslade, J. (2012). Positioning among the lines of force in schooling: An issue for psychologists and counsellors in schools. *Educational and Child Psychology, 29*(2), 20–31.

Winter, S. (1999). *Freud and the institution of psychoanalytic knowledge.* Stanford, CA: Stanford University Press.

Wittgenstein, L. (1922). *Tractatus Logico-Philosophicus.* London: Routledge.

Zaretsky, E. (2004). *Secrets of the soul: A social and cultural history of psychoanalysis.* New York: Alfred Knopf.

Chapter 2 Qualitative methodologies that give young people a voice: Grounded theory and interpretative phenomenological analysis

Julia Hardy & Karen Majors

Aims of this chapter

This chapter considers the importance of selecting appropriate methodologies when carrying out research with children and young people. We will describe two specific qualitative methodologies used frequently by educational psychologists (EPs): grounded theory (GT) and interpretative phenomenological analysis (IPA). We will reflect on the similarities and differences between various specific methodologies and techniques described. We will use illustrative examples to show how GT and IPA have been applied to researching with children and young people.[1]

Introduction

Much published research in developmental psychology has been primarily quantitative. It could be argued this reflects a research tradition in which individual children's experiences are not a valued focus for research. Greene and Hogan (2005) argue that developmental psychology has sought to 'homogenise' children's experiences. Children are the important sources of information on matters that concern them, and preferable to other sources which may not be orientated to the child's perspective (Kellet and Ding, in Fraser et al., 2005).

A key ethical question raised by Alderson and Morrow (2004) is whether the research can be explained to children in terms that they can understand sufficiently in order to give informed consent or to decline to be interviewed. EPs bring key skills to their role as researchers interviewing children and young people. These are the development of a rapport with the children in the research study, the use of language and questions that the children can understand, and listening and facilitating in the interaction (Greig and Taylor, 1999). EPs also have expertise in communicating with children who are vulnerable and/or where there are sensitive issues to explore. Spending time in the proposed research setting and talking with the children, as well as explaining the research to a group, can be a valuable way of enabling the child to decide whether or not they wish to participate in the research. In these situations, the child has knowledge of whom they would be talking to (the researcher) before giving consent. This is an effective process for finding child research participants who might otherwise be regarded as hard to reach.

---

[1] For consistency and brevity, this chapter uses the terms 'child' and 'young person', although some examples derive from those who see themselves as 'young people' or 'young adults'.

Similarities in qualitative methodologies

As Henwood (1996) reflected, 'to some extent, all discussions of methodology in the human and social sciences, not just in psychology, are influenced by the esteem afforded to detachment, objectivity and rationality – the guiding principles of western science – in industrialised democracies' (p.26). In qualitative research, when seeking to hear the voice of young people the focus is not on objectivity but on achieving successful interactions with children and young people that help them communicate genuinely and freely with others. This comes from a post-structuralist framework, which stresses the indeterminacy of language and meaning, and values the interpretative study of culture, symbolism and texts. Although the focus within diverse qualitative methodologies varies, all such researchers hold in mind how much the interpretative repertoires are historically and culturally created.

Henwood (1996) draws the distinction between quantitative research, which engages in 'manipulating, measuring and specifying relationships between specific variables in order to test hypotheses about causal laws' (p.27), and qualitative research, which argues 'for the importance of understanding the meaning of experience, actions and events as these are interpreted through the eyes of particular participants, researchers and (sub) cultures, and for sensitivity to the complexities of behaviour and meaning in the contexts where they typically or "naturally" occur' (ibid.).

Diversity of qualitative methodologies

It could be argued that a strength found in qualitative methodologies is the diversity of the underpinning epistemologies and related research methods. This diversity necessitates transparency and coherence about how the chosen methodology has been applied. The importance of transparency is particularly emphasised by qualitative researchers (Cresswell, 1998; Miles and Huberman, 1994). In part, this is in recognition that the stance of the researcher can never be value-free (Denzin & Lincoln, 2000) and also that epistemological and ontological perspectives have a direct bearing on the research process and outcomes (Crotty, 1998; Denzin & Lincoln, 2003). How to evaluate qualitative studies given this diversity and the limitations and relevance of applying quantitative measures of validity and reliability are issues that have been usefully explored elsewhere (Yardley, 2000). Elliott et al. (1999) very helpfully set out guidelines for the publication of qualitative research studies in psychology. These guidelines are useful to psychologists in the design stage of the research as well as in the final process of publishing the research.

Narrative approaches

These can be grouped into various methodologies, depending on the epistemological stance of the researcher. One such approach is critical realism (Bhaskar, 1978; Houston, 2001; Kelly, 2008; Matthews, 2003, 2010). This both assumes an objective reality and recognises that this reality is socially constructed and may be subject to error (Pawson & Tilley, 1997). Pawson and Tilley's four principles to apply in interviewing participants are as follows:

- Children contribute their views about what works for them and these ideas can be used to inform future interventions.
- Children are invited to comment on the theories of EPs and other participants.

- EPs bring expertise based on current research, which allows them to make interpretations that can inform interventions.
- Theories about 'what works for whom in what circumstances' are refined through cycles of intervention.

To some extent, the detailed research methods set out below fall beneath the umbrella of the narrative turn within psychology. However the analytic study of narrative, with its social constructionist foundations, has led to diverse research methodologies, including conversation analysis, discursive psychology and critical discourse analysis. The growth of narrative approaches within educational psychology has been apparent in recent years (Billington & Todd, 2012; Lewis & Miller, 2011). This chapter does not aim to detail all the complexities of the above-mentioned approaches but merely to illustrate two complex methodologies (IPA and GT).

Two qualitative approaches

Many qualitative methodologies utilise notes to the researcher (within a research diary) along with diagrams and pictures that illustrate the young people's ideas. A majority of IPA and GT studies employ semi-structured interviews as a way of seeking the views and perceptions of children about their own personal experiences and feelings about topics which are important and meaningful to them. Child research participants often respond very well to activities that support dialogue and communication, e.g. drawing and the use of timelines or other visual material. The use of structured activities to enable younger children to focus, rather than reliance solely on interview questions, is suggested by Harker (2002), and Greig and Taylor (1999). The use of 'member checking' is pervasive throughout qualitative research by EPs, where the tentative findings of research are shared with participants. Table 2.1 shows how IPA and GT take differing epistemological and ontological stances, ranging from a realist and relativist perspectives to that of critical realism. Table 2.1 also illustrates other distinctions between IPA and GT. So, for example, because IPA has a focus on individual experience and sense making, samples are typically small, though IPA has been used with larger samples.

Table 2.1: Comparison of two qualitative approaches

	Grounded theory (GT)	Interpretative phenomenological analysis (IPA)
Research purpose	Exploratory	Exploratory
Epistemology	Social constructionism	Critical realism
Questions	Open, and then focused	Open/general
Sample size	Flexible, depending on when 'saturation' is experienced	4–8 interviews typical
Time scale	Over months if not a year	One or more interviews
Levels of coding/ analysis	Three levels; then theoretical model proposed	Descriptive and interpretative
Member checks	Appropriate to give feedback but not to verify	Not appropriate
Findings	Proposes new, local, 'substantive' theories, rather than 'formal', large-scale theories	Claims rather than truths; theoretical/conceptual generalisation
Sample characteristics	Focus on specific, delineated area of research but can be heterogeneous	Homogeneous

Some methodologies overlap and are seen by some authors as compatible. Such authorities include Oliver (2012), who argued that critical realism and GT can be compatible, sharing as they do a focus on abduction (see below for further explanation), a commitment to fallibilism and an emphasis on the interconnectedness of practice and theory. Willig (2001) made the distinction between 'big Q' and 'little q' qualitative methodologies, where the 'big Q' approaches include discursive psychology, conversation analysis, IPA and GT, all of which share fundamental epistemological roots within constructionist psychology. The 'little q' methods, such as thematic analysis (Braun & Clarke, 2006), are less complex and prescriptive. The following section outlines two 'big Q' methodologies that are frequently reported in published research by EPs: GT and IPA.

Grounded theory (GT)

GT was described by Glaser and Strauss (1967) as an approach in which 'theory is derived from data and then illustrated by characteristic examples of data' (p.5). It is about inductive theory development, as opposed to the more usual deductive approach that was common within both the positivist stance and much quantitative epistemology. Glaser and Strauss were critical of colleagues within sociology who emphasised the verification of existing theories rather than a systematic approach to substantive theory development to explain real-world phenomena. Indeed they commented that much of the 'grand' theory work that colleagues had previously produced 'is generated from logical assumptions and speculations about the "oughts" of social life' (Glaser & Strauss, op. cit. p.35).

GT falls within Robson's (2002) definition of 'flexible' research design, which Robson noted need not necessarily preclude a 'scientific' character. Robson (2002, p.18) defines a 'scientific attitude' as one in which 'the research is carried out *systematically, sceptically* and *ethically*'.

The idea of discovery so fundamental to GT begins with discovering first the world as seen through participants' eyes. As Hutchinson (1988) comments, for the GT theorist 'the task is to discover and conceptualize the essence of specific interactional processes. The resulting theory provides a new way of understanding the social situations from which the theory was generated' (p.124).

Defining components of grounded theory
In a recent text describing the process of applying grounded theory, Charmaz (2006) summarises the defining components of GT, as described originally by Glaser and Strauss (1967), as follows:
- simultaneous involvement in data collection and analysis;
- constructing analytic codes and categories from data, not from preconceived logically deduced hypotheses;
- using the constant comparative method, which involves making comparisons during each stage of the analysis;
- advancing theory development during each step of data collection and analysis;
- memo-writing to elaborate categories, specify their properties, define relationships between categories and identify gaps;
- sampling aimed towards theory construction, not for population representativeness;
- conducting the literature review after developing an independent analysis (p.5–6).

GT as an iterative process
GT is often presented as comprising a series of steps (Hutchinson, 1988; Miller, 1995), from open coding (level I) to axial coding (level II) and on to level III codes and theory development. GT methodology is an essentially iterative cycle, in which many aspects of the process may be occurring simultaneously. Hutchinson (1988) demonstrated this in a spiral diagram showing the temporality of GT. This has been adapted to show how there is a continuous, iterative process during data collection, ending with saturation, which is then followed by literature review, writing and then publishing the new theory (see Figure 2.1). The aim is, through interpretative understanding of subjects' meanings, to generate a 'substantive theory' at the end of these simultaneous activities by moving through this iterative cycle.

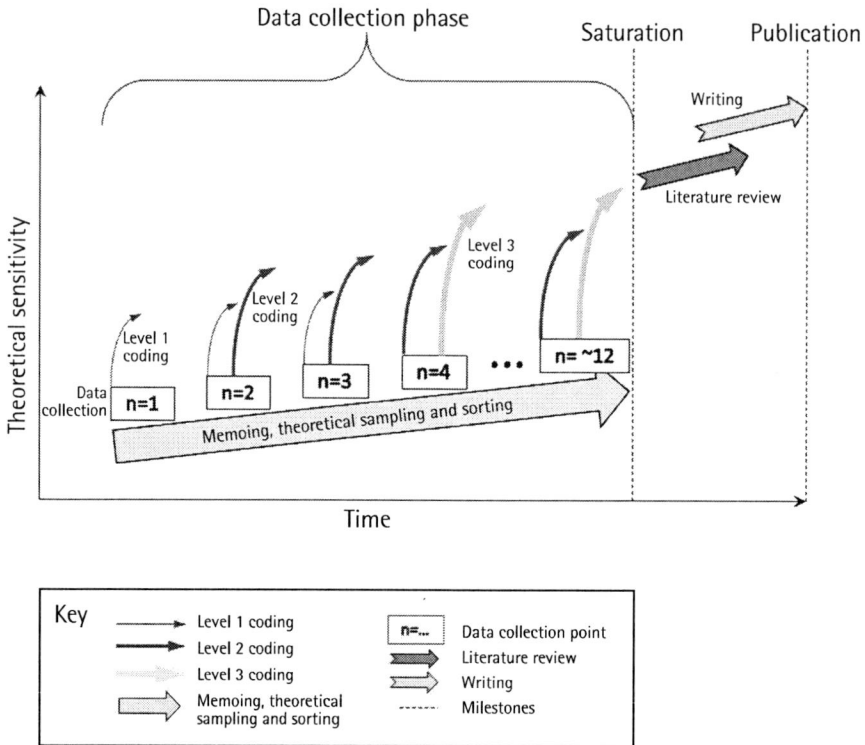

Figure 2.1: The temporality of GT

Glaser divides coding into two procedures: substantive and theoretical coding. Substantive coding has two phases, open and then selective coding; it is concerned with producing categories and their properties. Theoretical coding occurs at a theoretical level, weaving substantive codes into a hypothesis and theory. Glaser (1992) defined coding as 'conceptualising data by constant comparison of incident with incident, and incident with concept' (p.38). Many authors have used a variety of terms to describe the components of and processes within GT. It is a complex method, requiring support from an experienced practitioner to reflect on both methodology and the progress of the research. It includes a constant comparative method and the creative use of integrative diagrams to combine and consider categories and their properties, as a part of the need to develop and reflect upon the increasingly abstract process of generating an abductive theory (Charmaz, 2006; Glaser and Strauss, 1999). The use of abduction in contrast to deduction (a type of reasoning that starts with a general or abstract concept and reasons to specific instances) or induction (a type of reasoning that begins with the study of a range of individual cases and extrapolates patterns from them to form a conceptual category) is crucial in GT. Abduction is a type of reasoning that begins by examining data and after scrutiny of these data, entertains all possible explanations for the observed data, and then forms hypotheses to confirm or disconfirm until the researcher arrives at the most plausible interpretation of the observed data. GT methodology is often described as illuminative (Glaser 1978; Hutchison, 1988) and is certainly a process of discovery.

The use of GT with deaf adolescents

The first author undertook research into the question 'What awareness and ideas do adolescents (aged 13–16) with severe and profound hearing loss, attending mainstream schools, have about their developing deaf identity?' (Hardy, 2010). Interviews with 11 students, using a semi-structured questionnaire, were videotaped and transcribed. All the pupils were educated for the majority of their time with hearing peers, with exposure to Signed Supported English (SSE) at school, but all their parents were hearing. The first author was interested in this under-researched topic and was influenced by Wood et al. (1986) who asked why so many deaf young people leave school unable to communicate effectively, and who argued that the answer may lie not in the mode of communication but 'in the quality and productiveness of the processes of communication and teaching that deaf children experience' (p.xii). Knowing that 'deafness can be regarded both as an audiological disability and as a social and cultural construct' (Ohna, 2001), the focus of this study was on adolescents' individual reflections on their identity. The transcription data produced was analysed using GT.

The following section starts with the local emergent theory developed from the research and then uses 'particularised accounts' (Evensen et al., 2001) from four students to bring alive their stories for the reader and to outline the range of perspectives.

GT findings

This research combined issues of deafness with the theme of social identity. The emergent core variable within this GT research was group alignment. The analysis proposed that the ease or difficulty of communication combines with deaf adolescents' previous experiences of friendship and current preferences to influence their choices regarding group alignment. The adolescents identified themselves within one of three groups: deaf aligned, hearing aligned or the 'bridge between two worlds' group (see Figure 2.2).

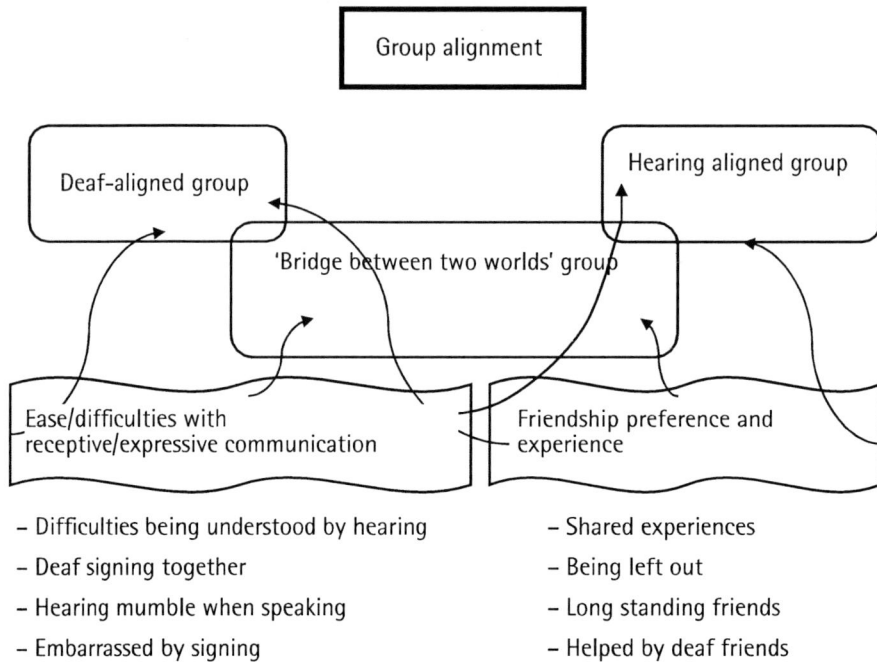

Figure 2.2: What influences group alignment for deaf adolescents
in mainstream schools?

Particularisation in GT accounts

The use of 'particularized accounts' to illustrate 'the uniqueness of the individual cases' was promoted by Evensen et al. (2001), who described their findings through case studies of 'individual learner identities', using 'quotations representing discovered concepts' that were 'woven together to form narratives' (Evensen et al., 2001, p.662). This is not a required aspect within GT but helps the reader access the rich interview data in a meaningful way. In the process of generating the proposed local theory the first author undertook line-by-line coding and then reviewed lower-level codes, grouping them into high-level codes in a constant iterative process, both while analysing each interview and when comparing codes from within and between interviewees. These codes, together with the ongoing process of memoing, led to the final generation of the local theory.

Pupil 1 (aged 15 years and 8 months) talked about the importance of inclusion and the need to develop hearing people's deaf awareness. This pupil was also interested in all the benefits of new technology and was irritated with his parents because they had not invested in a modern doorbell designed for the deaf. Some of the comments he made led the first author to reflect on the kind of comments any adolescent may make about their parents, such as those about his family's ignorance of technology and his need for privacy and independence. Some of his comments were deaf-specific, for instance when his parent observed his minicom communications by looking over his shoulder, saying 'They ought not to look'. This adolescent made poignant comments about how, when his parents did not talk to him when he was in the room with them, 'it feels like I'm not there, you know. It feels like I'm invisible'. He disagreed with his older brother who felt that being deaf should not make a difference, remarking 'that's not true, but when you conversate (sic), when you have a conversations with the hearing impaired, you need to be careful'. This adolescent talked at length about the importance of his friendships with other deaf people. He concluded the interview with a definite view that 'It's nicer being deaf really'.

Pupil 2, who had just turned 15 years old, had very strong and contrasting views to Pupil 1's. He was very clear and decisive in his preference for the term 'deaf'. Within the first minutes of the interview this adolescent talked about his first school in an inclusive provision:

> The other, the other deaf children they were around me. I didn't actually want to hang around with them, because they all act different, differently from all the hearing kids. So in the end I just find myself, like, regretting, regretting becoming deaf, like. That's all.

Pupil 2 continued:

> I mean, you know, in the whole way deafness has affected me in a sort of negative way, at school... because, umm. In each school there's like this umm, the whole deaf group and hearing group, and like the deaf group, like, nearly all of them act all different from you and, I thought, in the end I just, like, hang around with the hearing group ... Well, all the deaf kids, they all if you, if you see any of them around school, right, they're all, they're always, like in this big pack or something.

Pupil 2 actively chose to be with the hearing group: 'They don't really care that I'm deaf and they just, they just appreciate me like I'm a normal person.'

This adolescent talked about the individual differences between teachers, with the comments about how the good ones showed consideration in the treatment of the deaf. He disliked any obvious differences in the way others communicated with him that differentiated him from the hearing, describing how he could be embarrassed by signing adults and disliking being forced to sign at primary school or made to wear a radio aid.

Pupil 2 described how he was put off being with other deaf students at primary school and their 'weird actions'. He recollects how:

> They used to like force me to hang around with deaf, deaf students ... even when some of the hearing kids used to like, ask me to play with them at Primary ... the teacher would just, would just make me hang around with the deaf kids, like ... and every time, every time one of the deaf kids would see me walking away ... and just talking to some hearing kids, he or she would complain ... and just, I would just have to go just straight back.

Pupil 2 also had a deaf sibling and described how his parents had accepted his wish to be 'treated as normal' and not to sign. He indicated that the only deaf he would mix with were 'laid back people', objecting to those deaf who over-emphasise their deafness: 'some deaf kids, they're always like, make, trying to make everyone aware of being deaf... It's like, 'look at me I'm deaf, look at me!' Despite this negative attitude towards the way some deaf behave, Pupil 2 was also very appreciative of a teacher of the deaf who was herself hearing impaired, and 'understands all the kind of stuff that I go through, and stuff, that's, that's cool.' Pupil 2 finished the interview talking about being deaf 'it's just having a hard life, and just, all you have to do is try harder' and using the poignant phrase that deafness means to him 'being without.'

Pupil 3 is 14 years old and had a cochlear implant when she was 5. Early in the interview she spoke about how she had help from hearing support staff in school who signed what teachers had been saying, and the importance of seating position for lip-reading the speaker. Pupil 3 appreciated it when there was flexibility in the seating in class, in contrast to Pupil 1 who mentioned how the deaf were made to sit together at the front. She also talked about two teachers in particular who were easy to understand because they were 'teachers who speak clearly', and noted that 'some teachers act when they are taking the lessons, like in history my teacher acts a bit, like Hitler', concluding that this helps because 'the deaf act to communicate'. Pupil 3 is a sociable student who talked about her plethora of friends and how 'we like hanging around signing and talking together'. Pupil 3 made a distinction between the deaf friends she was close to and other hearing acquaintances. She noted that there were times when hearing students were 'rude to us' but she could describe strategies she used in response to perceived teasing because of her deafness.

This pupil spoke enthusiastically about how some other family members were learning to sign and went to signing clubs for hearing people her at school. However, she also described family gender differences in signing; admitting that at home 'I don't usually sign but if it's private, because of my Dad and my brother, they're men, and I'm a girl with my Mum, we sign and don't use our voices... so as my Dad can't understand what we're saying'. Pupil 3 talked about when she was out shopping with friends, adding that in order to understand each other while walking and signing in a big group when it's noisy, they employed the walking backwards communication strategy, so that they could see each other's faces to lip-read while walking. Pupil 3 appreciated the opportunity that a secondary school with inclusive provision for the deaf offered her, remarking 'here we've got lots of deaf students and lots of signers'. This is in contrast to the smaller numbers within similar primary school provisions where she had had the problem of having few friends. Pupil 3 went to both deaf clubs and deaf pubs; describing the first time she saw a large group of deaf together, she said 'I felt weird, strange, because they're all adults, they were signing different signs', and concluded 'I was like, mmm, cool, strange, yes but nice new people'. Although this pupil talked positively about many experiences relating to her deafness, she concluded the interview in response to the question 'what does deafness mean to you?' that 'I probably think it's not fair... Why am I the one that can't hear and they can?'

The last student in these particularised accounts was Pupil 4, who had just turned 15 years old and also had a cochlear implant. Her first memories of being aware she was deaf were when her family talked about the cochlear implant operation she would be having at around the age of five. This student described how she had an auditory oral start in a mainstream school and then from Year 4 to Year 9 attended a special school, where she was taught BSL. Pupil 4 also talked about being teased about her deafness. On one occasion she got very annoyed with this: 'I done, I done, I when, when he's finished talking about me, I sat up, I sat up and said to S... "Shut up! Will you grow up! Grow up!" And then he went out.'

She also talked about her hearing best friend and how they spend time together enjoying loud music and telling jokes. She described how her family choose not to sign with her, but she spoke of the benefits of 'having the two worlds'. When a signing deaf friend came home she described her role as interpreter: 'You are in the middle one. And if in deaf, deaf are signing to me, what my Mum, even my Mum she don't understand her, she signs me, I tell her'. Pupil 4 clearly enjoys her role as a bridge between two worlds. Pupil 4 had parental encouragement to play physical games with the deaf and went to Fulham deaf football club, through which she made many deaf friends. Clearly this pupil liked to hang around with hearing peers at school but also enjoyed being with a small deaf group playing football. This pupil concluded the interview with the comment 'So sometimes I feel "Oh damn I don't want to be deaf"', and remarked 'I would like to know what it's like being hearing'.

The essence of GT is to start with the data and move iteratively to any theory. After generating the local theory above, the first author reflected on how this methodology was an ideal approach to elicit findings from a potentially diverse group of young people. Tajfel (1978) defined social identity as 'that part of an individual's self-concept which derives from his knowledge of his membership of a social group (or groups) together with the value and emotional significance attached to that membership' (p.63). Tajfel (1981) also recognised the reciprocal (or dialectical) relationship between social settings and situations, and the reflection or expression of these in subjective group membership. Rather than undertake quantitative research (such as through a fixed questionnaire) imposing adult ideas and grand theories, the first author was interested in undertaking illuminative research to find out what young people had to say in this complex area of social identity.

Interpretative phenomenological analysis (IPA)

With its focus on people's sense-making of their lived experience, IPA has been prominent in health research with regard to a diverse range of health-related issues (e.g. Dean et al., 2005; Eatough and Smith, 2006; Mulveen and Hepworth, 2006). As Smith (in Brooks, 2015) comments IPA has become one of the best known and most frequently used approaches in psychology. It is a popular choice for qualitative researchers from a range of disciplines (Hefferon and Gil-Rodriguez, 2011) including educational psychology (Sugden, 2013). For example, Doutre et al. (2013) explored the experiences of young people caring for a parent with a mental illness. A contribution to this success may come from the clear guidance that exists for the novice IPA researcher (see Smith et al., 2009), a thriving email discussion forum that enables people interested in IPA to communicate with each other, and regional, national and now international IPA research groups which are held regularly to support those using IPA in their research (see www.ipa.bbk.ac.uk).

Ontological and epistemological perspectives of IPA

All phenomenological psychologists are concerned with the exploration of 'lived experience', a foundational concept laid down by Husserl (Landridge, 2007). Descriptive phenomenological psychology is closely related to the original philosophy of Husserl with its focus on seeking the essences of a phenomenon. Giorgi (e.g. 1971, 1975) is acknowledged as being a pioneer of such psychological research in the 1970s. In contrast, the more interpretative stance of Heidegger (1962) underpins IPA. This is because IPA has more of a concern with sense-making – attending to the research participant's perceptions and understandings to inform the researcher's interpretation. Thus IPA is more closely linked to existential philosophy, for example in its focus on hermeneutics – interpretation rather than the description emphasised in the early Husserlian tradition (Langdridge, 2007). IPA is a methodology that is compatible with the epistemological position of critical realism. For research in the social sciences, Sayer (2000) suggests that critical realism is an alternative to positivism and interpretivism in their exclusive forms.

IPA draws on an idiographic phenomenology (Smith et al., 2009) and aims to interpret the individual, subjective experience. It does not exclude noticing commonalities and shared experiences. This is in contrast to approaches such as GT, which has more of a concern in developing theories from a range of research participants. With IPA, the focus on individual experience and case uniqueness and the researcher's interpretation of this is time-consuming, and typically only a small number of cases are studied. Smith et al. (2009) suggest that the sample size for professional doctorates should be between four to ten interviews. A key feature of IPA is the view that participants are experts on their own experiences and can express their views and feelings in detailed accounts to the researcher (Reid et al., 2005). The researcher has an active role in interpreting participants' understandings of their experiences. This has been termed the 'double hermeneutic' (Smith and Osborne, 2003). IPA draws on psychological theory and research in interpretation. Careful attention is paid to the thematic analysis of each individual interview before combining main themes and sub-themes from all interviews. Psychological theory and research is then drawn upon in the interpretation and analysis of themes. Thus, IPA is good at dialogue with theory as this is an inbuilt part of the analysis.

Use of IPA with children

IPA was developed in the 1990s by Smith, primarily with adult research participants and with regard to health psychology. The procedures and processes for IPA have been clearly described in for example Smith et al. (2009) and Smith and Osborn (2003). The following is an example of how IPA has been used with child research participants. It is not the intention to give a comprehensive description of the research, rather to illustrate why IPA has been applied to carrying out research with a sample of children and to present illustrative examples of the analysis and interpretation. For full details of the research see Majors (2013) and (2009).

Children's perceptions of their imaginary friends and the purposes they serve: Rationale for using IPA and procedure

Several studies show that imaginary friends or imaginary companions are more prevalent in school-aged children than previously thought, although they may be unknown to others (Hoff, 2004–2005, 2005; Pearson et al., 2001). Pearson et al., in a study of 1800 school-aged children in the UK, found that 46 per cent reported experiences of imaginary friends and that they were not just a phenomenon of very young children. In this study, 19 per cent of 10-year-olds and 9 per cent of 12 year olds reported current imaginary companions. This finding opened up new possibilities for researching the phenomenon: school-aged children would be able to talk about their experiences of their imaginary companions and to express their views about them. Further, when reports of children's imaginary companions have been sought in research, the tradition has been to focus on the one main or most important imaginary companion, where the child has more than one imaginary companion. This study aimed for an in-depth exploration of children's perceptions of the range of imaginary friends they had, and necessitated a small sample of re-search participants. IPA was selected rather than other qualitative approaches, such as content analysis or discourse analysis, which do not attempt to explore human thought and perceptions of experience (Smith, 1996). The second author of this chapter posed two exploratory research questions in her research:

- What are the characteristics of children's imaginary companions?
- What purposes do imaginary companions serve for children?

It was expected that what was learned from the study would help our understanding of, and response to, the children who create them.

A pilot study revealed that children were happy to talk about their current im-aginary friends as they saw them as important and special. In contrast, children in the pilot study with previous imaginary friends showed much less interest in talking about them and some had difficulty recalling their interactions with them. Thus, criteria for selecting research participants for the main study included that they had current imaginary friends and were happy to talk about them. The research participants for the main study were eight children aged between 5–11 years (five girls and three boys) with current imaginary friends. The semi-structured interview is the primary research method used in IPA (Smith and Eatough, 2006) and was the main method used in this study.

Each child was asked about characteristics of the imaginary friend(s) and their interactions with them. They were invited to draw pictures of their imaginary friends and comment on any likes and dislikes about their imaginary friends and whether others knew about them. The children appeared to enjoy the opportunity to talk about their imaginary companions, which may be partly because the interview pro-vided validation of their experiences and of the importance of their imaginary com-panions. For the older children this was in contrast to their usual experience of keeping their imaginary friends concealed from others in anticipation of ridicule and/or disapproval.

Analysis and interpretation

Each interview was taped and transcribed. Analysis in IPA is an iterative and induc-tive cycle which includes close line-by-line analysis noting descriptive content but also noting language used and conceptual comments. The latter refers to a shift away from explicit claims of the research participant to attend to the participants' understanding of themselves and their situation (Smith et al., 2009). Themes, cluster themes and corresponding quotes were then grouped together to form a summary table for each participant, so that themes could be traced directly to what the research participant had said (Smith et al., 2009). Individual summary tables were then combined to form a summary table for all participants. IPA aims for a nuanced analysis, where the researcher is attempting to make sense of the participants making sense of their experience (Smith, 2011a). For the purposes of this chapter, rather than summarising main themes and sub-themes, aspects of the analysis and interpretation relating to two themes and the children's sense-making are presented together with examples of how themes have been related to theory and research to further develop understanding of the phenomenon. The children's names have been changed, though the names of the imaginary friends have been retained.

Theme 1: Children's feelings about their imaginary companions

All children felt that their imaginary friends were important and special and were able to say why. Harry, Lisa and Carmel felt that their imaginary companions were very important. Harry said this was because *Manager* guards the club. Harry, age 6, has a private club of which only he and his imaginary companions are members, and they 'are the only people who know how to come in.' Throughout the interview Harry talked about the clubhouse where all the imaginary companions and he met, reiterating that they guarded it and no one else could get in. It is possible that this private world provides a temporary retreat from the world and other people.

Carmel, age 10, said that her imaginary companions were very important and told me: 'yes, they're like family. I don't know what I could do without them if they weren't there.' Antonio, age 5, distinguished between his imaginary companions, saying that Britten was important because he was a playmate, but *Ridey* was not important because he was naughty: Antonio claimed not to like him. Britten is described as age 12; he wears smart clothes and rides a motorbike and 'is always good'. He was an important playmate for Antonio, who was an only child. This suggests to the second author that Ridey did also have significance as an imaginary companion and served a useful purpose. The second author's interpretation here is that there is a part of Antonio that wants to be grown up and well behaved, and which has a desire to comply with parental authority and to show increasing maturity. Britten serves here as a role model of how to think and behave. This aspect of Antonio would claim, as Antonio does, that Ridey is not important to him. However, there seems to be another side to Antonio that sometimes wishes to escape from being good and being compliant, such as by being naughty and rude instead. Ridey's characteristics and interactions with Antonio allow him to experience/express this vicariously. For example, it is Ridey saying rude names, not Antonio; it is Ridey that gets told off by parents, not Antonio. Antonio's claims not to like Ridey and that 'he is not important at all' are not entirely convincing. There is a sense of fun and freedom from control (hiding) that comes across in this quote:

Karen: Do you like him (Ridey) when he's naughty?
Antonio: No because when he's naughty and then when we'll both be naughty and we just laugh, we squiggle, we hide.

Theme 2: Child perceive imaginary friends meet their needs
The second author was particularly interested to see whether any of the children in the study were aware of, and could describe how, their imaginary companions met their needs – one of the main aims of the research being to find out what purposes may be served for children with imaginary companions, the children's own perceptions on this would therefore be illuminating.

There were five sub-themes, corresponding to functions fulfilled by imaginary friends:

- a friend to play with and talk to;
- provide entertainment/prevent boredom/overcome loneliness;
- support for problems;
- express upset feelings; and
- wish fulfilment.

Friend to play with and talk to (eight participants)
Imaginary friends for all children provided a companion to play with and talk too. Carmel, aged 10, on imaginary twin boys, Tinton and Dubbish, said 'They sit either under the pillow or on the duvet and I make a little cage for them, little dens and we play and talk sometimes.' Holly, age 11, describing her imaginary friend Dream, a horse, said 'I play this game with my friend, um we had this walk and we got lost in the forest and I used her for that and I used her for a lot of games as well'.

The second author was interested to learn that the imaginary friends of the older children were mostly not known to others. Children had contact with them when alone, or sometimes the imaginary friend was partially concealed in games with others. So, as with the case of Holly above, the game with others involves imaginary horses, though the other children didn't know that Holly's horses were also her imaginary friends.

Provide entertainment/prevent boredom or loneliness (six participants)
Six children spoke of how their imaginary friends protected them from boredom and loneliness. Ella, describing her imaginary friend Polly, said: 'Sometimes she makes me laugh and if I get bored at home – cos I've only got little siblings'.

Support for problems (six participants)
It was noted by Harry's mother and teaching staff that Harry initially had a problem with swimming lessons. Harry, age 6, seemed to have consciously created imaginary friend Ducky, a duck, when he was having difficulty with swimming lessons: 'I was swimming a width and then I thought I would do another one with my imaginary friend and I did and I needed it to be a swimming one so I chose a duck.' When asked to explain how Ducky helped him swim, he explained: 'When he tells me lots of things that have nothing to do with me even, and then that's the thing that helps me do it.'

Here the imaginary friend seemed to help the child by distraction, a self-soothing strategy. This appeared to be successful; Harry and his mother said that swimming was no longer a problem and Harry told the researcher that Ducky was mostly working at another pool.

Another indication that the imaginary friends were a source of support at times of difficulty was when Tara, age 11, was asked how she would feel if she didn't have imaginary friends. She commented:

> I don't think I'd mind really, because I wouldn't know that they ever really existed. So it wouldn't make much difference to me. I mean obviously when I was like, I mean that if the house was pitch black and I was going out every night or something, then obviously I might get a bit more scared. But um if I didn't have these imaginary horses then I'd probably have um other ones.

When asked how her imaginary horses helped her when she was scared at night she replied, 'Cos it's someone to be with you in the dark'.

There is an element of contradiction here, with Tara appearing to claim that her current imaginary friends were replaceable, suggesting that they were less important and also suggesting the power and control she has over them. Simultaneously, Tara's vulnerabilities are exposed; her childlike fears of the dark provide the driving force and need to conjure up other imaginary friends as a coping strategy to reduce anxiety.

Express upset feelings (six participants)

John, age 8, had pillow fights with imaginary friend Tom, a teenager who is similar to John: 'It makes letting my anger off but also I'm playing a bit of a game… It takes my anger out without actually hurting someone.' It was interesting to note that at the beginning of the interview with John about his imaginary companion Tom, his brother Carl commented 'I think Tom's an anger let-out.' John replied 'No, sometimes he can be friendly'. Later on in the interview, John said: 'Tom's not an imaginary human punchbag. He's friends.'

Tom had a fiery temper (as well as being a friend) – this was perhaps a projection of John's hidden angry feelings. John used his imaginary friend to release anger. Significantly, this anger and upset was not apparent to others. John's mother described him as easygoing and his school report commented that he had a large group of friends and was well liked and respected.

Wish fulfilment (six participants)

Some imaginary friends appeared to serve the purpose of wish fulfilment. Thus Holly, age 11, commented on her previous imaginary companion: twin Lily:

> I already had my imaginary twin because I didn't (have) an imaginary friend – I mean I thought – I already have friends – why do I need an imaginary friend, so I thought imaginary twin – I always wanted a twin… do everything with them… be exactly like you and so it was kind of something I could have.

Tara, age 11, has imaginary ponies *Fantasia* and *Tom*:

> But if like um you don't have an animal then it's like you can see why and you want an animal. Like I'm desperate to get an animal.

It is clear that the children's imaginary companions were significant to them. The second author suggests that this was because they served a range of important purposes for the children, including as a pleasurable retreat, dependable companions, wish fulfilment, entertainment and play. These situations provided a context where children could also express and explore feelings about themselves and issues that were important to them if needed, and seek support for problems and fears.

Dialogue with theory and research
IPA draws upon psychological theory and research in the interpretation of themes and to substantiate claims made: most of the children had a range of imaginary friends, with different characteristics and, the second author has argued, with a range of purposes being served. All children identified friend and playmate as a main purpose being served. This has been found in other research (e.g. Gleason et al., 2000; Kalyan-Masih, 1986; Manosevitz et al., 1973).

Harris (2000) is a British developmental psychologist who has been a pioneer in theory and research on childhood imagination. He conceptualises 'sustained role-play' as a form of high-level imagination facilitating emotional, social and cognitive growth in children. He theorises that through sustained role-play, children imagine different possibilities which ultimately lead to a developed concept of reality. Harris includes interactions with imaginary companions as one of three forms of sustained role play, the other two being impersonation, where a child takes on the character of another person for an extended period and personification, where a child has a relationship with a special toy, which becomes imbued with a personality.

Some children in the study drew on the imaginary friends for help with problem solving and support when there were difficulties in their lives. Contact with imaginary friends sometimes served as a welcome distraction and enabled the child to self-sooth and reduce anger or fear. Various psychologists and researchers have drawn on Winnicott's theorising on transitional phenomena to develop our understanding of the underlying mechanisms. Thus, Esplen and Garfinkel (1998) refer to the psychodynamic concept of self-soothing, which has its roots in Winnicott's (1971) notions of transitional phenomena. They suggest that imaginary friends serve the purpose of an intermediate object for older children. They can provide the self-soothing purposes of helping children overcome feelings of aloneness and anxiety, promoting self-development. Similarly Sugarman and Jaffe (1989), building on Winnicott's work, conceptualise the imaginary companion as a form of transitional phenomenon that enables children to reduce anxieties and emotional conflict and thus to cope with the numerous developmental transitions in child, adolescent and adult life.

These are examples of the psychological theory and research that were drawn upon to interpret the themes identified in this study, and to substantiate the claim that the children's imaginary companions served useful purposes and were a positive feature in the children's lives. The second author concludes that children's capacities for sustained imagination can be viewed as a strength.

Summary
The contribution of this study is that it has investigated the range and characteristics of imaginary friends that the children had had over time, how they interacted with them and how these interactions sometimes related to events in their lives. It enabled

the exploration of children's perceptions and feelings towards their various imaginary friends. These features have supported the identification of some of the purposes served by imaginary friends and shed light on how the children's interactions with imaginary friends seemed to meet their various needs. The detailed exploration of a small sample employing appropriate methodology, in this case IPA, has enabled the systematic analysis of both the similarities and distinctiveness of imaginary friends. This investigation might have been compromised by the search for general themes in a larger population. Further research may well reveal other purposes. Nevertheless, it is anticipated that this analysis will be of use to child practitioners and researchers in coming to an understanding of some of the purposes served by a child's imaginary friends.

Supervision: Time to think!

It is important to access appropriate supervision with IPA (see Hefferon and Gil-Rodriguez, 2011, for a discussion of related issues). The supervisor can provide feedback on the interview transcripts and the IPA analysis to confirm their agreement that the identification and categorisation of themes presents a plausible analysis. This strategy provides a 'credibility check', which is one of seven guidelines set out by Elliott et al. (1999) for evaluating the quality of qualitative research. For the novice IPA researcher there is a need to go beyond description to more interpretative levels and supervision is part of the process for developing this. Similarly, supervision from an experienced GT researcher is essential to ensure that all aspects of the method are understood and applied. Unlike IPA, there is a much smaller, dispersed community of GT practitioners; the danger here is that the methodology, which is designed to develop new theories using an abductive analysis over time, is misunderstood, rushed and used inappropriately.

This chapter has considered and illustrated IPA and GT, two of the 'Big Q' methodologies most commonly used by psychologists and sociologists (Willig, 2001, op. cit.). They share common ontological stances, under the wider narrative umbrella, with a commitment to social constructionism. They are both complex and systematic qualitative approaches which are ideal tools to explore the perspectives of individual children and young people. We hope that the readers have gained a sense of the subtle, nuanced differences in the two methodologies, whilst also hearing the specific accounts from particular children and young people that have illustrated their powerful, fascinating and informative perspectives.

References

Alderson, P. & Morrow, V. (2004). *Ethics, social research and consulting with children and young people.* Essex: Barnardo's.

Billington, T. and Todd, L. (2012). Narrative: Approaches in research and professional practice. *Educational and Child Psychology, 29*(2), 5–9.

Bhaskar, R. (1978). A realist theory of science. Brighton: Harvester Press. Brooks, J. (2015) Learning from the 'lifeworld'. *The Psychologist, 28*(8), 642–646.

Charmaz, K. (2006). *Constructing grounded theory. A practical guide through qualitative analysis.* London: Sage.

Cresswell, J.W. (1998). *Qualitative inquiry and research design: Choosing among five traditions.* London: Sage.

Crotty, M. (1998). *The foundations of social research. Meaning and perspective in the research process.* London: Sage.

Dean, S., Smith, J.A., Weinman, J. & Payne, S. (2005). Managing time: An interpretative phenomenological analysis of patients' and physiotherapists' perceptions of adherence to therapeutic exercise for low back pain. *Disability and Rehabilitation, 27,* 265–73.

Denzin, N. & Lincoln, Y. (2000). (Eds.) *Handbook of qualitative research.* London: Sage.

Doutre, G., Green R. & Knight-Elliott, A. (2013). Listening to the voices of young carers using interpretative phenomenological analysis and a strengths-based perspective. *Educational and Child Psychology, 30*(4), 30–43.

Eatough, V. & Smith, J.A. (2006). I feel like a scrambled egg in my head: An idiographic case study of meaning making and anger using interpretative phenomenological analysis. *Psychology and Psychotherapy, 79*(1), 115–135.

Elliott, R., Fischer, C.T. & Rennie, D.L. (1999). Evolving guidelines for publication of qualitative research studies in psychology and related fields. *British Journal of Clinical Psychology, 38,* 215–229.

Esplen, M. & Garfinkel, P. (1988). Guided imagery treatment to promote self-soothing in bulimia nervosa: A theoretical rationale. *Journal of Psychotherapy Practice and Research, 7,* 102–118.

Giorgi, A. (1971). Phenomenology and experimental psychology: I. In A. Giorgi, W. Fischer, & R. von Eckartsberg (Eds.) *Duquesne Studies in Phenomenological Psychology: Vol. 1* (p.9). Pittsburgh, PA: Duquesne University Press.

Giorgi, A. (1975). An application of phenomenological method in psychology. In A. Giorgi, C. Fischer and E. Murray (Eds.) *Duquesne Studies in Phenomenological Psychology, Vol. 2* (pp.82–103). Pittsburgh, PA: Duquesne University Press.

Gleason, T., Sebanc, A. & Hartup. W. (2000). Imaginary friends of pre-school children. *Developmental Psychology, 36,* 419–428.

Greene, S. & Hogan, D. (Eds.) (2005). *Researching children's experience: Approaches and methods.* London: Sage.

Greig, A. ,Taylor, J., & Mackay, T. (2013) *Doing Research with Young Children. A practical guide.* (3rd edn.) London: Sage. Harris, P. (2000) The work of the imagination. Oxford: Blackwell.

Hardy, J. (2010) The development of a sense of identity in deaf adolescents in mainstream schools. *Educational and Child Psychology 27*(2), 58–67.

Hefferon, K. & Gil-Rodriguez, E. (2011). Interpretative phenomenological analysis. *The Psychologist, 24*(10), 756–759.

Heidegger, M. (1962). *Being and time* (J. Macquarrie & E. Robinson, Trans). Oxford: Blackwell. (Original work published 1927).

Henwood, K.L. (1996). Qualitative inquiry: Perspectives, methods and psychology. In J.T.E. Richardson (1996). *Handbook of qualitative research methods for psychology and the social sciences.* Leicester: BPS.

Hoff, E. (2004–2005). A friend living inside me: The forms and functions of imaginary companions. *Imagination, Cognition and Personality, 24,* 151–69.

Hoff, E. (2005). Imaginary companions, creativity, and self-image in middle childhood. *Creativity Research Journal, 17,* 167–180.

Houston, S. (2001). Beyond social constructionism: Critical realism and social work. *British Journal of Social Work, 31,* 845–861.

Hutchinson, S. (1988). Education and grounded theory. In R.R. Sherman and R.B. Webb (Eds.) *Qualitative research in education: Focus and methods* (pp.123–140). London: Falmer.

Kalyan-Masih, V. (1986). Imaginary play companions: Characteristics and functions. *International Journal of Early Childhood, 18,* 30–40.

Kellet, M. & Ding, S. (2005). Middle childhood. In L. Fraser, V. Lewis, S. Ding & M. Kellet (Eds.) *Doing research with children and young people.* London: Sage.

Kelly, B. (2008) Frameworks for practice in educational psychology: Coherent perspectives for a developing profession. In B. Kelly, L.Woolfson and J. Boyle (Eds.) *Frameworks for practice in educational psychology: A textbook for trainees and practitioners* (pp.15–30). London: Jessica Kingsley Publications.

Langdridge, D. (2007). *Phenomenological psychology: Theory, research and method.* Harlow: Pearson Education.

Lewis, V. and Miller, A. (2011). Institutional talk in the discourse between an educational psychologist and a parent: A single case study employing mixed research methods. *Educational Psychology in Practice, 27*(3), 195–212.

Majors, K. (2009). *Children's imaginary companions and the purposes they serve: An interpretative phenomenological analysis.* Unpublished doctoral thesis, Institute of Education, University of London.

Majors, K. (2013) Children's perceptions of their imaginary companions and the purposes they serve: An exploratory study in the United Kingdom. *Childhood, 20*(4), 550–565.

Manosevitz, M., Prentice, N. and Wilson, F. (1973). Individual and family correlates of imaginary friends in pre-school children. *Developmental Psychology, 8,* 72–79.

Matthews, J. (2003). A framework for the creation of practitioner-based evidence. *Educational and Child Psychology, 20*(4), 60–67

Matthews, J. (2010). Realist consultation. *DECP Debate. No. 134,* pp.14–19.

Miles, M. & Huberman, A. (1994). *Qualitative data analysis: An expanded sourcebook.* London: Sage.

Mulveen, R. & Hepworth, J. (2006) An interpretative phenomenological analysis of participation in a pro-anorexia internet site and its relationship with disordered eating. *Journal of Health Psychology, 11,* 283–96.

Oliver, C. (2012). Critical realist grounded theory: A new approach for social work research. *British Journal of Social Work, 42,* 371–387.

Pawson, R. and Tilley, N. (1997). *Realistic evaluation.* London: Sage.

Pearson, D., Rouse, H., Doswell, S. et al. (2001). Prevalence of imaginary companions in a normal child population. *Child: Care, Health and Development, 27,* 13–22.

Reid, K., Flowers, P. & Larkin, M. (2005). Exploring lived experience. *The Psychologist, 18,* 20–23.

Robson, C. (2002) *Real world research: A resource for social scientists and practitioner-researchers.* Oxford: Blackwell.

Sayer, R.A. (2000) *Realism and social science.* London: Sage.

Smith, J.A. & Eatough, V. (2006) Interpretative phenomenological analysis. In G. Breakwell, S. Hammond, C. Fife-Schaw & J.A. Smith (Eds.) *Research methods in psychology.* London: Sage.

Smith, J.A., Flowers, P. & Larkin, M. (2009). *Interpretative phenomenological analysis: theory, method and research.* London: Sage.

Smith, J.A. & Osborn, M. (2003). Interpretative phenomenological analysis. In J. Smith (Ed.), *Qualitative psychology: A practical guide to research methods.* London: Sage.

Sugarman, A. and Jaffe, L. (1989). A developmental line of transitional phenomena. In M. Fromm and B Smith (Eds.) *The facilitating environment: Clinical applications of Winnicott's theory.* Madison, CT: International Universities Press.

Sugden, E.L. (2013). Looked-after children: What supports them to learn? *Educational Psychology in Practice, 29*(4), 367–382.

Yardley, L. (2000). Dilemmas in qualitative health research. *Psychology and Health, 15,* 215–228.

Willig, C. (2005) *Introducing qualitative research in psychology: Adventures in theory and method.* Maidenhead: Open University Press.

Winnicott, D. (1971). *Playing and reality.* London: Tavistock Publications.

Chapter 3 The history of research by educational psychologists into ascertaining the voice of the child and young person

Irvine Gersch, Anna Lipscomb & Anita Potton

Introduction and definitions

Listening to children is a key function for educational psychologists (EPs) and many have found various ways of doing this. Importantly they have helped others, such as teachers and parents, to do the same. This chapter aims to discuss the history of research and practice conducted by EPs concerning the voice of children and young people (CYP). Historically, there has been a view in education – and indeed more widely – that children 'should be seen and not heard'. Therefore EPs have had a social and cultural barrier to overcome when trying to promote the importance of listening to and respecting the child's voice. The first author remembers working as an EP some twenty years ago and reporting the child's view of certain events to a head teacher (of the old-fashioned disposition), who admonished him, saying 'that's the trouble with you EPs – you just believe what the child tells you'. He went on to say that the child's version should be treated with a pinch of salt! We hope we have travelled a long way from that attitude.

This chapter will commence with a definition of what we would argue counts as research, particularly qualitative. Our key thesis is that EPs have contributed positively to developments in listening to CYP in their everyday work, and in the development of resources that may also be used by others. Such activity has involved direct work with children as well as the promotion of this work, through, for example, training, consultation and interaction with other professionals. That said, the breadth and depth of the published research literature is relatively slight and perhaps understates both the actual work accomplished and its impact. It should also be noted that EPs have not been the only professionals to undertake such work, and credit must be given to the work of social workers, teachers and specialist therapists. This review, however, will be limited to published work and projects by EPs that indicate the tools and techniques that have been developed. We will review some key principles, dilemmas and challenges faced by EPs in promoting the voice of the child and then attempt to assess and evaluate their actual contribution to this field.

The history of research into the voice of CYP can be depicted as having three distinct stages as follows:
1. Observation/testing: children being seen, tested and observed, but in a passive way.
2. Listening with higher regard: listening and trying to understand the child's viewpoint and perspectives, respecting and learning, with the adult deciding upon actions.

3. Empowerment: taking the child's voice seriously and considering acting upon what the child says, if possible, wherever practicable and in the child's interest; the aim is to interpret, empower and translate the child's voice into direct and specific actions and plans.

It is also useful to construe listening to CYP as taking place along a continuum or dial from 'low' to 'high', such that one can listen 'a little' or 'a lot' to the voice of the CYP, and perhaps calibrate one's choice depending upon the child's needs and their level of maturity and ability, as elaborated by Gersch (1992).

Research is defined by the New Oxford Dictionary of English as 'the systematic investigation into and study of materials and sources in order to establish facts and reach new conclusions'. Mertens (2010) notes that research is conducted for many reasons, including understanding, describing, predicting, controlling and empowering others. Much of research conducted by EPs is of an 'applied' or 'real-world' type. This, according to Robson (2011), refers to 'applied research projects which are typically small in scale and modest in scope. They tend to be related to change and/or policy, often seeking to evaluate some initiative, service or whatever' (p.3). In contrast, more pure or academic research may be driven by the testing of theories.

Arguably, all work that EPs undertake with children, whether clinical or consultative, is part of their 'research' in the broadest terms, even though frequently conducted in an ad hoc manner in a natural problem-solving environment. Data collection is thus not always conducted in a scientifically controlled and rigorous way, and not necessarily exposed to stringent analysis. This information nevertheless provides a valuable knowledge base and backdrop, and historically has played a key part in the development of tools and techniques for listening to children. Indeed, the importance of such individual case-work study has been expounded and its importance demonstrated by Ravenette (1999), who utilised a Personal Construct approach. Ravenette has certainly made a significant and seminal contribution to the development of techniques for eliciting the child's views.

It is useful to note that EPs work at several levels with children and young people. They work directly with the CYP, consult with relevant adults (e.g. teachers, parents and other professionals), work with small groups of CYP, carry out interventions, and in addition offer systemic or organisational advice to schools and other organisations. They conduct research and contribute to local and national policy. These different roles carry with them opportunities for EPs to promote the voice of the child by using different methods. It is clearly important to apply different but relevant methods to fit the purpose of the work, but also to include children's views and ideas in all work, at all levels and types, and in all project development.

The general historical context: A brief pen picture

In order to place the work of EPs in respect of listening to CYP in context, it is helpful to at least briefly signpost some key developments in educational psychology generally. Key landmarks in the UK were perhaps the 1870 and 1944 Education Acts, which enabled universal and free education for all children but consequently led to assessments of those not able to progress, special schooling and thus EP involvement with children with special needs.

Pioneering work was carried out by the first EPs, led by Sir Cyril Burt, who was appointed to a part-time role by the London County Council in 1913. The focus was on psychometric testing, classification and the development of Child Guidance Clinics. Burt outlined his role in a speech to the Association of Educational Psychologists in 1964 as reporting on problem cases referred by teachers, doctors and magistrates for individual investigation, and assessing CYP with disabilities (for example those unable to read, spell, or learn arithmetic, or who had memory problems), gifted children, those who experienced emotional difficulties, and young people who were described then as maladjusted and/or delinquent. (As an aside, reading the transcripts of the time, it is startling to see how far the terminology used to describe special needs has changed in the past fifty years, and how negative some of the terms seem now). Burt stressed the importance of devoting 50 per cent of his time to clinical work, with the other 50 per cent committed to research (Rushton, 2002).

The Summerfield Report (DES, 1968) was the first to examine the role of EPs and to emphasise the need to apply psychology in order to support children and to increase the number of EPs. At the time of that report the number of EPs in the UK stood at about 400. By 2014 the number of EPs had grown to about 2,000, which represents a significant and steady increase over the past 50 years (Truong & Ellam, 2014).

By the 1970s the child's views were being sought directly and there was an interest by some, particularly Dr Tom Ravenette, in developing Personal Construct Theory (Kelly, 1955) and related techniques to gain an in-depth understanding of children's attitudes and core constructs. The first author, who was one of his students in those early days, noted that when Ravenette was at a large conference, the question posed of him by the chairperson about the child was not *'what is the child's IQ?'*, as it had been historically, but rather *'how does the child see things?'* Ravenette explained that he had spent time and energy educating other colleagues, services and schools in order to change the question they posed to the EP, and in so doing, had re-aligned and re-defined his role and what was expected of him.

The 1981 Education Act outlined a direct and prescribed role for EPs but was viewed by many as tying up much time in the assessment of children with special educational needs with a view to providing reports for Statements of Special Educational Needs. The child's views were meant to be included, and thus some EPs – as was the case with the first author – aimed to include such views directly and emphatically (Gersch & Holgate, 1991; Gersch et al., 1993). This emphasis on including the perspective of CYP has been even further strengthened in the Children and Families Act 2014 and the move from Statements to Education, Health and Care (EHC) Plans.

The widening of the role was depicted in further reports such as that of the Department for Education and Employment (DfEE, 2000) and the Farrell Report (Farrell et al., 2006) together with the Every Child Matters initiative (Department for Education and Skills [DfES], 2004), which all depicted evidence of EPs working with children in creative ways and developing ways of listening to them, and in particular to their emotional responses, for example in circle time, group work, systemic work and work on bullying.

A final development worth noting concerns the changes to the training format for EPs, which was initially six months, then a year, and finally became a three-year doctorate in 2001. This development gave the opportunity for an extended doctoral level thesis and research project that has enhanced EPs' confidence and skills in the whole area of research, with increased interest and skills in qualitative research. This approach has over the past twenty years gained significantly in academic respectability and popularity in educational psychology.

How attitudes and practice have changed over the years for EPs

The changes in the role of the EP are reflected by a gradual shift that can be traced through the legislative, political and educational movements over the past hundred years. Trends within EP practice have fluctuated over the years to emphasise the voices of different stakeholders. It has been argued that the role of early EPs was to identify and assess IQ for the purpose of allowing medical and educational professionals to categorise and label CYP (Farrell, 2009). The voice of the child was largely lost within this system where the emphasis was on promoting the agendas of adults. In an attempt to counteract this 'medical model' of disability, the consultation movement acknowledged that problems did not necessarily lie with the child but that emphasis should be on working with key adults in the child's life and the systems within which they operate (Wagner, 2000). However, this approach in its truest form also minimises the voice of CYP. More recently, renewed emphasis on directly seeking the views of CYP has resulted in a triangulation of approaches whereby more person-centred consultation methods are promoted. This central principle is promoted in the Children and Families Act 2014.

The changes in both the political and professional contexts then precipitated change in professional training routes. Promoting core skills in assessment work and concentrating on eliciting the views of CYP, conducting consultation and carrying out systemic practice are now all integral parts of EP training. In addition these are underpinned by a strong commitment to evidence-based practice and promoting research at a doctoral level. Much of this valuable and insightful practice-led research is not reflected in the published literature and therefore, although essential for the good practice of EPs, it is largely invisible within the wider literature on listening to children. The following literature review outlines the contribution from British EPs to ascertaining the voice of CYP. Although we acknowledge that this may not represent the full breadth of practice, the review will focus on qualitative contributions. It is acknowledged, however, that quantitative research also has a role to play.

Method for literature review

The literature review sought to identify research and practice by EPs in the UK that relates to listening to the voice of the child. A comprehensive search was performed of the following online databases: PsycARTICLES, PsycINFO, Academic Search Complete, Education Research Complete, Teacher Reference Center, CINAHL Plus, Communication & Mass Media Complete, Information Science & Technology Abstracts, Ingenta Connect, Wiley online library, Taylor & Francis online, Science Direct, Web of Science, Google Scholar. An initial search filter was set to 'educational psychology and listening or voice and children' but produced few results. The following keywords were then used in all possible combinations and without time limiters: education* psych*, young people, listening to children, children's views, voice of children, children's perspectives, participation, empowering, consulting, research. References of retrieved papers were scanned for relevant sources. Separate manual searches were conducted in the *British Journal of Educational Psychology*, *Journal of Educational Psychology, Educational & Child Psychology, Issues in Education, International Journal of Educational Psychology*, and *Educational Psychology*. In addition, all programme directors in Educational Psychology in the UK were contacted for information on published or unpublished projects and practices.

The development of tools and techniques for listening to CYP and more general research by EPs on the voice of the child

The importance of listening to children has been widely advocated by EPs from the 1960s and appears more directly in published work since the 1980s (e.g. Gersch, 1987, 1990, 1992, 1996, 2001; Gersch et al., 1996; Greig et al., 2014; Harding & Atkinson, 2009; Hobbs et al., 2000; Ravenette, 1999; Roller, 1998). The first author has argued that there are moral, legal and pragmatic reasons for involving children as fully as possible in assessment and education (Gersch, 1987, 1992, 2001). Direct work with children, though less frequently the subject of published articles, involves EPs in interviewing CYP, casework and reporting the views of children to other significant adults such as teachers and parents. Hobbs et al. (2000) provided a list of techniques that include interview approaches, letters to children, information about the EP role, the application of Personal Construct Psychology, solution-focused approaches in developing individual plans, videoing children's views about school, and students completing statutory advice appendices, with help if needed.

Two important, comprehensive books specific to EP practice in the UK that lead the field are Personal Construct Theory in Educational Psychology: A practitioner's view, by Tom Ravenette, and Educational Psychology Casework, by Rick Beaver. Ravenette, the first EP in the UK to apply the work of Kelly's (1955) Personal Construct Theory to children, outlines many techniques for use and, more importantly, his approach to this work. Ravenette describes the casework use of stories, metaphors, drawings, attitude interviewing, asking the child 'who are you?' and many other methods, which he argues can only be seen as a whole. In 1974, as a trainee EP, the first author had the privilege to work with Tom Ravenette in Newham, East London, and heard him emphasise that of all possible tools, the most important was the question. Ravenette was then a prime force in ensuring that EPs ask the right questions in order to help understand and empower children.

In the first edition of his excellent book based upon the work of Ravenette, Beaver (1996) provided a detailed practical guide for EP casework, demonstrating all the techniques, methods and ideas that EPs can and do use to elicit the views, ideas, thoughts and feelings of CYP. Included are techniques such as semi-structured drawings, talking exercises, family drawings, the use of opposites, three comments others would say about you, school situation cards, self-descriptive grids and many more.

Other work reported by EPs includes the use of computer-assisted interviewing to enhance communication (Barrett et al., 2011; Barrow & Hannah, 2012), the use of narrative analysis whereby children's detailed accounts are analysed carefully to enhance understanding (Hobbs et al., 2012) and the creative use of 'forum theatre', in which children create and discuss a performance of sensitive topics of importance to them as a method to facilitate communication (Hammond, 2012). Hobbs et al.

(2012) also mentioned use of video interactive techniques (Kennedy et al., 2010) as a useful method for discussions with children about their interactions. In a creative technique they describe as 'photo elicitation', Hill (2014) invited students with Autistic Spectrum Disorder (ASD) to take photographs of their school life and to discuss these.

Kittles and Atkinson (2009) consider motivational interviewing as developed by McNamara (1992, 1998), while Lubel and Greaves (2000) describe the development of an Educational Psychology Service (EPS) Information Booklet to ensure that children are carefully prepared for their meeting with an EP. This is particularly important in light of the findings reported by Armstrong and colleagues (1993) that children may have erroneous ideas about the EP role, and may not be clear about the whole process of assessment. Jelly et al. (2000) described an extensive project involving pupils in their education in Essex, listing ways of involving them specifically in negotiating personal learning targets, individual education plans, reviews, and seeking their views to influence school development. This project involved an EP working with head teachers and the LA as part of a team. EPs thus actively explore diverse ways of capturing children's views and experiences.

The first author of this chapter, as an EP in the London Borough of Waltham Forest, worked with colleagues between 1980 and 2000 on developing tools for increasing the involvement of CYP in assessment and supporting their voices to be heard. The Child's Report (Gersch, 1987; Gersch & Cutting, 1985), developed to allow CYP in care to record their views directly, was used regularly in a Social Services Observation and Assessment Centre and found to be of use to adults and throughout the entire assessment process. This led to a series of Student Reports, for use by children being assessed by EPs, which were updated and modified by the views of children on the report formats. The reports were evaluated over time and generally found to be useful and enjoyable, and were valued by both adults and children (Gersch, 1992; Gersch & Holgate, 1991; 1994; Gersch et al., 1993; Gersch et al., 1996; Gersch, 1996). This report was further extended to include an Excluded Student Report (Gersch & Nolan, 1994). All these projects are summarised in Gersch (2001). Similar work that reflects the importance of enabling children to record their views has been described by Harding and Atkinson (2009), while Mainwaring and Hallam (2010) used a novel method, called 'Possible Selves', employing semi-structured interviews and guided questions to assess children's motivations and aspirations for the future.

In systems work, children have been engaged in school systems projects and policy development. In one secondary school, for example, CYP offered their views about school, the building, the curriculum, teaching and activities. As a result, student representatives were given a permanent place on the School Council (Gersch & Noble, 1991). Using a single case study, Hall (2010) reported work by an EPS which assisted school change in Nottinghamshire and facilitated the expression of children's views by using focus groups. Similarly, Williams and Hanke (2007) explored the views of children with ASD about school provision in Dudley, using Personal Construct Theory and drawing techniques.

In recent years, there has been an attempt to listen more deeply to the views of children through spiritual or philosophical listening, and the development of a tool entitled 'The Little Box of Big Questions' (Gersch et al., 2008; Gersch et al.,

2014; Gersch & Lipscomb, 2012, 2013; Lipscomb & Gersch, 2012). Similar work was reported by Ruddock and Cameron (2010).

More generally, EPs have conducted research on groups of CYP, aiming to ascertain their actual views and ideas. Various interview methodologies have been used; EPs have worked with children as researchers, carried out research with young children, undertaken research with CYP who are hard to reach and invited feedback about their own practice. EPs have thus used a number of interesting interviewing methodologies in an attempt to elicit children's views in the most valid and meaningful way. This has been especially evident when researching the views of CYP with ASD who find the social, communication and interpersonal aspects of traditional interviewing challenging (Barrow & Hannah, 2012; Hill, 2014; Winstone et al., 2014). Barrow and Hannah (2012) described using computer-assisted interview technologies to listen to children with ASD. They investigated CYP views about the help and support they needed, as well as their role in decision making.

Hill (2014) reported another method to elicit the views of CYP with ASD, in which 'photo elicitation' was used to promote the views of six secondary-age CYP with ASD across two mainstream schools. The researcher asked the CYP to take photographs of aspects of school that were important to them and this formed the basis of further discussions. By doing this, the researcher felt that the CYP's subjective meanings derived from the photographs drove the subsequent discussions and thereby shaped the research.

Winstone et al. (2014) took a different stance again when researching the views of CYP with ASD by using 'activity orientated' (AO) interviews. This was a comparative study within a special school population of boys aged 12–14 years. The authors concluded that AO interviews were more effective at eliciting CYP views and that the traditional interviews reinforced a deficit perception of ASD. The researchers felt that the focus should not be on what people cannot do but instead on participation along a continuum, adopting creative and individualised methods to elicit the most meaningful data.

Other researchers within the EP field have used creative methodological procedures to elicit the views of CYP without special educational needs and disability (SEND). McCallion and Trew (2012) carried out a one-year study with 104 children aged 5–9 years, focusing upon their hopes, dreams and aspirations for the future. The researchers developed an innovative and creative technique called a 'me tree' to allow the children to explore their hopes and fears for the future by putting different coloured leaves on their tree, which had branches for different aspects of life (e.g. school). A method used to gather the spiritual, philosophical and metaphysical ideas of children uses the 'Little Box of Big Questions', which was developed by the first two authors of this chapter and has been used in several research projects (Gersch et al., 2014; Lipscomb & Gersch, 2012).

The literature thus indicates the important part EPs have played in advocating working with children as researchers. Burton et al. (2010) discussed the role of EPs in working with teachers in order to conduct pupil-led research and argued that involving children in research has a number of social, cognitive and personal benefits for the children. Davies and Lewis (2013) described the use of an appreciative enquiry model with children acting as joint researchers. The first two authors of this chapter have reported working with children as an 'advisory group' to help with the evaluation and product development of the 'Little Box of Big Questions' (Gersch et al., 2014; Lipscomb & Gersch, 2012).

In an international project that included the UK, Canada and Australia, Yardley (2014) discussed the notion of empowerment that arose from conducting research with children. This project involved carrying out a series of workshops with children to support them in the development of their own research designs, methodological frameworks and analysis. The application of creative approaches such as drama, movement and intergenerational dialogues were used. Yardley argued that if children are fully empowered within the research process, the focus becomes less on adults trying to understand children's worlds and more the other way around. Some projects have drawn on the methodological approaches proposed by Clark (2003, 2005), called the 'mosaic approach'. Although this approach was not developed by EPs, its influence is notable within research by EPs who conduct research with young children. In a study with 36 children aged between 3 and 5, Gray and Winter (2011) used the mosaic approach to generate a 'toolkit' of data-gathering approaches aimed at enabling children to design and carry out their own research in their setting. This involved using a puppet to help the children to generate research questions and then offering selected methods such as interviews, photographs, drawing and putting 'thumbs up' and 'thumbs down' signs on things in the setting to investigate the children's chosen topic. Day (2010) also adapted the mosaic approach to explore how children aged 20 months to 4 years experienced their sessions at children's centres. In order to piece together the children's views the researchers conducted full-day observations, interviews with parents and key workers, and direct work with children that included interviews, tours, photos and role play, and was tailored to children's individual skills and strengths.

EPs have also made contributions to research which aimed to elicit the views of other hard-to-reach groups of CYP, including those who are deemed to be disaffected (Hartas, 2011) and children not in education, employment or training (NEET) (Crichton & Hellier, 2009; Currie & Goodall, 2009). Hartas (2011) points out that many of the institutional methods for gathering pupils' views (e.g. school councils, student bulletins, etc.) only tap into one demographic and miss out the disaffected who choose not to contribute. Having gathered disaffected CYP's views (aged 13–15) through focus groups and individual interviews, Hartas argued that these children choose not to access such opportunities because they see them as irrelevant to their individual needs. As a result more informal and meaningful and less hierarchical methods for contributing their views are suggested. Both Crichton and Hellier (2009) and Currie and Goodall (2009) conducted research with NEET children in Scotland. These researchers used an action research model to gather the views of CYP who were NEET.

Harding and Atkinson (2009) investigated how EPs represent children's views in written reports. They used content analysis of Year 9 transition reports to determine key themes within the 'pupils' views' section. Focus group interviews were also carried out with EPs to explore the range of methods they used to capture children's views. Techniques from this study included discussion-based methods (e.g. direct questioning), task-related procedures (e.g. 'myself as a learner' scale), therapeutic approaches (e.g. personal construct psychology), and using measures specific to children in special schools.

Woolfson et al. (2006) describe a different model that includes consulting with children as well as key adults; they explore children's views about the process of consultation and the experience of being consulted. In four focus groups it emerged that children generally felt they should be involved as long as certain conditions were met. These conditions were that (a) consultations should be tailored towards their individual needs, (b) children should know all key adults present during the consultation, (c) children should be able to choose where consultations take place, and (d) the need for confidentiality was stressed.

This section has explored the trends and variety of methodologies that have been used by EPs to elicit the views of CYP. It has shown that EPs have made a significant contribution to research into the views of children, a group that historically has been underrepresented in the literature. The breadth of creative and child-centred research within the profession is inspiring, and it is reassuring to see the current trend towards celebrating and publishing work of this nature.

There is insufficient space in this chapter to do justice to all EP work, published and unpublished, undertaken in listening to children. This section therefore can only indicate examples of the scope and diversity of such work; the interested reader is encouraged to use the references at the end to explore the work in more detail. Furthermore, the March 2014 edition of the journal *Educational and Child Psychology* was devoted entirely to the topic of 'Empowering young people'. To conclude, then, the literature reveals a slow but steady progression in hearing the voice of CYP, and in increasing their participation in assessment, learning and school life generally; EPs have played a significant and positive part in this process.

Key principles, dilemmas and challenges for EPs

The previous section has indicated the significant contribution EPs have made to the area of listening to CYP. However, in considering this work, it would be remiss not to mention some of the principles and complexities that arise from research and work in this field. In terms of key principles, it is obviously paramount that any work respects and dignifies the voice of the child, that time and space is given to collecting such information properly, and that researchers and practitioners abide fully with the BPS Codes of Conduct that cover such matters as confidentially, anonymity, informed consent, parental consent and the use of data, whilst being alert to child protection issues and the best interests of CYP.

With regard to dilemmas and challenges, it is fair to say that listening to CYP and sharing their views, and – even more so – acting upon their views, is not value free. The messenger can be criticised, as in the anecdote mentioned in Section 1, for being gullible; parents and children may see things differently and indeed may have different views from teachers, professionals and other significant adults. The adults need to distinguish 'discussion with a child' from allowing the child completely free choice. Children need to learn how to put forward their views in a dignified and acceptable way. There may be many ways of seeing the same event and psychologists have needed to disentangle and make sense of the qualitative data. The EP role in the system needs to be carefully considered. Overall, the atmosphere and relationship must be appropriate and safe if children are to be encouraged to speak in a truly free and open way.

These complex ethical and professional issues have been considered in depth elsewhere (e.g. Gersch et al., 1996; Hobbs et al., 2000; Ingram, 2013) as part of a continuing debate. Importantly, listening should be linked to action, so that we don't just hear the voice of the child but rather, as professionals, jointly with the children themselves integrate and utilise their ideas and views in forming understandings and plans.

EP contribution: Commentary and critique

It might be argued that whilst the contributions of EPs to the UK-based qualitative literature on ascertaining the views of CYP has been significant, the published literature may not capture the full breadth and depth of practice that is carried out on a daily basis by EPs. However, the contribution that has been made to date may be summarised in three ways: use and promotions of key research methodologies; the development of key practical tools and techniques; and contributions to what the authors call the 'big ideas' within the field, for example the concepts of *empowerment, ethics* and *inclusion.*

With regard to the development of 'big ideas' in listening to CYP, EPs have clearly been engaged in debate and critical discussion of the roles of empowerment, ethics and inclusion. Earnshaw (2014) unpicked the ideas and assumptions around empowerment and argued that unless conversations are versatile, open and thoughtful, CYP will often not engage effectively. The ethical aspects of listening to CYP have also been scrutinised and discussed by EPs (e.g. Gray & Winter, 2011; Harding, 2009; Hartas, 2011). Issues such as obtaining consent and the limits of participation in respect of very young children, and those with disabilities, require careful thought. Further issues such as the context of the conversation have been given consideration. EPs have also contributed comprehensively to the inclusion debate, ensuring that the participation of CYP is a central theme (e.g. Lindsay, 2003).

Finally, it is worth noting that other disciplines and professionals (as well as EPs) can demonstrate examples of publications and work in the area of listening to children. The voice of the CYP has been the subject of study and development in the practice of social care workers, educationalists other than EPs, charities, social policy professionals and others involved in various psychotherapies, including creative arts therapies. It is outside the scope of this chapter to review that literature, but important to acknowledge the work that has been conducted by those professionals.

Conclusions

In summary, over the past hundred years the voices of children have been given greater attention and weight, and EPs have contributed positively to the research, practice, development of tools and techniques and, importantly, to the promotion of this advance. Their own work has progressed from observation and testing to more creative ways of interviewing, eliciting the child's views and thoughts, and to translating such views into action plans for children. EPs have to ensure that such plans are proportionate, useful, evidence-informed, workable and of course negotiated sensitively with relevant adults and other professionals.

We believe that EPs have made a special contribution to this field but that there is further to go (in depth and breadth) in developing deeper listening techniques and ensuring that all CYP are included to their highest levels of participation and empowerment.

Acknowledgements

We would like to thank Barbara Gersch for her invaluable, patient work in editing this chapter; all the children, young people, schools and teachers who have participated in our research; and colleagues, including the group of Programme Directors of training in educational psychology, for their ideas and suggestions. The views and ideas of the writers, however, remain their responsibility alone.

References

Armstrong, D., Galloway, D. & Tomlinson, S. (1993). Assessing special educational needs: The child's contribution. *British Educational Research Journal, 19*(2), 121–131. doi: 10.1080/0141192930190201

Barrett, W., Dent, J. & Rodgers, S. (2011). Using computer-assisted self-interviewing (CASI) systems to obtain the views of looked-after children: A pilot study. *Educational & Child Psychology, 28*(3), 81–88.

Barrow, W. & Hannah, E.F. (2012). Using computer-assisted interviewing to consult with children with autism spectrum disorders: An exploratory study. *School Psychology International, 33*(4), 450–464. doi: 10.1177/0143034311429167

Beaver, R. (1996). *Educational psychology casework: A practical guide.* London: Jessica Kingsley Publishers.

Clark, A., McQuail, S. & Moss, P. (2003). *Exploring the field of listening to and consulting with young children.* Thomas Coram Research Unit Research Report. London: DfES.

Clark, A. & Moss, P. (2005). *Spaces to play: More listening to young children using the Mosaic approach.* London: National Children's Bureau.

Crichton, R. & Hellier, C. (2009). Supporting action research by partners: Evaluating outcomes for vulnerable young people in negative post-school destinations. *Educational & Child Psychology, 26*(1), 76–83.

Currie, R. & Goodall, L. (2009). Using collaborative action research to identify and support young people at risk of becoming NEET. *Educational & Child Psychology, 26*(1), 67–75.

Davies, O. & Lewis, A. (2013). Children as researchers: An appreciative inquiry with primary-aged children to improve 'Talking and Listening' activities in their class. *Educational & Child Psychology, 30*(4), 59–74.

Day, S. (2010). Listening to young children: An investigation of children's day care experiences in Children's Centres. *Educational & Child Psychology, 27*(4), 45–55.

DES (1968). *Psychologists in Education Services: The report of a working party appointed by the Secretary of State for Education and Science: The Summerfield Report.* London: Author.

DfEE (2000). *Educational Psychology Services (England): Current role, good practice and future directions.* Report of the Working Group. London: Author.

DfES (2004). *Every Child Matters.* London: The Stationery Office.

Earnshaw, O. (2014). Learning to be a child: A conceptual analysis of youth empowerment. *Educational & Child Psychology, 31*(1), 13–21.

Farrell, P. (2009). The developing role of school and educational psychologists in supporting children, schools and families. *Papeles del Psicólogico, 30*(1), 74–85.

Farrell, P., Woods, K., Lewis, S. et al. (2006). *A Review of the functions and contribution of educational psychologists in England and Wales in light of 'Every child matters: Change for children'.* Nottingham: DfES Publications.

Gersch, I.S. (1987). Involving pupils in their own assessment. In T. Bowers (Ed.), *Special educational needs and human resource management.* London: Croom Helm.

Gersch, I.S. (1992). Pupil involvement in assessment. In T. Cline (Ed.) *The assessment of Special Educational Needs: International perspectives.* London: NFER Nelson.

Gersch, I.S. (1996). Involving children in assessment: Creating a listening ethos. *Educational and Child Psychology, 13*, 31–40.

Gersch, I.S., Dowling, F., Panagiotaki, G. & Potton, A. (2008). Listening to children's views of spiritual and metaphysical concepts: A new dimension to educational psychology practice? *Educational Psychology in Practice, 24*(3), 225–236. doi: 10.1080/02667360802256782

Gersch I.S. & Holgate, A. (1991). *The student report.* London: London Borough of Waltham Forest.

Gersch, I.S., Holgate, A. & Sigston, A. (1993). Valuing the child's perspective: A revised student report and other practical initiatives. *Educational Psychology in Practice, 9*(1), 36–45.

Gersch, I.S. & Lipscomb, A. (2012). *Little box of big questions: Philosophical conversations with children and young people.* Syresham, Northants: Small World.

Gersch, I.S. & Lipscomb, A. (2013). Listening to children's views about life's 'big questions': Is there a role for spiritual and philosophical questioning within educational psychology practice? *DECP Debate. No. 46,* pp.15–23.

Gersch, I.S., Lipscomb, A., Stoyles, G., & Caputi, P. (2014). Using philosophical and spiritual conversations with children and young people: A method for psychological assessment, listening deeply and empowerment. *Educational & Child Psychology, 31*(1), 32–47.

Gersch, I.S., Moyse, S., Nolan, A. & Pratt, G. (1996). Listening to children in educational contexts. In R. Davie, G. Upton & V. Varma (Eds.) *The voice of the child: A handbook for professionals* (pp.27–48). London: Falmer.

Gersch, I.S. & Noble, J. (1991). A systems project involving students and staff in a secondary school. *Educational Psychology in Practice, 7*(3), 140–147.

Gersch, I.S. & Nolan, A. (1994). Exclusions: What the pupils think. *Educational Psychology in Practice, 10*(1), 35–45.

Gersch, I.S., Pratt, G., Nolan, A. & Hooper, S. (1996). Listening to children in educational contexts. In R. Davie, G. Upton & V.P. Varma (Eds.) *The voice of the child: a handbook for professionals.* London: Falmer.

Gray, C. & Winter, E. (2011). Hearing voices: Participatory research with preschool children with and without disabilities. *European Early Childhood Education Research Journal, 19*(3), 309–320. doi: 10.1080/1350293x.2011.597963

Greig, A., Hobbs, C. & Roffey, S. (2014). Guest editorial: Empowering young people. *Educational & Child Psychology, 31*(1), 6–12.

Hall, S. (2010). Supporting mental health and wellbeing at a whole-school level: listening to and acting upon children's views. *Emotional & Behavioural Difficulties, 15*(4), 323–339. doi: 10.1080/13632752.2010.523234

Hammond, N. (2012). Introducing Forum Theatre to elicit and advocate children's views. *Educational Psychology in Practice, 29*(1), 1–18. doi: 10.1080/02667363.2012.733309

Harding, E. (2009). Obtaining the views of children with profound and multiple learning difficulties. *Educational & Child Psychology, 26*(4), 117–128.

Harding, E. & Atkinson, C. (2009). How EPs record the voice of the child. *Educational Psychology in Practice, 25*(2), 125–137. doi: 10.1080/02667360902905171

Hartas, D. (2011). Young people's participation: Is disaffection another way of having a voice? *Educational Psychology in Practice, 27*(2), 103–115. doi: 10.1080/02667363.2011.567088

Hill, L. (2014). 'Some of it I haven't told anybody else': Using photo elicitation to explore the experiences of secondary school education from the perspective of young people with a diagnosis of Autistic Spectrum Disorder. *Educational & Child Psychology, 31*(1), 79–89.

Hobbs, C., Durkin, R., Ellison, G. et al. (2012). The professional practice of educational psychologists: Developing narrative approaches. *Educational & Child Psychology, 29*(2), 41–52.

Hobbs, C., Todd, L. & Taylor, J. (2000). Consulting with children and young people: Enabling educational psychologists to work collaboratively. Educational and Child Psychology, 17(4), 107–115.

Ingram, R. (2013). Interpretation of children's views by educational psychologists: Dilemmas and solutions. *Educational Psychology in Practice, 29*(4), 335–346. doi: 10.1080/02667363.2013.841127

Jelly, M., Fuller, A. and Byers, R. (2000). *Involving pupils in practice: Promoting partnerships with pupils with special education needs.* London: David Fulton.

Kelly, G. (1955). *The psychology of personal constructs.* New York: Norton.

Kennedy, H., Landor, M. & Todd, L. (2010). *Video Interaction Guidance: A relationship-based intervention to promote attunement, empathy and well-being.* London: Jessica Kingsley.

Kittles, M. & Atkinson, C. (2009). The usefulness of motivational interviewing as a consultation and assessment tool for working with young people. *Pastoral Care in Education, 27*(3), 241–254. doi: 10.1080/02643940903133870

Lindsay, G. (2003). Inclusive education: A critical perspective. *British Journal of Special Education, 30*(1), 3–12. doi: 10.1111/1467-8527.00275

Lipscomb, A. & Gersch, I. (2012). Using a 'spiritual listening tool' to investigate how children describe spiritual and philosophical meaning in their lives. *International Journal of Children's Spirituality, 17*(1), 5–23. doi: 10.1080/1364436x.2011.651713

Lubel, R. & Greaves, K. (2000). The development of an EPS information booklet for primary age pupils. *Educational Psychology in Practice, 16*(2), 243–248. doi: 10.1080/713666049

Mainwaring, D. & Hallam, S. (2010). 'Possible selves' of young people in a mainstream secondary school and a pupil referral unit: A comparison. *Emotional & Behavioural Difficulties, 15*(2), 153–169. doi: 10.1080/13632752.2010.480889

McCallion, A. & Trew, K. (2000). A longitudinal study of children's hopes, aspirations and fears for the future. *The Irish Journal of Psychology, 21*(3–4), 227–236. doi: 10.1080/03033910.2000.10558255

McNamara, E. (1992). Motivational interviewing: The gateway to pupil self-management. *Pastoral Care in Education, 10*(3), 22–28.

McNamara, E. (1998). *The theory and practice of eliciting pupil motivation: Motivational interviewing – a form teacher's manual and guide for students, parents, psychologists, health visitors and counsellors.* Ainsdale: Positive Behaviour Management. Available via www.positivebehaviourmanagement.co.uk

Ravenette, T. (1999). *Personal construct theory in educational psychology: A practitioner's view.* London: Whurr.

Robson, C. (2011). *Real world research: A resource for users of social research methods in applied settings.* Chichester: Wiley.

Roller, J. (1998). Facilitating pupil involvement in assessment, planning and review processes. *Educational Psychology in Practice, 13*(4), 266–273. doi: 10.1080/0266736980130408

Ruddock, B. & Cameron, R.J. (2010). Spirituality in children and young people: A suitable topic for educational and child psychologists? *Educational Psychology in Practice, 26*(1), 25–34. doi: 10.1080/02667360903522751

Rushton, J.P. (2002). New evidence on Sir Cyril Burt: His 1964 speech to the Association of Educational Psychologists. *Intelligence, 30*(6), 555–567.

Truong, Y. & Ellam, H. (2014). *Educational psychology workforce survey 2013. National College for Teaching and Leadership report.* London: DfE.

Wagner, P. (2000). Consultation: Developing a comprehensive approach to service delivery. *Educational Psychology in Practice, 16*(1), 9–18. doi: 10.1080/026673600115229

Williams, J. & Hanke, D. (2007). 'Do you know what sort of school I want?': Optimum features of school provision for pupils with autistic spectrum disorder. *Good Autism Practice (GAP), 8*(2), 51–63.

Winstone, N., Huntington, C., Goldsack, L. et al. (2014). Eliciting rich dialogue through the use of activity-oriented interviews: Exploring self-identity in autistic young people. *Childhood, 21*(2), 190–206.

Woolfson, R.C., Harker, M., Lowe, D. et al. (2006). Consulting about consulting: Young people's views of consultation. *Educational Psychology in Practice, 22*(4), 337–353. doi: 10.1080/02667360600999468

Yardley, A. (2014). Children describing the world: Mixed-method research by child practitioners developing an intergenerational dialogue. *Educational & Child Psychology, 31*(1), 48–62.

Chapter 4 From the problematisation of children to the celebration of difference

Antony Williams & Dan Goodley

Introduction

This chapter reviews the increasing focus placed by modern western societies on children and childhood. This focus has brought a growing awareness that childhood – the period of life before adulthood, from birth to the end of adolescence – is a period of great physical and psychological change. The modern socio-political response is to develop child-centred processes and an increasingly child-centred culture. Educational psychology theory and practice has followed these trends. Childhood is recognised as a period of relative dependence and of great opportunity: these ideas underpin the requirement on adults to protect children and prepare them for adulthood.

The recognition of dependencies is multifaceted. The obvious physical dependence during infancy and childhood is tied also to notions of legal and financial dependence through childhood and adolescence. Families, communities and societies are made up of mutually dependant relationships, but there is a particular recognition and understanding of the dependence inherent in childhood that has framed the social construction of childhood in modern western societies. This shifting recognition can be seen in Winnicott's famous aphorism 'there is no such thing as a baby' (Winnicott, 1964). This emphasises in a powerful way that a baby or child is inevitably described in relation to those who care for them within a given social context. 'The baby' is a relational phenomenon. This description emphasises to a lesser or greater extent the importance of such care. The way we talk about and understand children reflects contemporary social concerns that transcend childhood. Childhood is a phase of life we all experience, and as adults we go on in various ways to create the context within which childhood is lived out by others. To a certain degree, and in a range of ways, we are all recursively experiencing childhood. So from this perspective are the problems attributed to children their problems, or are there broader issues to be teased out?

In thinking through the ways in which children in modern societies are understood Elisabeth Young-Bruehl (2012) suggests that the term 'Childism' should be used to *'highlight the fact that prejudice is built into the very way that children are imagined'* [p.5]. 'Childism', Young-Bruehl (2012) suggests, is an appropriate term to reflect the prejudice that informs the routine and systematic way in which children are problematised or recognised as problematic. This recognition justifies, rationalises and normalises harm to children that would not be accepted if suffered by other groups in society. In arguing for the usefulness of the concept of childism, Young-Bruehl (2012) calls for a concept that could guide the systematic exploration of 'how and why adults fail to meet children's needs or respect their rights' (p.7).

While such a systematic exploration is beyond the scope of this chapter, we do aim to offer a critical and historical perspective on the problematisation of children, and reflect upon educational psychology's role in creating the concepts that are drawn upon when talking and thinking about children as a problem. Psychological language has its role to play in the language that structures childism, in much the same way that psychological discourse has been used at points throughout the 20th century to construct sexism, racism and disablism (discrimination against people with physical, sensory or learning impairments). Take, for example, the ways in which disablism collides with childism (the situating of children as less than adult and therefore less than human). Disabled people are often infantilised and children's cognitive development is often viewed as deficient when compared with the reasoning of adults. In this way both processes rely upon one another for existence. Add to this the increased pathologisation of childhood, the psychological framing of deficits within children as evidenced through an exponential rise in categories of childhood disability, and one comes to recognise the dependence of the 'child' upon 'disability', and vice versa. Such an analysis also highlights the way in which particular groups of children and children in particular circumstances have been the target of normalised harm.

Recognising difference and the emergence of educational psychology

Following the advent of industrialisation in the 19th century and the social changes it initiated, by the 20th century children were observed and classified in an ever increasing number of ways. Schools became an important site for the observation and classification of children. Following the Education Act of 1870 and a series of educational reforms in the early 20th century the requirement to attend school was introduced for children between 5 and 10 years of age (1880) and then extended to cover an increasing proportion of the child population. Local Education Authorities were introduced in the 1902 Education Act to offer local management of the developing school system. It was at this cultural point that schools became important sites for the examination of all the significant characteristics of childhood.

In 1904 the London County Council became a local education authority: it was this authority's need in 1913, following the Mental Deficiency Act of that year, to find a way to classify children that led to their employment of psychologist Cyril Burt. The Act of this year heralded the category 'feeble-minded', and noted:

> In the case of children, they [the feeble-minded, with an IQ of between 50 and 70] appear to be permanently incapable by reason of such defectiveness of receiving proper benefit from the instruction in ordinary schools. (Rendle-Short, 1967, p.374)

London County Council required a psychologist to identify, or rather confirm the identity of, feeble-minded children alongside those identified as idiots and imbeciles. Taking on this role in 1913, Burt became the first employed applied psychologist in the United Kingdom. He was throughout his career strongly influenced by Eugenics Society founder (in 1908) Sir Francis Galton, serving as a member of the Consultative Council of the Eugenics Society in 1937 and 1957.

Burt's 1959 paper 'The Examination at Eleven Plus' pays tribute to Galton, noting that 'the idea of assessing the ability of children by means of experimental test is due to the versatile genius of Galton' (Burt, 1959, p.109). The relationship between Galton and Burt proved influential in the early shaping of UK educational psychology as Burt's educational psychology was heavily influenced by Galton's concepts, methods and values. Reflecting Galton's theories, Burt was to contend throughout his career that intelligence was innate and easily measured.

The 20th century psychometric psychology of the individual, with its focus on measurement and differentiation, depended on an accurate measure of what was conceived as intellect and the relative stability of that concept over time. Although such a view of intelligence was contested (Binet, 1909, p.54; Lippmann, 1922, in Block & Dworkin, 1976), Burt's contention that intelligence was largely innate and genetically determined would appear to validate the concept of the intelligence quotient (IQ) and underscore the utility of standardised tests that claimed psychometric properties as powerful tools for ascribing fundamental differences between children:

> By the term 'intelligence' the psychologist understands inborn, all-round intellectual ability. It is inherited or at least innate, not due to teaching or training; it is intellectual, not emotional or moral and remains uninfluenced by industry or zeal; it is general, not specific, that is to say it is not limited to any particular kind of work, but enters into all we do say or think... it can be measured with accuracy and ease. (Burt, 1933, pp.28–29)

Burt is clearly an important figure in the development of educational psychology in Britain (see Arnold & Hardy, 2013). His model of working was employment in a Local Authority, and this became the dominant mode of employment for the profession of educational psychology. Burt's favoured psychological tool, psychometric intelligence testing, became a standard procedure within the developing profession.

From his early work to the present day, applied educational psychology has been in the forefront of recognising individual differences in children from a psychological perspective. Educational psychology has provided a vocabulary to enable people to recognise and think about difference, and such psychological concepts have become firmly embedded in the language of schooling and in everyday talk. The early work of Burt drew upon a eugenic understanding of personhood, that is the innateness of a range of human qualities and from this assumption the assessment and categorisation of children was both possible and necessary. Indeed Burt's early work was to identify which children were educable and which were not.

In contrast to the eugenic conception of psychological difference, as located in genes and improved through selective breeding and/or sterilisation, the early work of the French Psychologist Alfred Binet focused on the development of assessment materials that would give insight into children's learning capacities. Like Burt, Binet reflected a significant strand of thinking of the period: for Binet the challenge was to understand and explore the malleability of the developing mind. In reviewing Binet's contribution Gould (1996) notes that Binet was suspicious of making any claims about the aetiology of the capacities he sought to measure, his aim was rather to create an assessment that could aid teachers in their professional task:

> The scores are a practical device; they do not underpin any theory of intellect. They do not define anything innate or permanent. We may not designate what they measure as 'intelligence' or any other reified entity. (Gould, 1996, p.185)

Early educational psychology was framed within the governmental project of the age. Industrialisation demanded a form of governmentality that maintained the smooth running of state institutions, and educational psychology was recognised as an important tool for the maintenance, management and structuring of the developing education system. The new social problem of the time, of particular consideration in the construction of an education system, was the concept of mental defectiveness. Educational psychologists' role in recognising difference was from the very early days motivated by two seemingly mutual but ultimately contradictory impulses, 'to know and predict' and 'to offer insight in the hope of facilitating change'.

Emergent psychological understanding of the relational dimension of childhood development

A further strand of psychological thinking in the first half of the 20th century offers a context to the significant changes to educational psychology in the late 20th and early 21st centuries. These changes have led to innovations in practice, as a number of the assumptions embedded within the early practice of educational psychology have been challenged. Susan Isaacs wrote a number of influential books on child development in the early 1930s. Her 1930 *Intellectual Growth in Children* was based on her experience between 1924 and 1927 as head of Malting House School in Cambridge. She trained and practised as a psychoanalyst and was a close colleague of Melanie Klein, who developed a psychoanalytic 'play therapy' with children in the 1920s. In 1933 Isaacs became the first Head of the Child Development Department at the Institute of Education at the University of London (an appointment that followed by two years Burt's installation as the chair of Psychology at University College London). Isaacs was clear on the potential value that a psychological perspective could bring to the understanding of children, though wary of the narrow perspective offered by experimental studies. While not rejecting the experimental insights of the day, she remained cautious, emphasising in her 1930 text 'the importance of watching the child's intelligence actually at work in his everyday practical and social relations' (p.5). She was also alive to the recognition that knowledge about children was a result of social interactions, and that this fact needed to be carefully considered by those working with children:

> With young children, no adult can under ordinary circumstances be minimal stimulus... The children are psychologically orientated towards him as an adult. Their world hangs upon him, and his slightest sign is full of meaning. (Isaacs, 1930, p.9)

In the shift to recognising difference as a fact to be accepted and celebrated without needing to be marked out as a problem or a signpost to poor outcomes, Isaacs articulates a further strand in early psychological thinking about children and childhood. She is an example of an early educational psychologist who, like Binet, was cautious about reifying processes when completing psychological assessment with children. We also see in her work the recognition of the social construction of knowledge, which was to become an increasingly important consideration for educational psychologists critical of normative testing as the dominant mode of knowledge production in their discipline.

Recognising difference, but in whose best interests?

Although educational psychology was for many years allied to the psychometric testing of children, unease about the unquestioning application of such tests, their rationale and their consequences grew. The most noteworthy articulation of this unease produced by the profession came in the 1978 publication Reconstructing Educational Psychology (Gillham, 1978). Here a number of the relevant traditions of practice were challenged. David Loxley, then Principal Educational Psychologist for Sheffield, reflects the unease with assumptions about practice:

> If a child is 'identified' by school or by a survey as a 'problem', who is really the client? Was Burt's client, 'the backward child' or 'the young delinquent' or was it in fact, the LCC? I think it is evident that it was the latter and that much intervention by psychologists today, whether LEA or school initiated, and directed at populations, groups or individual children, is of very much the same kind. (Loxley, 1978, pp. 97–98)

Loxley's rhetorical question and his reflective answer are insightful and illuminating: he highlights important aspects of how and with what intent the psychologist becomes involved in the life of a child. This is the starting point of the definition of the child as a 'problem' (a theme developed by Billington, 2000). From this starting point there comes the question 'who is the client?' – in whose best interests is the psychologist working? This question can be traced back to Ingleby's 1974 chapter in *Reconstructing Social Psychology*. In a chapter titled 'The job psychologists do', he asks 'for whom does the psychologist work? What interests is he paid to further and what value judgements does his work embody as a consequence?' (1974, p.316).

This question remained crucial throughout the 1980s and 1990s, following the Warnock Report of 1978 and the subsequent Education Act of 1981. In this new legislative era educational psychologists were challenged to emphasise within their practice their role as advocates for the 'voice of the child' (Davie, 1993; Hobbs et al., 2000), and dilemmas inevitably arose related to the ongoing tensions inherent in recognising individual difference. The perceived 'needs' of the child were increasingly recognised as rights. The United Nations Convention on the Rights of the Child frames in terms of rights those duties that children should expect from the adults who organise the environment in which they grow up, and it is the most widely ratified international human rights treaty in history. The UK ratified the convention in 1990, and it came into UK law in 1992. In the context of cultural shifts that reflect contemporary concerns about the treatment of children, educational psychologists are commissioned by parents, head teachers and local authorities in an increasing variety of ways, and EPs themselves draw upon psychological knowledge from a number of paradigms. But as educational psychology continues to operate in the discursive space in which children's differences are both problematised and celebrated, how can EPs, whose work draws on their psychological knowledge of children in this space, avoid reproducing forms of knowledge which perpetuate 'childism'?

What are the consequences of recognising and naming such differences and in whose best interests do such consequences operate? These questions, particularly the latter, led to the reconsideration of the structural location of educational psychology services (as part of the local government that funds placements)[1] and of the ways this location influences psychological knowledge. The Lamb Inquiry (Lamb, 2009), commissioned in the UK in 2008, can be seen as a contemporary resurfacing of concerns related to the political nature of psychological knowledge, not unlike those articulated by educational psychologists in 1978.

So how is educational psychology and its practice to be judged? This perennial problem has led to much discussion about identifying a unique contribution, and what is proposed here is that psychological experts, those trained to offer a psychological gaze, must be challenged to 'hold political realities and psychological problems in focus at the same time' (Ingleby, 1974, p.327). This call is not new, but one that periodically needs to be renewed. It can be seen to echo Mills's (1959) insistence that personal troubles must be understood in terms of public issues and that the social sciences and the practice of social science must include both troubles and issues, as well as an analysis of their intricate relations.

Psychological practitioners are being challenged about the degree to which they practice in a tradition that propagates childism. However, practitioners draw upon psychological language to challenge childism and work in situ to support the recognition of the hopes, fears and wishes of the children they work with, trying to ensure that those with some power over the child bear in mind such hopes, fears and wishes. As educational psychology continues to focus on the identification of difference as a prelude to recognising and celebrating it, there is a responsibility to recognise the power and influence of psychological explanations.

Psychological explanations always exist within, and are always to a lesser or greater degree a function of a social situation: the following points are made in respect of the increasing trend for psychological explanations of children's apparent difference.

- Empirically based psychological explanations do not offer a truth that is outside of ideology, but rather a set of signifiers that with the human propensity for sense-making may become important reference points for the understanding of self/others.
- Such diagnoses/categories are used as a way of managing finite resources and pursuing these may be a tactic that is employed to gain access to services. The issue here becomes how the tactic is used and whether the person labelled knows it is a tactic or comes to believe it is a life sentence (Parker, 2007).
- Is the resource/service one that the person themselves actively desires (with a reasonable understanding of the implications of access) or is it one which they are attempting to resist?
- Is your participation (or desire to participate) in labelling processes part of your 'responsibility in accord with the best interests of social government' (Billington, 2006, p.151)? If so, how are the particulars of the individual human situation acknowledged within the process of applying psychological knowledge?

---

[1] The Lamb Inquiry was commissioned in the UK in 2008. This inquiry focused on parental confidence in the processes that identified and provided provision for children recognised as having special educational needs. The 2010 report *Improving Parental Confidence in the Special Educational Needs System* was a governmental response to the recommendations of the Lamb Inquiry leading to 2014 Children and Families Act.

Acknowledging and celebrating difference

In order to think about childhood difference in politicised and affirmative ways, we would argue that it helps to keep in mind lives of disabled children and the theoretical and political responses emerging from Critical Disability Studies (CDS) literature. CDS is a contemporary trans-disciplinary space that (i) accounts for childhood difference as embodied and categorised in relation to disability; (ii) interrogates those social, cultural and political practices implicated in the constitution of disability and (iii) seeks to celebrate the disruptive potential of disability in everyday life. As Goodley (2011, 2012) has argued, one key element of Critical Disability Studies is the idea that the bodies of disabled people, including disabled children, do matter. This notion of bodies that matter recalls the work of Judith Butler, who was keen to think about the ways in which bodies are materialised through many discursive and material practices. Her work has shown that bodies do not appear out of nowhere, as simple biological entities untouched by the social world. In contrast, bodies are made, or materialised, in and through the cultural and social spaces in which they are recognised, felt, experienced and responded to. At the same time, Butler's work has been absolutely crucial to a growing recognition of the potential of different, atypical and diverse bodies to disrupt taken-for-granted and normative ideas around what a body should be. As a key influencing voice in the emergence of queer theory, Butler celebrates the transformative potential of queer, non-heteronormative and trans bodies to rethink and rematerialise what counts as a body that matters. Indeed, in *Bodies That Matter: On the discursive limits of sex,* Butler (1993, see also 1999, p.243) asked a number of questions of bodies, to which one of us (Goodley, 2011, 2012) has add a number of linked questions to disability:

1. How, then, can we think through the matter of bodies as a materialisation governed by regulatory norms in order to ascertain the workings of heterosexual hegemony in the formation of what qualifies as a viable body? *How are non-disabled bodies made more viable than disabled bodies?*

2. How does materialisation of the norm in bodily formation produce a domain of abjected bodies, a field of deformation, which, in failing to qualify as the fully human, fortifies those regulatory norms? *How do societal practices uphold the precarious higher status of non-disabled people through the abjection (rejection) of disabled people?*

3. What challenge does the abjected realm offer to a symbolic hegemony that might force a radical re-articulation of what qualify as 'bodies that matter'? *In what ways do disabled bodies rearticulate what qualifies as a body that matters?*

Let us briefly consider these three areas of contestation. How are non-disabled bodies made more viable than disabled bodies? While there are many answers to this question, we will consider the following:

First, 'being disabled' becomes known as the conspicuous object of lack, while 'being non-disabled' remains unquestioned, untroubled and implicitly valued. So disability increasingly enters the school as a category of deficiency, a marker of trouble and a phenomenon that risks undoing the normative workings of schools. As more and more psychological knowledge becomes known about the psychopathologies of childhood, less and less is known about the markings of those assumed to be normal. We urgently need then an interrogation of the educational processes that permit some bodies to be known as damaged and damaging, while other bodies are simply and implicitly assumed to be unproblematic and therefore acceptable.

Second, how do societal practices uphold the precarious higher status of non-disabled people through the abjection (rejection) of disabled people? These practices work in a number of ways but are demonstrated by the way schools locate their own failings (in terms of lacking the institutional practices and philosophies) within the bodies of disabled children. While schools struggle to meet the performative standards forced on them by governments and inspection processes, that is to say, they remain precarious places of education, precariousness is ignored (perhaps repressed and disassociated from institutional consciousness) and disabled children are evoked as the real markers of failure.

Third, in what ways do disabled bodies rearticulate what qualifies as a body that matters? An answer might be found in the ways in which the presence of disability in schools demands new, imaginative and inclusive approaches to pedagogy. Rather than viewing disability as a drain on educational resources or by the teachers as an inconvenience in the classroom, we should ask what disability contributes to an educational context. One answer is that pedagogical practices have to shift and change to ensure that disabled children are included as valued members of the classroom. At their very best, these practices work also to promote a sense of belonging for disabled children; at the same time, those non-disabled children in the classroom will, more often than not, also benefit from the development of more inclusive pedagogies. It is an old adage to say that all children benefit from forms of inclusive education and we might add that disability's disruptive potential may be harnessed in order to seek new forms of inclusion. Disability appears, then, not as a marker of lack but as an arbiter of change for good.

Conclusion

In this chapter we have uncovered some of the ways in which childhood and disability reproduce one another. There is no doubt that childhood is marked more and more by categories of disability and this phenomenon reflects the historical and contemporary input of educational psychology. Two tasks for critical educational psychology relate to (1) the historicisation of childhood, disability and forms of professional practice, while (2), at the same time, unpacking the ways in which all of these relate to one another. Furthermore, we would want to ask questions about the affirmative ways in which 'the child' and 'disability' disrupt normative ideals embedded in psychological practice and language. At the heart of much educational psychological theory and practice is a normatively developing child, following a linear path of educational attainment, sound of mind and body, ready, willing and able to learn and then eventually earn. By bringing disability to the centre of our deliberations we have an opportunity to disrupt these normative ideals of childhood. Rather than viewing disability as a marker of lack we would want to ask what disability brings to the party in terms of rethinking pedagogical practices, reshaping educational spaces and revisioning the ideal goals of educational psychology practice. Disability actually might be the disruptive and critical friend of educational psychology.

References

Arnold, C. & Hardy, J. (Eds.) (2013). *British educational psychology: The first hundred years (History of Psychology Centre Monograph No. 1)*. Leicester: British Psychological Society.

Billington, T. (2000) *Separating, losing and excluding children: Narratives of difference*. London: RoutledgeFalmer.

Billington, T. (2006). *Working with children: Assessment, representation and intervention*. London: Sage.

Binet, A. (1909). *Les idées modernes sur les enfants*. Paris: Flammarion.

Block, N. J. & Dworkin, G. (1976). *The IQ controversy*. New York: Pantheon.

Burt, C. (Ed.) (1933). *How the mind works*. London: George Allen & Unwin.

Burt, C.L.S. (1959). The examination at eleven plus. *British Journal of Educational Studies, 7*, 99–117.

Butler, J. (1993). *Bodies that matter: On the discursive limits of sex*. London:

Butler, J. (1999). Bodies that matter. In J. Price and M. Shildrick (Eds.) *Feminist theory and the body* (pp.235–245). Edinburgh: Edinburgh University Press.

Davie, R. (1993). Listen to the child: A time for change. *The Psychologist, 6*(6), 252–257.

Gillham, W.E.C. (Ed.) (1978). *Reconstructing educational psychology*. Beckenham: Croom Helm.

Goodley, D. (2011). *Disability Studies: An interdisciplinary introduction*. London: Sage.

Goodley, D. (2012). Dis/entangling critical disability studies. *Disability & Society* [Advance online publication]. doi: 10.1080/09687599.2012.717884

Gould, S.J. (1996). *The mismeasure of man*. New York: Norton.

Hobbs, C., Todd, L. & Taylor, J. (2000). Consulting with children and young people: Enabling educational psychologists to work collaboratively. *Education and Child Psychology, 17*(4), 107–115.

Ingleby, D. (1974). The job psychologists do. In N. Armistead (Ed.) *Reconstructing social psychology*. Harmondsworth: Penguin Books.

Isaacs, S. (1930). *Intellectual growth in young children*. London: Routledge & Kegan Paul.

Lamb, B. (2009). *Lamb Inquiry: SEN and parental confidence. Report to the Secretary of State on the Lamb Inquiry Review of SEN and Disability Information Department for Children Schools and Families*. Retrieved 20 June 2015 from http://webarchive.nationalarchives.gov.uk/20130401151715/https://www.education.gov.uk/publications/standard/publicationdetail/page1/dcsf-01143-2009

Loxley, D. (1978). Community psychology. In W.E.C. Gillham (Ed.) *Reconstructing educational psychology*. Beckenham: Croom Helm.

Mills, C.W. (1959). *The sociological imagination*. New York: Oxford University Press.

Parker, I. (2007). Revolution in psychology: Alienation to emancipation. London: Pluto Press.

Rendle-Short, J. & Gray, O.P. (1967). *A synopsis of children's diseases*. Bristol: Butterworth-Heinemann.

Winnicott, D.W. (1964) 'Further thoughts on babies as persons'. In D.W. Winnicott, *The child, the family and the outside world* (pp.85–92). Harmondsworth: Penguin. (Original work published 1947).

Young-Bruehl, E. (2012). *Childism: Confronting prejudice against children*. Chicago: Yale University Press.

Chapter 5 A participatory research approach to understanding the experiences of pre-verbal children and young people and those with complex needs in residential settings

Vivian Hill, Rhiannon Yates, Scot Greathead,
Abigail Croydon, Lorcan Kenny & Liz Pellicano

Introduction

This chapter describes the development of techniques to elicit details of the experiences and preferences of pre-verbal children and young people with complex needs. This account reflects one element of a larger study that was funded by the Children's Commissioner for England, in 2014. The aim of the study was to explore the experiences of children living and being educated in residential special schools, with a particular focus on how their wellbeing and rights were being promoted and facilitated by their schools. A full account of all aspects of the study is provided in Pellicano et al.'s *My Life at School* (2014).

Children's rights and entitlements

The focus of the study reflected an interest in ascertaining how well the United Nations Convention on the Rights of the Child (1989) is being delivered for children and young people with special educational needs within their residential school contexts. The UN Convention makes provision for all children to access an education that helps them to develop to their full potential. It recognises that children and young people with special educational needs and disabilities are likely to experience significantly greater challenges in achieving this aim and it consequently affords them additional protection under Article 23. It states that children with disabilities have the same rights and entitlements as all children, namely to live a full and decent life in conditions that promote independence and the opportunity to participate in their community.

Article 12 of the UN Convention explicitly states that children have the right to participate in decision-making about their lives. These rights extend to all children, and it is required that adults must facilitate all young people to have their views, feelings and aspirations elicited and placed at the centre of plans for their future. However, Shier (2001) has observed that Article 12 of the UN Convention has been 'one of the provisions most widely violated and disregarded in almost every sphere of children's lives' (p.108). It is without doubt that children and young people with special needs, and in particular those with complex, severe, profound and multiple needs that are accompanied by major challenges in communication are those who face the greatest difficulties in accessing these rights. The focus of this chapter will be on the development of techniques to investigate the ways in which residential special schools were helping to support these requirements for children and young people with complex needs.

There has been surprisingly little research conducted with children attending residential special schools. This is a concern due to their obvious vulnerabilities, and may reflect the challenges in ascertaining their views and perspectives. Furthermore, some researchers had concluded that it was not possible to elicit views and perspectives from the children with the greatest learning and communication needs (Rabiee et al., 2006). However, the UN Convention places a clear responsibility on adults to engage in creative and developmentally appropriate ways of facilitating children's communication. During this study it was critical that we developed methods and approaches to ensure that we were able to elicit insights into the experiences and preferences of all children and young people.

Participatory research techniques

The processes and techniques that informed the study were derived from the use of participatory research (PR) and aimed to ensure that the voices of all of the children attending residential special schools were heard, and that the issues and concerns that were of highest priority for them were not subsumed by those of adults. This was of central importance since the study embraced a multi-informant approach to data collection, and the focus was on the voice of the children and young people.

The literature that describes the uniqueness of PR methods accentuates the value of empowering participants in the research process. Examples of PR have shown how participants are encouraged to make decisions about and guide the topic of research; have control over the collection of data; and assist in the interpretation of that data (e.g. Thomas & O'Kane, 1998). Applying PR methods with children with severe learning difficulties (SLD) and profound and multiple learning difficulties (PMLD), however, requires more thoughtful and deliberate consideration.

In 2001 Shier produced a refinement of Hart's (1992) eight-rung ladder of participation, describing a five-step model of participatory approaches that reflected:
1. children being listened to;
2. children being supported in expressing their views;
3. children's views being taken into account;
4. children being involved in decision making processes; and
5. children sharing power and responsibility for decision-making.

An adaptation of the work of Cornwall (1996) and Truman and Raine (2001), described by Kindon et al. (2007), sets out six degrees of participation that reflect movement from traditional researcher-led work toward a more radical approach. These degrees of participation begin with *co-option*, a tokenistic approach wherein users are represented but are not actively involved in the research. In the next stage, *compliance*, users are assigned tasks but researchers decide the research agenda and processes. The *consultation* level seeks participants' opinions but has researchers still leading the analysis and research agenda, whereas at the *co-operation* level users work alongside the researchers to determine priorities, though responsibility for the research process remains with the researchers. The *co-learning* level reflects a process whereby users and researchers share their knowledge in order to develop new and shared understandings, and in partnership develop and conduct the research activity. At the final stage, *collective action*, users set the research agenda and conduct the research without outsider involvement.

In our study we aimed to engage children and young people in working at the levels of consultation, co-operation and co-learning. We did this through the development of a Young Researchers' group. Davis (2009) highlights the challenges of developing a 'gold standard' of participatory techniques and advocates a pragmatic approach based on what is possible within time, ethical and budgetary constraints. There were many challenges in operationalising the present project, particularly in terms of the timeframe for the study, which was restricted to a single academic term. This timeframe posed challenges for building effective relationships with our Young Researchers, and for developing and piloting creative techniques to enable the full involvement of all participants. Despite these time pressures, the findings indicated that the approaches developed and described in Hill et al. (in press) and below, particularly through co-operation and co-learning, have considerable potential for providing greater insight into the rights, entitlements, experiences and opportunities provided for our most vulnerable learners within their school settings.

The Young Researchers' group

From the inception of the study we developed a Young Researchers' group to advise, support, steer and report on the study. The group included children and young people aged 13 to 19 years of age and with a wide range of special educational needs and disabilities, including those with severe learning difficulties and those experiencing challenges with communication. The young people were all attending one of two different special residential school provisions. The diversity of the group meant that some Young Researchers were more able to verbally communicate their experiences than others, but all were able to support the research agenda. The Young Researchers' group advised on all stages of the study, including helping to identify key issues for investigation and advising on and piloting appropriate methodologies. They verified the themes emerging from the data and led on the development of an accessible form of the report, helping to disseminate the findings at the UK House of Lords in December 2014. The Young Researchers also made a short film of their experiences.

Promoting children's voices when they challenge powerful lobby groups

Children and young people do not always endorse the views of parents and lobby groups: there is, then, a considerable issue in ensuring that their voices are heard and not suppressed. Tisdall and Bell (2006) found that when planning was underway for new legislation, the Education (Additional Support for Learning) (Scotland) Act 2004, children's views were side-lined when there was a conflict with some high profile parents' organisations. During this study similar issues were experienced: many disability lobby groups operating in the post 'Winterbourne View' climate were most resistant to hearing about positive experiences of life in residential special schools. Lobby groups were very keen to ensure that children should remain with their families and access necessary support within their local authority. Whilst this is a positive aim, and is based on the evidence of many negative experiences, it does not necessarily consider the constructive contributions made to the lives of children and families that participated in this study. As researchers it was important that we ensured the voices and experiences of the children and young people who contributed to the study were heard and that they informed the debate about both the positive and negative consequences of a residential school placement.

Developing techniques to use with children and young people with complex needs

The primary focus of this chapter is the development of techniques and approaches to better understand the experiences of pupils with SLD and PMLD at their respective residential schools. We aimed to include all children and therefore carefully considered how we could effectively work with children with SLD and PMLD to ensure that their unique experiences were represented.

Children with SLD and PMLD are defined as having significantly delayed cognitive and intellectual functioning, and often cannot verbally express their views (Bellamy et al., 2010; DfCF, 2009). Professionals have also questioned whether children with PMLD are able to develop 'views' more complex than simply expressed preferences (Ware, 2004). Such definitions and descriptions of children with complex needs may portray these individuals to be 'helpless and lacking in volition and intention ... [persons who] are largely believed to have little agency, ability to voice experiences, or opportunity to participate in society' (Simmons & Watson, 2014, p.19). Simmons and Watson (2014) further comment that these descriptions have considerable influence over the way in which professionals and adults work with and perceive young people with complex needs. This influence operates in particular on expectations about what these children can achieve and how they can participate in sharing their views and experiences and contribute to plans for their future.

These perceptions perhaps contribute to the scarcity of research with children with SLD and PMLD. Indeed, one study explicitly documented the exclusion of children who are pre-verbal and have a lower level of cognitive ability (Rabiee et al., 2006). Despite developing a range of creative techniques to engage and include children in a research study about their life aspirations, Rabiee et al. (2006) reported that they were not able to access the views and experiences of 17 participants. Although children and young people with complex needs may not be able to overtly express their experiences and views, we still have a responsibility under Article 12 of the UN Convention to find methods and means which will enable us to develop a deeper understanding of the experiences of these children, and to ensure that their rights are being protected. It was therefore an aim of this study to develop methods to capture and represent the experiences of young people with complex learning needs.

A previous research study observed young children with learning difficulties and the interaction between their agency and the structure and culture of the different early years settings they attended (Nind et al., 2010). The authors found that the age of the children combined with their developmental level of need meant that it was not possible to directly and explicitly ask them to share their narratives and interpretation of their experiences, yet Nind et al. nonetheless argue that they were still able to engage in 'active listening based on ethnographic involvement in their lives' (p.656). The techniques developed here extend the work of Nind et al. (2010). Based upon both structured and unstructured observations of communication and interactions, we employ ethnographic methods to explore how children expressed their preferences and had their choices elicited.

Ethnography and detailed observation techniques

These techniques were discussed with our Young Researchers. It was agreed that observing children and young people through their transition from a care setting to an educational setting and then back again would make it possible to see how they were given opportunities to express preferences and make choices, and indeed would enable us to observe where these factors were less evident or absent. It was decided that to gather this data it would be crucial to develop a detailed observation schedule and to collect evidence of what was happening for the young person throughout the day.

We endeavoured to ensure that the research aims were conducive to investigating the children's rights and wellbeing. These aims were devised with the intention of identifying whether and how the children were listened to, empowered and supported by those who worked with them. To address these aims, an ethnographic approach and techniques similar to those adopted by Nind et al. (2010) were used. Nind et al. accompanied one child, Mandy, across different early years settings: her playgroup and a Children's Centre. They observed the interactions that took place and that gave rise to a range of contrasting experiences. The authors noted that in one setting the interactions Mandy experienced fostered a sense of competence, yet those in the other constrained her ability to make a choice effectively. The ethnographic data that was collected yielded rich descriptions and examples of how the diversity of a child's communicative experiences can influence outcomes.

Indeed, Schiller and Einarsdotir (2009) state that 'we need to understand how children's lives are co-constructed by the actions of key adults because child-adult relations and spatial practices are central in deciding which children's voices get heard, what they can speak about and what difference it makes' (p. 127). It is therefore important to analyse the interactions that young people experience with their carers in different contexts and to consider how this impacts upon their ability to communicate and express their needs.

Consequently, we specifically investigated the presentation of the communicative behaviours of children with complex needs in context, including in the context of (1) the nature of the support provided by their adult communicative partners and (2) the organisation of their environment. In addition, we examined the extent to which young people were involved in choosing the activities they are offered throughout the day.

Methodology and measures

Ethnographic techniques

The adoption of ethnographic methods emerged from the new paradigm research movement active within sociology during the 1970s. The technique has been widely used with people with learning disabilities to 'ground studies in the experience and views of respondents' (Kiernan, 1999, p.43) Ethnography is described as a reflexive and flexible qualitative methodology (Hammersley & Atkinson, 1995) in which the researcher observes from the perspective of the individual and the system under review.

Adopting an ethnographic approach in this project enabled the researcher to work with a number of children and their one-to-one supports for a period ranging from 5 to 12 hours during a school day, seeing the children across contexts in the 'home' and 'educational' parts of the school and with a variety of communication partners. By spending extended periods of time with the children involved, we were able to encounter the school day as the children did. This particularly relates to the PR model, in that the methods chosen were those that are in tune with the way in which children see and experience the world (Thomas & O'Kane, 1998); it echoes Nind et al.'s (2010) concept of 'active listening' through means that are suitable and appropriate for children with a high level of need.

Furthermore, the flexibility that the ethnographic approach values meant one researcher worked as a one-to-one support with some of the children in the study. This enabled the researcher to move from the role of 'researcher' into the role of 'learner', thereby equilibrating the power imbalance between the researcher and the child and adult participants in keeping with the PR framework. This is an excerpt taken from a day working with a Sarah, an 11 year old with PMLD. Transferring into this role enabled the researcher to gain a deeper appreciation and understanding of the experiences of staff that support these children, in addition to more actively learning about the individual children.

Participatory research endorses the use of the local knowledge of the community who are part of the context (Cohen et al., 2011). Throughout the days spent with these children, the researcher worked with staff to help with interpreting the children's communicative signals, therefore further reducing the portrayal of the 'expert researcher'. The flexibility of the ethnographic approach, together with the length of time the researcher spent with the children, enabled the researcher to work collaboratively with familiar adults, construct shared understandings, and equilibrate power dynamics (Clark, 2004; Cornwall & Jewkes, 1995).

Structured observation

To focus our observations and attend to the research aims throughout the day, we developed and used a range of measures (see Greathead et al., 2016 for further details). To examine the extent to which young people were involved in choosing their activities, a brief cover sheet was completed for each activity observed. This detailed certain variables, including:

- the length of the observation;
- group size (one-to-one; small; large);
- the nature of the activity (must do; must do with preferences; child directed); and
- the child's communication partner (how long they have known the child; how frequently do they work with the child).

Furthermore, a structured observation schedule was devised. It specifically captured information regarding how a child's initiated communication – what their initiation consisted of (sounds, symbols, or gestures, for example) and how the adult responded – as well as noting the adults' interaction, the supports they used to facilitate the child's understanding of the interaction and how the child responded. This information was filled in minute-by-minute and therefore rates and frequency of child and adult initiation were assessed. Moreover, the observation schedule provided space for field notes, to write detail about activities and resources and note informal discussions with staff throughout the day. This schedule supported the researchers in writing a narrative of the day they had observed and been a part of.

To analyse the presence of young peoples' communicative behaviours in the context of their environment and adult support, the Social Communication Emotional Regulation Transactional Support (SCERTS) model (Prizant et al., 2007) was applied. SCERTS is a multi-disciplinary model that aims to enhance the communication and socio-emotional abilities of children with autism and children with varying degrees of difficulty in cognitive, communicative, sensory processing and regulatory capacities (Prizant et al., 2003). The underlying principles are based on theories of and research into children's learning and language development and, corresponding with this particular research aim, the model emphasises the key role that the environment and interactions play in child development.

SCERTS focuses on three stages of socio-emotional development. First, is the 'social partner' stage, which refers to children who are at the pre-symbolic stage of communication development. Next comes the 'language partner' stage, wherein young people are able to communicate intentionally, with symbols, words, phrases and signs. Finally, the 'conversational partner' stage includes children who are able to use language to generate sentences to tell stories. For each stage, SCERTS offers developmentally appropriate targets for:

- the child, to enhance social communication and emotional regulation;
- transactional support to promote an environment that is conducive to socio-emotional growth and
- adults, to adapt their interpersonal style so that they are meaningful and consistent with the child's developmental level.

Consequently, four SCERTS checklists were selected specifically for children at the social partner stage and were used to gather information about the nature of transactional supports used by adults and the child's communicative behaviour within each activity. Transactional support was assessed through two checklists: one for learning support, with items such as 'partner uses augmentative communication systems to foster development', and one for interpersonal support with items such as 'partner respects child's independence'. The child's communicative behaviour was examined by developing one checklist which amalgamated certain behaviour from the 'social communication' and 'emotional regulation' SCERTS checklists, which are indicative of social-emotional growth (concerning e.g. happiness, sense of self). The checklists were completed at the end of each activity. An additional checklist, the Expression of Intentions and Emotions worksheet, allowed researchers to record the presence of a range of 16 socio-communicative behaviours used by the young person to express themselves (i.e. requesting food, making comments, showing happiness etc.,) and whether those behaviours were symbolic (signs, pictures, spoken words) or pre-symbolic (eye gaze, pointing etc.,) The checklists were completed at the end of each activity, by endorsing the observed items on the checklist.

Combining detailed field notes, consistent with the ethnographical approach, with the data yielded from the SCERTS checklists and the structured observation schedule captured a rich portrait of the child's experiences across a variety of activities within the school day. A unique picture emerged for each child; these can be used to build evidence of the degree and nature of support to which the individual children responded best. This personalised understanding of each child is a vital step to accessing their world by being able to appreciate and learn about what motivates, interests and, ultimately, engages them. Engagement and learning are inextricably interlinked and from revealing how to connect the child with their environment, achievement and development will follow (Carpenter et al., 2011).

Participants

For this element of the project the participants included ten young people aged between 8 and 16 years, including four girls and six boys, who attend a 52-week placement at a residential special needs school in England. The participants all had complex learning needs and their statements indicated that they had a diagnosis of autism or were described to have PMLD, and were currently working at P scales (attainment targets for pupils with SEN) 2–4.

Results

To determine the extent to which children direct their own activities, the data from ten observed children demonstrated that 56 per cent of their activities were categorised as 'must-do with preferences built into the activity'. Another 22 per cent were based purely on 'child preferences', with 14 per cent categorised simply as 'must-do' activities and only 8 per cent described as 'child-directed'. Including child preferences within must-do activities may make the activity more meaningful and purposeful for the child and therefore encourage motivation and participation. Lacey (2011) places more emphasis upon enabling children to direct their activities. This perspective argues that adults responding to children's needs and initiations, rather than focusing on attempting to make activities more accessible to children, is more appropriate and beneficial for the developmental stage of children with PMLD. Despite this, child-directed activities were the least frequently observed in our study.

The ethnographic methods, combined with the SCERTS checklists, captured rich data about the interactions between children and their adult supports, including the offering and communication of choices within activities. For example (see Table 5.1), observing the morning routine of one young person, Adam, revealed an individualised system that enabled him to communicate his choices at breakfast. The narrative data in Table 5.1 describes the observations.

Table 5.1: Ethnographic narrative data with associated SCERTS communication data: Adam, Activity 1

Ethnographic data	SCERTS checklist	
Narrative	Adam's communication (checklist items bracketed)	Adult supports (checklist items bracketed)
Adam had his own breakfast menu that had been individually designed for him with photographs of a range of food and drink. His teacher placed the pictures around him on the table and immediately as these were laid out, Adam picked a picture of cranberry juice and gave it to his teacher.	Sense of self Makes choices when offered by partners (mutual regulation 2.6) Social membership and friendships Looks towards people (joint attention 2.1)	Uses AAC* to foster development Uses AAC to foster communication and expressive language (learning support 2.1) Partner is responsive to child Responds appropriately to child's signals to foster a sense of communicative competence (interpersonal support 1.3)
His teacher left the table to pour the cranberry juice as he had requested and held it in front of him, with the photograph, and stated; 'Here's your cranberry juice'. Adam then tapped the visual and the teacher gave him the juice. Through this method, Adam also chose toast and chocolate spread.	Sense of self Makes choices when offered by partners (mutual regulation 2.6) Social membership and friendships Looks towards people (joint attention 2.1) Social membership and friendships Engages in extended reciprocal interaction (joint attention 1.4)	Uses AAC to foster development Uses AAC to foster communication and expressive language (learning support 2.1) Partner sets stage for engagement Uses appropriate proximity and nonverbal behaviour to encourage interaction (interpersonal support 4.3)
While waiting for the breakfast Adam looked at his teacher, moving his head closer to him and looking directly into his eyes. He repeated this five times; every time his teacher would reciprocate and copy his movement, with a smile and sometimes with a nod of the head. After Adam ate his breakfast, he reached for his book, turned the page	Independence Responds to visual cues (symbol use 2.6)	Partner is responsive to child Imitates child (interpersonal support 1.6)

Table 5.1 (continued)

Ethnographic data	SCERTS checklist	
Narrative	Adam's communication (checklist items bracketed)	Adult supports (checklist items bracketed)
and chose cereal and toast, to which his teacher responded that he needed to choose just one of these. To support Adam's understanding of his teacher's expectations, he held both pictures up in front of Adam and Adam chose the cereal. He was then shown pictures for options to put on his cereal: Adam chose honey.	**Independence** Makes choices when offered by partners (mutual regulation 2.6)	**Partner is responsive to child** Responds appropriately to child's signals to foster a sense of communicative competence (interpersonal support 1.3) **Uses AAC to foster development** Uses AAC to foster understanding of language and behaviour (learning support 2.2)

*Augmentative and Alternative Communication (AAC) provides ways to support communication other than only through the use of speech

Following breakfast, Adam went to his bedroom with his carer and pointed to a picture of a blanket that was amidst a group of photos on his wall. The carer indicated that it was time for us to leave Adam's room explaining that Adam was requesting privacy so he could sexually stimulate himself. In the past, when members of staff had not understood what Adam had wanted to do, this had resulted in Adam becoming frustrated, demonstrating challenging behaviour and disengaging from his activities. Over time, those working with Adam have developed a way for him to understand his feelings and to communicate his needs, thus enabling him to exercise control and make choices, further helping him to be settled and calm in school.

This sequence of events details how developing a meaningful communication system with Adam is key to giving him autonomy over his day-to-day living, in addition to recognising the importance of responding to his sexual needs and representing this option to him in a safe and socially appropriate way.

In using the SCERTS checklists to examine children's communicative behaviour in context with the transactional support they receive, there was a considerable amount of variety observed over a day. Table 5.2 details just two of the activities that one young person with PMLD, Mary, experienced in relation to the variety of support that she received. It is interesting to note the difference in Mary's communicative behaviour between activity 1 and 4; not only did she register a higher percentage of communicative behaviour that is indicative of social-emotional growth in activity 4, she was also observed in this activity to initiate more interaction and experience greater reciprocal interaction with her adult support (as assessed by structured observation schedules).

Table 5.2: Mary's communicative behaviour and
adult's transactional support across two activities

	Activity 1	Activity 4
Location	Home	School
Duration (minutes)	52	60
Child's communicative behaviours associated with social-emotional growth indicators (percentage of total number possible)	50%	70%
Adult's interpersonal support (percentage of total number possible)	69.7%	90.9%
Adult's learning support (percentage of total number possible)	48%	80%
Communicative bids from young person (rate per minute)	0.08	0.93
Communicative bids that led to reciprocal interaction (rate per minute)	0	0.13

These data are further enriched and complemented by the detail in the narrative table 5.3. Activity 4 was led by Mary's teacher, with whom Mary has worked for two years on a daily basis. By contrast the support staff working with her during activity 1 did not work consistently with any particular child on a regular basis. In addition to noting the high level of transactional support that Mary experienced in activity 4, the narrative data highlights the responsive and attuned relationship Mary and her teacher have developed.

Table 5.3: Ethnographic narrative data with associated SCERTS communication data: Mary, Activity 4

Ethnographic data	SCERTS checklist	
	Mary's communication (checklist items bracketed)	Adult supports (checklist items bracketed
When Mary joined her class, she seemed unhappy. Firstly, she started to make sharp, small noises, but these progressively lengthened, became louder and then she started to cry. The staff member who was now working with Mary was empathetic towards her, asking 'What's the matter? I know, I know', 'Did you not like coming out of the pool?' Mary continued crying for 19 minutes, in which time the member of staff walked her around the school for a 'change of scenery', which she was reported to sometimes enjoy, and brushed her hair to try to soothe her.	**Independence** Protests undesired actions or activities (joint attention 4.4) **Co-operation and appropriateness of behaviour** Soothes when comforted by partners (mutual regulation 2.1) **Sense of self** Uses appropriate rate of communication for context (joint attention 7.1)	**Partner is responsive to child** Recognises signs of dysregulation and offers support (interpersonal support 1.5) **Partner is responsive to child** Offers break from interaction or activity as needed (interpersonal support 1.7)
On return to the class, Mary's class teacher focused his attention on comforting Mary. He pulled a chair next to her and imitated her noise, which became a brief reciprocal interaction between them, and she looked closely at his face during this time. Her class teacher wondered aloud whether Mary was hungry, and held a banana out to her saying, 'Hm, banana?'	**Social membership and friendships** Responds to bids for interaction (mutual regulation 2.3) **Social membership and friendships** Engages in extended reciprocal interaction (joint attention 1.4) **Happiness** Shares positive emotion using facial expression and vocalisations (joint attention 3.2)	**Partner is responsive to child** Recognises and supports child's behavioural strategies to regulate arousal level (interpersonal support 1.4) **Partner is responsive to child** Facilitates reengagement in interactions and activities following breaks (interpersonal support 1.8)

Ethnographic data	SCERTS checklist	
Narrative	Mary's communication (checklist items bracketed)	Adult supports (checklist items bracketed)
Her teacher waited for a response from Mary and she smiled after a short pause. During this time, Mary's teacher sat next to Mary and they made eye contact for extended periods of time whilst Mary was eating.	**Social membership and friendships** Looks towards people (joint attention 2.1)	**Partner sets stage for engagement** Uses appropriate proximity and nonverbal behaviour to encourage interaction (interpersonal support 4.3) **Partner is responsive to child** Imitates child (interpersonal support 1.6) **Partner structures activity for active participation** Creates turn taking opportunities and leaves spaces for child to fill in (learning support 1.2) **Partner fosters initiation** Offers choices non verbally (interpersonal support 2.1) **Partner respects child's independence** Provides time for child to solve problems/complete activities at own pace (interpersonal support 3.2) **Partner is responsive** Responds appropriately to child's signals to foster a sense of communicative competence (interpersonal support 1.3) **Partner sets stage for engagement** Uses appropriate proximity and nonverbal behaviour to encourage interaction (interpersonal support 4.3)

The quantitative data provided by the SCERTS checklists offer frequency figures, enabling a comparison of data across settings, contexts and communicative partners, as Table 5.2 demonstrates. Whilst it is acknowledged that there are a range of factors which impact a child's communicative behavior, these data can provide opportunities for the analysis of the activities during which a child demonstrates more communicative behaviour in combination with the supports that were available at the time. This information, together with the qualitative data that were received through employing ethnography, enabled the researchers to tell a more in-depth story of the lives and experiences of these young people, detailing specific and individual communicative systems which support a child's autonomy and the significance of long-lasting and attuned relationships.

The following excerpt was taken from a day working with Sarah, an 11 year old with PMLD. This excerpt portrays another example of the importance for children, like Sarah, to have the opportunity to build long-lasting relationships with staff, so that they can respond sensitively to communicative behaviours and foster emotional regulation.

Table 5.4: Ethnographic narrative data with associated SCERTS communication data: Sarah, Activity 2

Ethnographic data	SCERTS checklist	
Narrative	Sarah's communication (checklist items bracketed)	Adult supports (checklist items bracketed)
Sarah demonstrated to staff that she was unhappy by frowning and saying 'Ah' repetitively. Staff wondered whether Sarah was uncomfortable in her chair. Her vocalisations became progressively louder and more persistent towards the end of the activity and she was therefore taken upstairs to the residential lounge where she was placed face down on a soft 'wedge', with her head over the edge.	**Independence** Protests undesired actions or activities (joint attention 4.4) **Co-operation and appropriateness of behaviour** Soothes when comforted by partners (mutual regulation 2.1)	**Partner is responsive to child** Responds appropriately to child's signals to foster a sense of communicative competence (interpersonal support 1.3) **Partner modifies goals, activities, and learning environment** Modifies sensory properties of learning environment (learning support 4.3)

Ethnographic data	SCERTS checklist	
Narrative	Sarah's communication (checklist items bracketed)	Adult supports (checklist items bracketed)
This position is thought to help her to feel more comfortable and settled and she did indeed seem calmer; she was vocalizing less, although she was still frowning. A member of staff joined Sarah and sat next to her on the floor. She started reading her a 'Gruffalo' book, with buttons to make the noises of the characters and animals in the book. 'Scary Sid' followed this, which has a puppet combined with the story. Sid, the puppet would sometimes try to 'eat' Sarah's fingers and this was incorporated into holding and jiggling Sarah's arms. Sarah lifted her head up and smiled when this happened. Throughout the reading session, the member of staff stroked Sarah's back and held her hand.	**Flexibility and resistance** Responds to partners attempts to re-engage in interaction or activity (self regulation 4.3) **Flexibility and resistance** Re-engages in interaction or activity after recovery from extreme dysregulation (self regulation 4.3) **Happiness** Responds to sensory and social experiences with differentiated emotions (self regulation 1.7) **Happiness** Shares positive emotion using facial expression and vocalisations (joint attention 3.2)	**Partner modifies goals, activities, and learning environment** Arranges learning environment to enhance attention (learning support 4.4) Partner structures activity for active participation Offers repeated learning opportunities (learning support 1.4) **Partner structures activity for active participation** Provides predictable sequence to an activity (learning support 1.3) **Partner sets stage for engagement** Uses appropriate proximity and nonverbal behaviour to encourage interaction (interpersonal support 4.3) **Partner modifies goals, activities, and learning environment** Infuses motivation materials and topics into activities (learning support 4.7)

Conclusions

Despite the challenges in eliciting the views and experiences of children and young people with complex needs, this study is evidence of a technique that helps to provide insights into the preferences and abilities of children with complex needs to experience and make choices. Furthermore it affords the level of detail to support planning to extend and facilitate the individual's communication skills and provides insights into the life and experiences of those young people with the greatest challenges in communicating.

The techniques are further evidence that all children have the ability to express preferences and give insight into factors that enhance their wellbeing. The findings endorse the view that there is a challenge for researchers to find creative and innovative ways to help provide insights into the inner world of pre-verbal children and young people, and think about how to develop and extend their communication skills. The data generated gave valuable insights into the daily experiences of these children and young people and the systems and structures that best support them.

The data provides some evidence that suggests that these young people communicate best with people who know them well and that when the child and adult are attuned the process of interaction and understanding and promoting their wellbeing works best. Many schools expressed a degree of ambivalence about whether staff should be building strong relationships with the children, questioning the boundaries of a professional carer's relationship. For those children with the greatest needs, who attend 52-week placements, not to do this would deny them the basic human right to a warm and continuous relationship in which mutual satisfaction is experienced. This is not to replace parents but to ensure that in cases where parents cannot fulfil this role, due to the distance of the school from the family home and the consequent amount of contact that is possible, someone does.

The formation of a Young Researchers' group helped to engage a wide range of children and young people with significant needs in a PR process. Their unique insights and experiences helped to shape the focus of the study, by facilitating our understanding of their context. By working closely with the group over the duration of the project they were able to help guide the process of the project, advise on the materials and the areas that we should investigate and explore. The engagement of the group was far from tokenistic and they had a very active role in each stage of the project and engaged with passion and enthusiasm. It provided a powerful and mutually beneficial learning and process. The Young Researchers had a strong presence at the dissemination event at the House of Lords. It is hoped that the Office of the Children's Commissioner and Government will make good use of this group to consult on policy development and follow the logical progression of the participation agenda. What was refreshing for the research team was that the children and young people were able to give their personal accounts of the advantages and disadvantages of life in residential special schools free from the constraints of political and ideological dogma. They have given a clear and strong message, not necessarily reflecting the views and perspectives of powerful lobby groups. The challenge is, in the spirit of the UN convention, to hear the children's voices and work with these young people on policy development.

Finally, much of the literature describing PR techniques considers how to support individuals who are cognitively able in becoming active participants in the research process. There is still currently a dearth of documentation detailing how this model can be applied to children who have SLD and PMLD. Cornwall & Jewkes (1995) argue that a key element of PR is the attitude of the researchers. This is particularly relevant to researching and working with children who have not yet reached the developmental level of making informed decisions about the research process. The PR model encourages researchers to be flexible and reflective about how they are working ethically with a vulnerable population, through attending to power imbalances and ensuring that the participants' rights and needs are consistently being met. The mixed methodology approach, which applied ethnography as guided by SCERTS principles, captured the experiences of children with autism, SLD and PMLD in a residential school. It pursued a focus on how these children's rights are being met and how their voices are being listened to, and on how their wellbeing and participation are enhanced through the creative work undertaken by these schools.

References

Bellamy, G., Croot, L., Bush, A. et al. (2010). A study to define: Profound and multiple learning disabilities (PMLD). *Journal of Intellectual Disabilities, 14*(3), 221–235.

Carpenter, B., Egerton, J., Brooks, T. et al. (2011). *The complex learning difficulties and disabilities research project: Developing meaningful pathways to personalised learning* (final report). London: Specialist Schools and Academies Trust (now The Schools Network). Available via http://complexld.ssatrust.org.uk

Clark, J. (2004). Participatory research with children and young people: Philosophy, possibilities and perils. *Action Research Expeditions, 4*(11), 1–18.

Cohen, L., Manion, L. & Morrison, K. (2011). *Research Methods in Education* (7th edn.). Abingdon: Routledge.

Cornwall, A. (1996). Towards participatory practice: Participatory rural appraisal (PRA) and the participatory process. In K. de Koning & M. Martin (Eds.) *Participatory research in health: Issues and experiences* (pp.94–107). London: Zed Books.

Cornwall, A. & Jewkes, R. (1995). What is participatory research? *Social Science and Medicine, 41*(12), 1667–1676.

Davis, J.M. (2009). Involving children. In K.M. Tisdall, J.M. Davis, & M. Gallagher (Eds.) *Researching with children and young people: Research design, methods and analysis.* London: Sage.

Department for Children, Schools and Families (2009). *Schools, pupils and their characteristics.* Nottingham: DCSF Publications.

Department of Health (2012) *Transforming care: A national response to Winterbourne View Hospital* (final report). Retrieved 21 January 2016 from http://www.gov.uk/government/uploads/system/uploads/attachment_data/file/213215/final-report.pdf

Greathead, S., Yates, R., Hill, V., Kenny, L., Croydon, A., & Pellicano, E. (2016) Supporting Children with Severe and Profound Learning Difficulties and Complex Communication Needs. *Topics in Language Disorders, 36*(3), 217–244

Hammersley, M. and Atkinson, P. (2007). *Ethnography: Principles in practice.* London: Routledge.

Hart, R.A. (1992). *Children's participation: From tokenism to citizenship.* Florence: UNICEF.

Hill, V., Pellicano, E., Croydon, A., Greathead, S., Kenny, L., & Yates, R. (in press). Research methods for children with multiple needs: Developing techniques to facilitate all children and young people to have 'a voice'. *Educational & Child Psychology, 33,* 26–43.

Kiernan, C. (1999). Participation in research by people with learning difficulties: Origins and issues. *British Journal of Learning Disabilities, 27*(2), 43–47.

Kindon, S.L., Pain, R. & Kesby, M. (2007). *Participatory action research approaches and methods: Connecting people, participation and place.* London: Routledge.

Lacey, P. (2011). Developing a curriculum for pupils with PMLD. *The SLD Experience,* Autumn, 4–7.

Nind, M., Flewitt, R. & Payler, J. (2010) The social experience of early childhood for children with learning disabilities: Inclusion, competence and agency. *British Journal of Sociology of Education, 31*(6), 653–670.

Pellicano, E., Hill, V., Croydon, A. et al. (2014). *My life at school: Understanding the experiences of children and young people with special educational needs in residential special schools.* London: Office of the Children's Commissioner.

Prizant, B.M., Wetherby, A.M., Rubin, E. & Laurent, A.C. (2003) The SCERTS model: A transactional, family-centred approach to enhancing communication and socioemotional abilities of children with autistic spectrum disorder. *Infants and Young Children, 16*(4), 296–316.

Prizant, B., Wetherby, A., Rubin, E. et al. (2007) *The SCERTS Model: A Comprehensive Educational Approach for Children with Autism Spectrum Disorders.* Baltimore, MD: Paul Brookes Publishing Co.

Rabiee, P., Sloper, P. & Beresford, B. (2006). Desired outcomes for children and young people with complex health care needs, and children who do not use speech for communication. *Health and Social Care in the Community, 13*(5), 478–487.

Schiller, W. & Einarsdottir, J. (2009). Special issue: Listening to young children's voices in research – changing perspectives/changing relationships. *Early Child Development and Care, 179*(2), 125–130.

Shier, H. (2001). Pathways to participation: Openings, opportunities and obligations. *Children and Society, 15*(2), 107–117.

Simmons, B.R. & Watson, D.L. (2014). *The PMLD ambiguity: Articulating the life-Worlds of children with profound and multiple learning disabilities.* London: Karnac Books.

Thomas, N. & O'Kane, C. (1998). The ethics of participatory research with children. *Children and Society, 12*(5), 336–348.

Tisdall, E.K.M. & Bell, R. (2006). Included in governance? Children's participation in 'public' decision making. In E.K.M. Tisdall, J.M. Davis, M. Hill & A. Prout (Eds.) *Children, young people and social inclusion.* Bristol: Policy Press.

Truman, C. & Raine, P. (2001). Involving users in evaluation: The social relations of user participation in health research. *Critical Public Health, 11*(3), 215–229.

United Nations (1989). Convention on the Rights of the Child. Retrieved 18 July 2014 from http://www.unicef.org.uk/Documents/Publication-pdfs/UNCRC_PRESS200910web.pdf

Ware, J. (2004). Ascertaining the views of people with profound and multiple learning disabilities. *British Journal of Learning Disabilities, 32,* 175–179.

Chapter 6 Educational psychologists involving young people in planning for their own learning: A person-centred planning approach

Sarah Philp & Fiona Brown

> Fundamentally, we need to find ways to position ourselves so we can hear children's stories and so that these stories can challenge the narrative of our own practice with them. We need to work so that children and young people feel they can own and direct their own story. (Hobbs et al., 2000, p.114)

While children and young people are the real consumers of education (Costley, 2000) they have often lacked the opportunity to be involved in the planning and development of their own educational pathways (Lansdown et al., 2014; Roller, 1998), especially if they have communication or learning difficulties (Franklin & Sloper, 2009; Harding & Atkinson, 2009). However, fully involving children and young people in matters affecting them is so important that it is enshrined in international and national law (The United Nations Convention on the Rights of the Child, 1989; Children and Young People (Scotland) Act, 2014).

Promoting the involvement of children and young people in assessment, planning and research is a central concern of educational psychologists (EPs) working across the UK (Harding & Atkinson, 2009; Hobbs et al., 2000; Lansdown et al., 2014). This is particularly true in relation to young people who have additional support needs (Roller, 1998). This chapter explores an approach often used by EPs to facilitate learner participation in planning their learning which recognises that all learners have a unique way of learning, communicating and engaging.

Person-centred planning

Person-centred planning (PCP) was developed in the USA and Canada in the late 1980s within the inclusion movement, and was intended as an effective way of putting the person with disabilities at the centre of the planning process (Murray & Sanderson, 2007). It originated from the Solution-Focused Brief Therapy approach, with its focus on the active involvement of all participants and its emphasis on developing solutions (Roller, 1998). Adopted in the UK in the 1990s, PCP quickly became widespread in education and social care for engaging individuals in planning for their futures (Sanderson, 2000). The approach is rooted in positive psychology, and uses a solution-oriented, strengths-based methodology to identify the strengths of the current reality and the skills and support necessary to realise an individual's desired future (Murray & Sanderson, 2007; Sanderson et al., 2013).

Effective PCP occurs when people listen carefully to what the focal person says and seek to understand the importance of this from the person's perspective (O'Brien &

O'Brien, 1998). The process relies on the engagement of all professionals in a continuous cycle of listening and learning in order to focus on what is important to the learner now and in the future. The fundamental aspect of the PCP approach is the learner's place in the centre, with the implicit assumption that they and those closest to them have the most knowledge about their own life (Roller, 1998, Sanderson, 2000). This shifts control towards learners as it is they who take a lead role in planning (Sanderson, 2000). The dynamic, visual nature of person-centred plans allow for this shift of control and the emergence of a powerful, truly collaborative plan.

Sanderson (2000) identifies the following five key features of PCP:

1. **The person is at the centre**
    PCP incorporates a range of features which ensure that the person stays at the centre of the planning process. This also enables the control and power in the process to shift from the professionals towards the learner and their family. This principle is demonstrated in three key ways: the person is consulted throughout the planning process; the person chooses who to invite; and the person chooses the time and place of the meeting.

2. **Family members and friends are partners**
    PCP is about getting to know the person and their situation, therefore it is important that the process takes into account their family, community and relationships. PCP is about contributing to the person's life and those that know them best have a lot to offer in this respect. It is assumed that families want to make a positive contribution to the life of the person. Their understanding of the issues, hopes and fears may be different to those of professionals and others; this difference must be embraced as adding to the richness of our understanding. Through partnership families and professionals can make a positive difference.

3. **The plan reflects what is important to the person, their capacities and the support that they require**
    PCP opens up a better understanding of the person in terms of their capacities, strengths and skills. The support they require to achieve their goals is clearly identified within the plan to ensure that they can achieve what is important to them.

4. **The plan results in actions that are about life, not just services, and reflects what is possible, not just what is available**
    The gap between where a person is now and what is important to them facilitates a discussion about the support that is required to create the needed change. This leads to action planning that is individual and that does not default to existing packages or known solutions. It challenges us to work together to develop creative approaches to supporting the person.

5. **The plan results in ongoing listening, learning and further action**
    PCP is not a one-off event and is based on the assumption that as the person grows and develops, their hopes will change and that as a result their supports will also need to change.

Person-centred planning tools

Within the PCP approach there exists a range of practical planning 'tools' that have been developed to support thinking, improve communication and understanding, and capture high-quality information to inform the planning process (Murray & Sanderson, 2007; Sanderson et al., 2013). Although the tools differ in how they gather information they all place the person at the centre and lead to clear actions. They are visual in approach, using short phrases or pictorial representations of key concepts, and focus on the day-to-day support of longer term planning. Most tools address two key questions:

- Who are you, and who are we in your life?
- What can we do together to achieve a better life for you now and in the future? (Sanderson, 2000)

The most commonly used tools are MAPs (Making Action Plans), PATH (Planning Alternative Tomorrows with Hope) and giftedness posters.

MAPs, PATHs and giftedness posters

A MAP (Snow et al., 1996) is a useful tool to get to know a person better and find out more about their life, in turn creating a full picture. The MAP is designed to help individuals, organisations and families decide how to move into the future effectively. In some situations it can be helpful to review the past; the MAP starts with this before building a picture of the person and their future. The process explores the person's history and their dreams and nightmares before considering their skills, strengths, needs and available resources to construct an action plan that will move away from the nightmare and towards the dream.

A PATH is a focused planning tool which sharpens the details of a preferred future and plans the steps that need to be taken. It often requires support from people around the person over a period of time to achieve this (Pearpoint et al., 1993). The process encourages the person and those closest to them to (1) identify their future vision, (2) identify a long-term interim goal that would help to achieve that vision, (3) establish where they are now and (4) develop a detailed action plan to get them from where they are to their interim goal. The stages of the PATH are outlined below.

Box 1: PATH stages

Step 1 – The dream

Personal vision for the future. This may be general or very specific.

Step 2 – Sensing the goal

Breaking down the dream into smaller goals.

Step 3 – Now

Where are we now? What parts of the dream are already happening? Where are the tensions?

Step 4 – Enrol/ Who's on board?

Who needs to help?

Step 5 – How are we going to build strength?

What are the individual and those around them going to do to maintain strength and commitment to the goals?

Step 6 – Three-/six-month goals

Set interim goals.

Step 7 – First steps

Identify first steps and set date for another meeting.

(Sanderson, 2000)

Giftedness posters are used to identify all the positive skills, attributes and capacities of the person. Creating a giftedness poster can support the person to develop a positive sense of self and of how they contribute to the community around them (Sanderson et al., 2013). The poster is a useful starting point in employing PCP approaches and can be used to inform other planning tools.

Using PCP to involve learners in planning for their own learning in a special school

With its focus on a person's strengths and interests, PCP is an ideal planning format for ensuring that education meets the learner's needs (Harding & Atkinson, 2009; Hobbs et al., 2000; Roller, 1998; Sanderson et al., 2013), especially in the case of learners with additional support needs and communication difficulties (Murray & Sanderson, 2007). For this reason, the EPs working with a special school in Scotland introduced the approach for pupils in the senior phase in the school, seeking to develop effective post-school transition planning and ensure that the learning opportunities offered to young people in school were meaningfully related to their hopes for the future. The impact of this change to the review process was monitored through focus groups with staff and pupils, held at the end of the spring term.

Due to the long-established fact that appropriate training is key when gathering the views of young people with communication difficulties (Franklin & Sloper, 2009), the EPs ran professional development sessions with key members of staff in the senior (15–18-year-old) phase of the school. These sessions introduced the philosophy of the PCP approach and the key tools involved. Staff then decided, with the offer of support, how to implement the approach across the senior phase and explanatory leaflets were shared with parents. The PATH (see Figure 6.1) was chosen as a framework for the young people's review meetings, which were held early on in the academic year; the intention was to ensure meaningful, collaborative discussion around each young person's post-school vision and therefore help to clarify how the school year could be best utilised to move towards this vision. EPs further supported the process by facilitating the initial meetings.

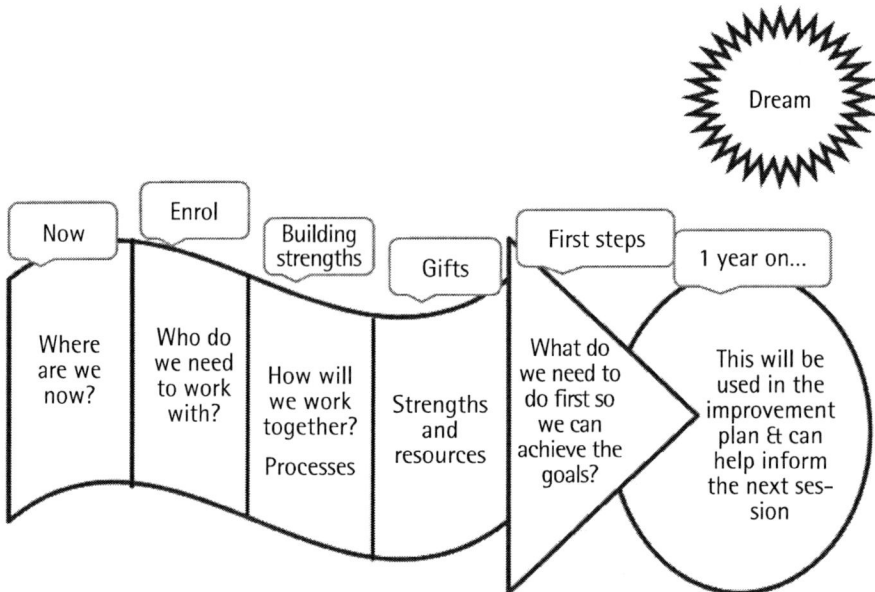

Figure 6.1: The PATH

To prepare pupils, giftedness posters were completed as a whole-class activity before the round of review meetings began. Many young people can be reluctant to discuss their strengths and successes, often because they are unused to the process (Sanderson et al., 2013). Having their peers, teachers and learning assistants contribute and identify their skills and abilities before choosing which comments would remain on their posters allowed the young people to develop their concepts of self (Sanderson et al., 2013) before participating in their review.

Learner involvement

It is vital to involve young people with additional support needs actively in their review meetings as this ensures that their perspective is fully represented, increases their motivation and offers a greater opportunity for change, allowing for informed and effective decisions to be made (Lansdown et al., 2014; Roller, 1998). To ensure that there was active participation within the special school, EPs advised that review meetings start with the young person talking through their giftedness poster, with support where necessary. This placed the learner firmly at the centre of the process while giving them a concrete, tangible focus for the meeting. Indeed, Forest and colleagues (2001) argue that we should be encouraging young people to facilitate the process with adults as they may even do it better. Speaking later in the year, pupils described how they had valued having their poster with them; one young person noted that while she had felt nervous about talking in the meeting, her poster had reassured her because it had reminded her of the positive things she had to relate (see Figure 6.2).

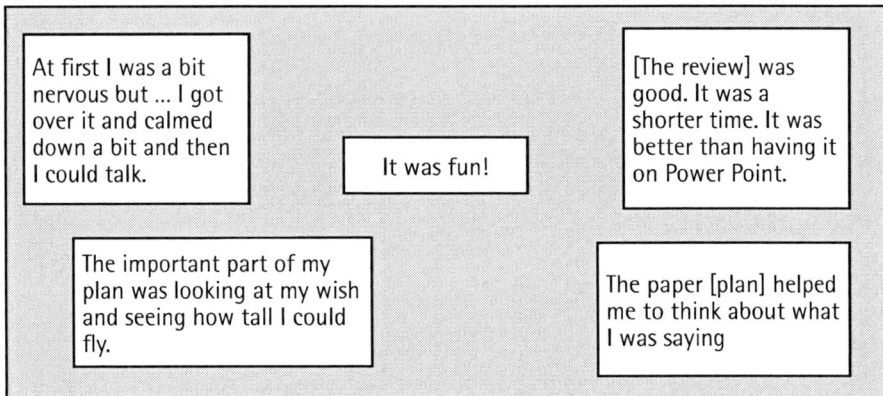

> At first I was a bit nervous but ... I got over it and calmed down a bit and then I could talk.

> It was fun!

> [The review] was good. It was a shorter time. It was better than having it on Power Point.

> The important part of my plan was looking at my wish and seeing how tall I could fly.

> The paper [plan] helped me to think about what I was saying

Figure 6.2: Young persons' quotes from focus groups

The use of the PATH meant that the planning process started with the young person, and their parents and carers where appropriate, describing a personal vision for the future in terms that were as simple or elaborate, as concrete or abstract as the young person wished. This allowed all the participants in the review – which included teachers and other involved professionals such as therapists and community nurses – to understand the pupil's dreams for the future. For example, did they want to live independently or with their family? Did they want to go to college? What type of job did they wish to pursue? The importance of taking account of the unique perspective of the young person (Lansdown et al., 2014; Sanderson et al., 2013) was highlighted as several pupils mentioned dreams of which even their parents had been unaware.

Once the dreams had been established, the young persons and their parents or carers chose positive, achievable goals in line with the vision to be attained within the year. These included having chosen between college and a work programme, to have completed a bus journey independently or have developed independence in self-care routines at home. As well as placing the young person's views at the centre of the process, staff felt that choosing interim goals that led directly to the vision helped parents feel reassured during discussion about post-school transition. In this school, pupils often start at the age of five and make no significant transition until they leave at the age of 17 or 18. Senior phase reviews have therefore often proven difficult as, for the first time, parents are faced with the reality that their child will leave the protective environment of the school. However, teachers reported that the reviews felt more relaxed when using the PCP approach; parents were able to see how the post-school options fed into what their children wanted for their future and were better able to make sense of the plethora of options and services that were on offer for post-school life.

All participants then worked together to develop a clear plan of action for the young person's year-group for their final year in school to help them work towards achieving these goals. The actions were concrete and directly related to the goals, making it clear to pupils, parents and staff what the young person would be doing, and – perhaps more importantly – why. The dynamic, visual approach of the PATH helped all participants maintain their focus on the goals and how they might be achieved. The graphic creation allowed the young people to be active throughout the meeting. Some drew pictures on the PATH; some wrote, while others instructed the meeting's facilitator. All pupils later reported enjoying this review more than their previous meetings because they had the 'big paper' and knew exactly what it meant. Some young people explained that they had liked drawing out their dreams; others had preferred the dynamic nature of the discussion in this review compared with previous years' meetings. The completed PATH was photographed at the end of the meeting as a record of the review and the young people kept their PATHs in their classrooms for the year.

Follow-up

Research suggests that when young people are fully engaged in a process they are more motivated (Roller, 1998) and that this is particularly evident in learning (Clarke, 2014; Hattie, 2009). While it is evident that PCP is effective in engaging young people in their meetings (Murray & Sanderson, 2007; Sanderson, 2000; Sanderson et al., 2013), for the process to be seen as truly worthwhile the motivation should extend into their future life and learning. Research suggests that when plans truly involve the people whom they concern they are more likely to be followed (Cochrane, 2001); coupled with the visual nature of the plan, this aspect of PCP ensures that it will not be lost as 'just another plan'. The fact that the young people in this example were able to talk positively about their meetings several months later suggested that these meetings had been memorable. More interesting, however, was the apparent impact they had had on their learning.

The completed PATHs, which remained on display in the classrooms for the year, supported both teachers and learners in making the links between the pupils' dreams for their future and the learning experiences offered in the classroom. Pupils noted that having their posters on the walls helped them remember their own targets and those of their peers, while their teachers reported having greater clarity and purpose when planning class activities across the year. The teachers felt that they were able to make the learning fully pupil-centred; one teacher noted that 'in the life skills class, it's offered… a much more individual way of working'. Each learning opportunity provided throughout the year related directly to the action plan for at least one pupil in the class.

While the timetable was learner-centred, many of the activities, such as college visits, practising using public transport, shopping and other life skills, were established parts of the curriculum. They represented key skills that the pupils generally needed to acquire in the senior phase and were activities that young people with additional support needs often find anxiety-provoking. However, the teachers reported that there was a very different feel to the year; while the teachers would usually provide the activities because they felt that the students should do them, this year the pupils had chosen them and knew how they related to their action plans for the year and their long-term visions. Over the year the teachers observed that the pupils were more willing to try challenging and potentially stressful activities and, even when they were initially reluctant, when the teacher reviewed their plans with them and reminded them of the links to their dream, the pupils would then have a go.

It is well established in recent literature on learning that learners' knowledge of what they want to achieve and what next steps they must take to do so is the factor with the greatest influence on engagement and achievement (Clarke, 2014; Hattie, 2009, 2012, 2013). The PATHs allowed the pupils to see clearly how the learning experiences were linked directly to their own targets or those of their peers. This was in turn observed by the teachers, who described how the young people appeared to be more confident about tackling new or difficult tasks as they understood the purpose of the activities and their direct relevance to their own lives.

An example in practice: The senior school café
A clear illustration of how the young people were able to engage fully in purposeful learning activities lay in the establishment of a school café. During the reviews, 'Sophie' expressed an interest in working in a cafe when she was older, while 'Kayleigh' indicated that she liked baking cakes and that her dream would be to bake. Other pupils had mentioned that they would like to work in retail environments, talking to customers and taking money at tills. Staff therefore set up a spring term enterprise project in the form of a café, to allow the pupils to develop the skills that they needed. The senior pupils worked together to plan their café's appearance and menu, and staff negotiated additional home economics classes with specialist teachers in the nearby mainstream secondary school.

The young people engaged well and were able to reflect on the skills they had developed. Sophie described how she could take orders from people and make the drinks they had requested; another pupil explained that he had used his counting skills to find change for customers, while Kayleigh had enjoyed baking a wide range of different products.

While enterprises such as the café were not novel in the school's history, staff felt that on this occasion the pupils were clearer about what the learning experience offered them in terms of skills development and how these skills would benefit them in their future. There was greater clarity about the long-term purpose of these learning experiences.

Throughout the academic year, the staff noted that the young people's greater engagement in learning extended beyond the classroom. The review meeting had created synergy between home and school and parents were able to see why the school were offering the learning opportunities that formed the curriculum and what they could do to support their child's learning. Many parents and carers suggested practical activities that they could do at home to complement the work being done in school and work towards their child's outcomes for the year. In some cases, the circle of support was widened to include other family members; one family enlisted the support of the young person's brother to help meet his fitness goal, which had an additional benefit of boosting the sibling relationship. Staff reported increased contact with the senior phase parents compared to previous years and felt that parents were invested in their children's learning to a greater degree.

An example in practice: 'Jamie' and his dad

In his review meeting, Jamie explained that he would like to live independently as an adult. His father was surprised by this admission and said that he had always assumed that because of Jamie's additional support needs he would have to stay in the family home. While exploring what living independently might mean for Jamie, it became clear that his dad was overly involved in the day-to-day aspects of Jamie's personal care. Jamie's father immediately suggested that a target of Jamie choosing his own clothes for the following day and setting them out would be a good first step in developing appropriate self-care skills.

Jamie's dad's commitment to his son's journey to greater independence ensured that Jamie's learning developed across all spheres of his life. At parents' evening towards the end of the year, the father explained to the teacher that Jamie was currently learning to do his own laundry at home and they were going to continue to develop his self-care skills over the school holidays.

Impact of the PCP approach

Teachers felt that the greatest strength in the PCP approach was the way in which it engaged parents; they felt that parents were able to see their children's dreams and aspirations, what the school could do to support them and what they could do at home to support their child's move towards post-school life. Rather than basing the meetings on a choice between the available post-school services and options, the focus was on deciding how to build the life that the young person wanted. Responsibility for achieving the dream was shared fully between all partners to the plan, resulting in meaningful actions.

In the academic year following the PCP reviews, teachers noted that creating Individual Education Plans (IEPs) for this cohort of senior-school pupils was a simpler process than usual as they were able to draw directly on the action plans created in the PATH. Forest and Pearpoint (2001) are very clear that a MAP, though not an alternative to an IEP, can provide useful information and direction for an IEP. For this reason, and with the support of the Educational Psychology Service, the school planned to incorporate a PCP approach for all learners and therefore build consistency across the school. Using the approach at an organisational level can build the capacity of the school to deliver a person-centred curriculum which meets the individual needs of learners and can transform the delivery from timetabled lessons to a whole-school experience (Murray et al., 2007).

Conclusions and implications for EP practice

PCP is a simple tool that can have a powerful effect. It can unstick 'sticky' situations, give people hope and can help them see a future. It also creates a starting point for action. The interactive and visual nature of PCP can facilitate learners' engagement in planning for their own futures. Galloway et al. (1994) researched the views of 24 children and found they were generally unaware of how decisions had been reached and felt powerless to influence decision-making. The process of PCP allows children to be involved in and witness how and why decisions are being made.

Using PCP approaches in the senior phase of a special school proved to be a positive and worthwhile experience for pupils, their parents and carers and staff in the school. It created a new purpose and energy in ensuring that young people's learning needs were planned for and met and that they had a smooth transition into appropriate post-school placements. PCP has the capacity to ensure that learner voice is heard and truly listened to, that learners are able to talk about how they want their futures to look and how they might get there with the help of those around them. The exploration of learners' hopes and dreams can often uncover surprises for the adults involved, proving that 'Adults do not always have sufficient insight into children's lives to be able to make informed and effective decisions … Many rights can only be effectively fulfilled, respected and protected with children's active participation. Creating opportunities for individual children to be heard is vital to ensure that appropriate decisions are made in respect of the child's perspective' (Lansdown et al., 2014, p.6).

To empower children to take greater control and responsibility for their learning, we need to develop ways of genuinely collaborating with children, which includes creating a genuine listening ethos. This should help ensure that approaches to eliciting children's views are not tokenistic and therefore meaningless. There is a need to emphasise active and effective listening so that children's views are not based upon adult misinterpretation or assumptions about how the child thinks or feels (Todd et al., 2000). The PCP approach offers a structured approach to engaging learners and adults in planning.

References

Clarke, S. (2014). *Outstanding formative assessment: culture and practice.* London: Hodder Education.

Cochrane, G. (2001). *Hope restored with PATH.* Retrieved 24 March 2015 from http://www.inclusion.com/arthoperestored.html

Costley, D. (2000). Collecting the views of young people with moderate learning difficulties. In A. Lewis & G. Lindsay (Eds.) *Researching children's perspectives* (pp.13–172). Buckingham: Open University Press.

Forest, M. & Pearpoint, J. (2001). *Common sense tools: MAPS and CIRCLES for inclusive education.* Retrieved 16 March 2015 from http://www.inclusion.com/artcommonsensetools.html

Forest, M., Pearpoint, J., McBride, M. & Hollands, J. (2001). Who says MAPS and PATH facilitators have to be 'Adults'. Retrieved 20 March 2015 from http://www.inclusion.com/artwhosays.html

Franklin, A. & Sloper, p.(2009). Supporting the participation of disabled children and young people in decision-making. *Children and Society, 23,* 3–15.

Harding, E. & Atkinson, C. (2009). How EPs record the voice of the child. *Educational Psychology in Practice, 25*(2), 125–137.

Hattie, J. (2009). *Visible learning: A synthesis of over 800 meta-analyses relating to achievement.* Abingdon: Routledge.

Hobbs, C., Todd, L. & Taylor, J. (2000). Consulting with children and young people: Enabling educational psychologists to work collaboratively. *Education and Child Psychology, 17*(4), 107–115.

Lansdown, G., Jimerson, S.R. & Shahroozi, R. (2014). Children's rights and school psychology: Children's right to participation. *Journal of School Psychology, 52,* 3–12.

O'Brien, J. & O'Brien, C.L. (Eds.) (1998). *A little book about person centred planning.* Toronto: Inclusion Press.

Pearpoint, J., O'Brien, J. & Forest, M. (1993). *PATH: A workbook for planning positive possible futures: Planning alternative tomorrows with hope for schools, organizations, businesses, families.* Toronto: Inclusion Press.

Roller, J. (1998). Facilitating pupil involvement in assessment, planning and review processes. *Educational Psychology in Practice, 13*(4), 226–273.

Sanderson, H. (2000). *Person centred planning: Key features and approaches.* York: Joseph Rowntree Foundation. Retrieved 18 July 2016 from www.familiesleadingplanning.co.uk/documents/pcp%20key%20features%20and%20styles.pdf

Sanderson, H., Goodwin, G. & Kinsella, E. (2013). A guide to using person-centred practices in schools. Stockport: HSA Press. Retrieved 18 July 2016 from www.personalisingeducation.org/wp-content/uploads/2012/09/Person-centredpracticesinschools.pdf

Chapter 7 Young people's wellbeing in schools: Student voice and agency

Sue Roffey

Introduction

The advent of positive psychology has seen an increase in the focus on wellbeing and what it means to flourish, function well and have a fulfilling life. Rather than identifying difficulties and responding to problems, positive psychology studies the conditions and processes that enable people and organisations to perform optimally and individuals to thrive. It addresses questions of meaning, relationships, positive emotions and engagement – everything that makes life worth living.

Those who study topics in positive psychology fully acknowledge the existence of human suffering, selfishness, dysfunctional family systems and ineffective institutions. But the aim of positive psychology is to study the other side of the coin – the ways that people feel joy, show altruism and create healthy families and institutions – thereby addressing the full spectrum of human experience (Gable & Haidt, 2005, p.105). Positive psychology is, therefore, not an alternative to more traditional approaches in the field but an effort to add to the knowledge base and offer new insights and ways of working.

This chapter explores what young people themselves say about their wellbeing and describes an intervention in Australia that provides a rich example of putting student voice and agency into practice.

Student voice on wellbeing

Article 12 of the United Nations Convention on the Rights of the Child (UNCRC) sets out the right of children and young people to express an opinion and to have that opinion taken into account on any matter that affects them. This convention was ratified by the UK in 1991, but putting it into practice is not a straightforward process.

What do we know of students' views on their wellbeing? What do they want from their educational experiences? What enables them to learn best? Here we give a brief overview of a few larger-scale studies eliciting the views of children and young people on these important issues.

The New South Wales Commission for Children and Young People (2007) interviewed 126 children and young people to discuss what wellbeing meant for them. Although there is complexity in their responses, three overarching themes were identified:
- Agency: having the power to make your own decisions in everyday life.
- Security: feeling safe and being safe – especially having people who will look out for you. Without this you cannot engage fully with life.
- A positive sense of self: seeing yourself and being seen by the people around you as a good person.

In 2007 UNICEF published Report Card 7 – 'An overview of child wellbeing in rich countries'. Responses were gathered from 21 OECD nations; the UK was bottom of the league table overall and ranked lowest in three out of six critical measures of wellbeing: family and peer relationships, subjective wellbeing and risk-taking behaviours. Other indices of wellbeing (both educational and material) were also very low. Health and safety was the measure on which the UK ranked best, coming 12th out of the 21. As a result of this, UNICEF UK commissioned a scoping study that led to a qualitative exploration of the links between inequality, materialism and experienced wellbeing in children (Ipsos-MORI & Nairn, 2011). They interviewed 250 children aged 8–15 years and from a range of backgrounds in the UK, Spain and Sweden, the latter two countries having received high scores on the Report Card. Findings were strengthened by filmed observations of 24 families and focus group interviews with 14 year olds in each country. Although participants were recruited within schools, this study was not immediately concerned with children's educational experiences but highlighted factors that contributed to children's rights and wellbeing, in particular materialism and equality.

The message from all the children and young people in the study was unanimous: Their wellbeing depended on time with a happy, stable family, and on having good friends and plenty of things to do, especially outdoors. Issues that contributed to a 'bad day' included family conflict and problems with friends. The notion of 'being bullied' featured strongly with UK children. A stark difference between the three countries was that family time was a priority in Sweden and Spain but many UK children appeared deprived of this, with parents who were often too busy or too tired to actively and positively engage. In Sweden children are also expected to contribute to household chores and see this as training for their independence:

> In line with a strong culture of equality, Swedish children were expected from an early age to play an active role in the running of the household, from laying the table, cooking and gardening to saving money and deciding rules. (Ipsos-MORI & Nairn, 2011, p.32)

Although some children in the UK were asked to help at home, most of the time they were left (literally) to their own devices:

> Members of a family may well all be in the home at the same time but they co-exist rather than share time and space. Indeed, for younger children, television was often used as a babysitter, keeping children occupied while parents got on with other things. (Ipsos-MORI & Nairn, 2011, p.34)

All the children acknowledged that family time was more important than material goods, except for the poorest in the UK for whom designer labels and the newest version of technological goods assumed a particular importance.

In 2013 the Children's Society published the Good Childhood Report, which encapsulated the views of 42,000 children and young people. Three factors – choice, family and enough money – were consistently cited as integral to wellbeing. The most deprived children, in comparison with the 71 per cent who are not seen as living in poverty, were also thirteen times more likely to feel unsafe at home, nine times less likely to feel that they had a lot to be proud of, and six times less likely to feel positive about the future. The report states that, although wellbeing had been improving up until 2009, there had since been a sharp fall, with a particular concern for teenagers, the lowest scores for wellbeing being reported at age 15. Members of this age group were worried about school and about how they look. Beyond this, a significant proportion of young people were neglected:

> We often underestimate the number of older children experiencing neglect at home, encountering neglect by professionals and institutions as well as by our wider society. What's more, the impact of adolescent neglect is underrated. This widespread failure to understand, acknowledge and address fully the neglect experienced by adolescents means that too often their poor treatment goes unnoticed or is dismissed. Meanwhile this neglect blights their experience of adolescence, stunts their capacity to flourish later in life, and in some cases results in serious harm. (Children's Society, 2013, n.p.)

The Australian Child Wellbeing Project is a child-centred study in which young people's perspectives are being used to design a major, nationally representative survey of wellbeing among 8–14 year olds. In the first phase, researchers talked to around 100 Australian young people aged 8–14, most belonging to groups often considered to be marginalised. Respondents consistently named family as the primary domain for wellbeing. Other domains mentioned frequently included friends, school, health, community, feeling good about yourself, money and material goods (though these domains often meant different things to different groups). Young people with disability viewed school as a precarious place associated with bullying and exclusion. Some young people reported being stressed or anxious about school as a result of pressures associated with excessive amounts of homework (ACWP, 2014).

Formal studies are often mirrored and extended by informal research and interesting accounts of practice on websites and YouTube clips. For instance, Edutopia posted an article from a teacher (Wolpert-Gawron, 2014) who asked her 220 Year 8 students what enhanced their engagement. Their responses included working with peers, having choice, getting out of one's seat, having teachers who love what they do and connecting learning to the real world.[1]

'Double-whammy' kids

Children and young people who come from supportive backgrounds are more likely to make the most of learning opportunities available to them, regardless of school values, relationships and practices. It is these pupils that governments would seem to have in mind with their emphasis on normative testing, although there is evidence that even academically able students do not necessarily have good mental health or positive relationships. Children who are neglected, abused or struggle with chronic adversity are less likely to be able to concentrate, be intrinsically mo-

---

[1] Other examples of student voice on issues of wellbeing can be accessed from www.wellbeingaustralia.com.au/wba/category/swan/student-voice/

tivated, be compliant, or have good social skills or confidence. They need an educational environment that cares for their social and emotional needs in order to maximise their learning potential (Noble et al., 2008). This was starkly illustrated in a discussion with young people in an alternative UK provision:

> I do want to know stuff. They have helped me with spelling here cos you have these worksheets and you have as much time as you want and they help you... there is someone to help if you get stuck.
>
> You feel loved here – I do anyway. They make you feel you are part of something. At your old school you don't feel comfortable. Here you are comforted, you get along with other people, you don't have nagging teachers, they like you and they tell you they like you. They make you feel like you're their own child and look after you. It helps with your learning. (Roffey, n.d., n.p.)

Although there are many mainstream schools where wellbeing is core business, and even more where individual teachers build positive relationships with challenging young people, no pupil should have to be excluded before they feel cared for in an educational setting (Noddings, 1992; Spratt et al., 2006). It is clear from the research cited above that positive relationships both at home and at school are critical for the wellbeing of young people and their future contribution to society. Without a focus on wellbeing more pupils are likely to end up as NEET (not in education, employment or training). Unless educators pro-actively and positively intervene for these 'double-whammy' kids there is a risk of reinforcing a cycle of disadvantage for the next generation.

The intervention described below was initiated to address the risk to these 'double-whammy' kids – not just for the individuals involved but also for their communities. With a focus on developing more confident, resilient and empathetic students, we were also aiming to grow leaders and agents of change. After four years the evaluation indicates that we are at least heading in that direction (Dobia et al., 2014).

The Aboriginal Girls Circle (AGC)

The Aboriginal Girls Circle (AGC) grew out of the National Association for Prevention of Child Abuse and Neglect (NAPCAN)'s preventative and long-term approach to issues of child neglect and abuse. In Australia in 2004–2005, 1.2 billion Australian dollars were spent on child protection services, yet only 4.2 million dollars were spent on child abuse prevention in the same period (Australian Government Productivity Commission, 2006).

Evidence suggests that children are more likely to be nurtured well where parents are positively connected and supported, and where women have a higher level of education, a positive self-concept and more confidence in themselves (Azar, 2002; Friesthler et al., 2006; Mosco & O'Brien, 2012). Many Aboriginal communities have experienced cultural breakdown and disconnection and as a result there have been increased levels of dysfunction, mental illness, violence and addictions (Purdie et al., 2010). However, evidence shows that Aboriginal women can be strong leaders in determining future culture:

When we invest in the education of Australian Aboriginal women and girls we are investing in the leadership capacity of future generations and a more inclusive Australian society. (Nereda White, director of the Centre for Indigenous Education and Research, Australian Catholic University, in Doyle and Hill, 2012, p. 29)

Based on research on resilience (Werner, 2004), connectedness (Blum & Libbey, 2004), social and emotional learning (CASEL, 2010) and behaviour change (Roffey, 2011), the AGC objectives are to empower young women aged 11–16 to discover and use their own strengths; identify, develop and be proud of positive personal and community attributes; learn how to make positive decisions; take action together; and find a sense of healthy belonging to both their own community and wider Australian society. Issues addressed are intended to inhibit child abuse over the longer term and provide for inter-generational change. These include:

- increased self-worth and self-respect;
- cultural pride;
- empowerment to make positive choices;
- emotional literacy and strategies to manage strong negative emotions;
- resilience and coping skills;
- better understanding of relational needs for self and others;
- development of empathy;
- problem-solving skills;
- higher levels of educational aspiration; and
- social connection and support.

The pedagogy is based in the Circle Solutions framework (Roffey, 2014), which operates through the principles of respect, agency, positivity, inclusion, democracy and safety. All staff involved in the project are trained so they understand the philosophy and facilitate circles appropriately. Without this there is a risk that teachers may exert too much control in the running of circles and focus on problems rather than positive solutions (Roffey & McCarthy, 2013).

Within circles, adults and students are seen as equal. Everyone sits within the circle and participates in all activities. No-one puts another person down either verbally or non-verbally; people listen to each other; adults facilitate decision-making rather than making decisions for the girls; having fun is an important component of what happens; no-one is ever pressured to do or say anything they don't want to and everything possible is done to keep girls included and give them choices. This includes a set of guidelines for when disruptions occur. Girls are regularly mixed up into different groups so that everyone works with everyone else, to discourage cliques and promote cooperation. People rarely work individually and work instead in pairs, small groups and with the whole circle. Most activities require no academic skills and the focus is on collaboration rather than competition.

A wide variety of games and stimulus materials are used to structure discussion, reflection and feedback. These include photographs, strengths cards, collage-making activities, focusing on commonalities and role-play scenarios. Circle sessions often finish with a reflective sentence completion in the round, beginning 'today I learnt', or by participants simply turning to the next person in the circle and saying 'I would like to thank you for…'. In one game the girls identify their strengths by imagining they have been stranded as a group in the bush. They consider the knowledge, character strengths and interpersonal skills that would help them survive. This also gives the girls a way of valuing what they may have learnt from elders in their community and encourages them to find out more. Personal disclosure is discouraged, with a focus on the positive and the third person. This responds to some justifiable critique of social and emotional learning and ensures that the circle is a safe place for both students and staff (Ecclestone and Hayes, 2008).

As the school saw the benefits of this pedagogy all school staff had professional training so they could facilitate circles in other lessons. Several teachers have become trainers to ensure that all new staff are confident with the approach as soon as possible after joining the school. This has therefore become a way of initiating whole-school change from a single intervention.

As with most action research projects in education, we learnt as we went along and the programme developed organically in response to contextual circumstances. Although it takes place within the school there is regular liaison with the local community, especially the Aboriginal elders, to elicit their active support.

Over the four years of the pilot over 50 girls participated in the AGC. Girls volunteer to join in Year 7, though they can express interest later. They stay until the end of Year 10. After this exams set in and time is more limited. Several girls have joined because their older sisters, cousins or other relatives have been part of the AGC and given positive feedback. There are indications, however, that some girls were strongly 'encouraged' in school to join the AGC with a view to changing their behaviour or because they had had particularly challenging experiences.

The AGC runs two overnight camps a year; otherwise the girls meet weekly with the AGC co-ordinator and Aboriginal education officers. The first overnight camp takes place early in the school year and is intended to promote a sense of connection between the girls and to illustrate the circle principles. The girls also engage in activities that show them what resilience means. One of these introduces inspiring Aboriginal women who have made a difference to their communities despite serious adversity. In the evening there is a fun activity and on the second afternoon family and community members are invited to share food with the group, who talk about what they have been doing.

Figure 7.1 depicts a card given by a group of 18 girls to the facilitators at the end of the first camp. It is notable that it appears that, for many, this was the first time they felt that they had a voice, a right to that voice and that others were hearing them.

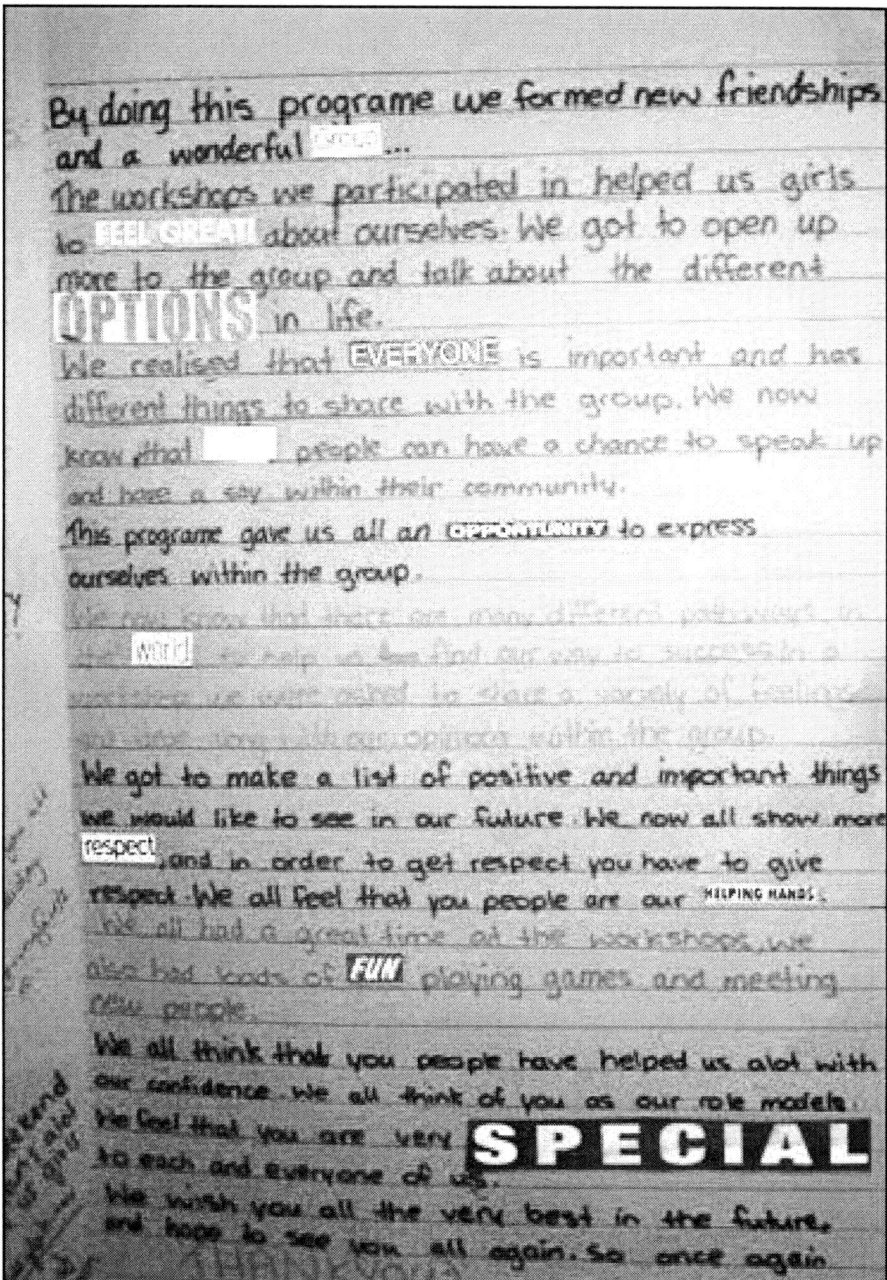

Figure 7.1: Card created by AGC camp participants

These are some of the words on this card:

> We formed new friendships and a wonderful group.
> The workshops helped us feel great about ourselves.
> We got to open up more to the group and talk about the different options in life.
> We realised everyone is important and has different things to share with the group.
> We now all show more respect and in order to get respect you have to give respect.
> We now know that young people can have a chance to speak up and have a say in their community.
> We all had a great time…we had loads of fun playing games and meeting new people.
> It helped us a lot with our confidence.

The second camp explores what the girls are proud of in their community and what they would like to change – what is useful for them to take into their future and what is not. By the end of the two days they will have decided on a project to carry out over the next year (or longer, if necessary). So far groups have chosen very different areas of concern and ways of doing things: these include 'What hurts and what heals racism' (interviews and a book), 'My community' (PowerPoint presentations about cultural identity and family history), 'Friendship and fighting' (a play and dance routine), 'Aboriginal health – with a focus on Diabetes' (an expo) and 'Creating safer communities' (comprising photographs and film). The girls have also raised funds and hosted an elders' lunch. The girls are formally accredited for their community service and this appears on their Record of School Achievement.

A university research team has evaluated the impact of the pilot intervention (Dobia et al., 2014). Support for the initiative from the girls, the community and participating staff was clear and enthusiastic, with increases in the girls' confidence, social skills and leadership being the most frequently cited outcomes. Resilience, connectedness, self-concept and cultural identity were also impacts for the majority of girls who participated.

All stakeholders commented on the growth in the girls' confidence derived from the AGC programme. Specific gains were also reported for self-esteem and leadership ability:

> I was surprised how making the workshops fun, the girls were engaged and were then able to discuss some deep/serious issues. (Adult participant in camp)

Reports of more positive attitudes and improved capacity to take a more considered approach to conflict suggested greater resilience:

> Probably if someone spoke badly to me, I'd probably go back at them. Now I just don't.(AGC participant)

There were multiple reports from the participants of feeling more connected to each other:

> You feel like you're a part of something; and like we all respect each other and respect others', like, ideas and stuff. (AGC partipant)

> I think a lot of these girls walk around feeling like they're not connected to anyone or anything… So for them to come to the circle and feel – and you can just see it – their eyes light up. They feel like a family and they know that they're allowed to say – it's not wrong, whatever they say. Just having that connection. I don't think they've ever had with anyone else. Same with myself. It's a good feeling. (Aboriginal liaison officer)

Both students and Aboriginal staff highlighted the value of the girls coming together in shared acknowledgement of their cultural identity. Particularly notable were the very positive responses from both Aboriginal and non-Aboriginal staff who had participated in circles training and in implementing the programme. Staff felt they had learned valuable practical skills and gained substantially from their understanding of the circles philosophy and framework. All of the components of the programme – including the circles workshops, the camps, meetings with elders and mentors, ongoing regular meetings with the school-based coordinator, the project work and the trips – were highly valued by the girls and by school staff. The extension of the Circle Solutions programme into everyday use in classrooms provides a notable affirmation of the value of the approach taken and the engagement of school staff. For the AGC in particular, the decision to extend it to a new group of girls, to provide specially timetabled sessions and to structure student involvement developmentally from Year 7 indicates the school's commitment to the AGC model and provides a sound basis for further development of the programme.

The positive focus of the AGC sessions was strongly appreciated by the girls:

> You can go to AGC sad and you'll leave it like really happy. (AGC participant)

In addition, the relational focus of the AGC facilitators appeared central to the programme's success. This included their ability to create a safe, non-judgmental atmosphere that allowed the girls to express themselves and gain support for dealing with problems:

> You can talk to, like, [the facilitators] about your problems and stuff and they'll help you with it. (AGC participant)

The sense of trust cultivated within these relationships enabled girls to learn to reflect on and handle difficulties that might otherwise have remained bottled up:

> You can share stuff that you can't share really with anyone else and they'll like help you with it. I would say not even a best friend – I wouldn't be able to share. (AGC participant)

Sustaining such an initiative is a challenge. School personnel have commented many times that the availability and support of outside agencies has made a big difference. As well as facilitation for the two camps, support has taken the form of email and phone contact as well as occasional site visits. This has been critical in keeping to the principles of Circle Solutions. Wanting to do the best for the girls can easily be translated into knowing what is best for them and risks undermining the sense of on-going agency. Teachers want to be helpful and at times this can lead to doing things for the girls instead of with them. Time is a factor especially when the end product becomes the central focus rather than the process. To support the maintenance of an authentic student voice a steering group including AGC representatives has been established, alongside a checklist for on-going circle facilitation.

Despite the challenges, the seeds we have sown are bearing fruit and others can see the differences that are coming about. We are now writing a trainer programme and seeking funding to roll out the initiative in other communities.

> … in this program the girls are given a chance to talk and their opinion is valued and that's made quite clear, in the expectations of the circle where everyone is allowed to say something, there are no put downs, it's a safe environment. … So it's definitely given them a voice – I'd say this is one of the strongest things – plus boosted their confidence as well, definitely. (Teacher)

Although originally designed for a specific group in Australia, this initiative could easily be adapted for other populations. On one level it addresses the needs of a target group, but the outcomes in this instance have rippled across the whole school and beyond.

Conclusion

Many pupils are at risk of either chronic or acute adversity, and we do not necessarily know who these children and young people are. There are things that schools can do – and need to be doing at a universal level – to promote the protective factors that support resilience and wellbeing for all. In so doing they enhance educational opportunities as well as promote more pro-social behaviour. Sadly there has been an increase in educational policies and practices that risk undermining children's social and emotional wellbeing, especially for more vulnerable students. Despite the socio-political climate, or perhaps because of it, we all have a responsibility to encourage and support schools to promote wellbeing wherever and whenever we can, not just as individual practitioners but as services and as a profession. Educational psychologists have a wealth of knowledge and skills that impact positively on the lives of many young people. Add to this courage and creativity and we can extend our commitment to the wellbeing of all.

The true measure of a nation's standing is how well it attends to its children – their health and safety, their material security, their education and socialisation, and their sense of being loved, valued, and included in the families and societies into which they are born. (Unicef, 2007, p.1)

References

ACWP (2014). *Australian Child Wellbeing Project*. Retrieved 25 July 2014 from http://australianchildwellbeing.com.au

Australian Government Productivity Commission (2006). *Report on Government Services 2006, Vol. 2*. Canberra: Author.

Azar, S.T. (2002). Parenting and child maltreatment. In M.H. Bornstein (Ed.) *Handbook of Parenting* (pp.361–388). Hillsdale, NJ: Lawrence Erlbaum.

Blum, R.W. & Libbey, H.P. (2004). Executive summary: Issue on school connectedness – strengthening health and education outcomes for teenagers. *Journal of School Health*, 74(7), 231–232.

CASEL (2010). *The benefits of school-based social and emotional learning programs.* Retrieved 25 August 2014 from www.innerresilience-tidescenter.org/documents/Meta-analysis3-pagesummary7-5-10%282%29.pdf

The Children's Society (2013). *The Good Childhood Report.* Retrieved 25 July 2013 from www.childrenssociety.org.uk/what-we-do/research/well-being/good-childhood-report-2013

Dobia, B., Bodkin-Andrews, G., Parada, R.H. et al. (2014). *The Aboriginal Girls' Circle: Enhancing connectedness and promoting resilience for Aboriginal girls. Final Report.* Penrith, NSW: University of Western Sydney.

Doyle, L. & Hill. R. (2012). *The best of every woman: An overview of approaches to philanthropic investment in Aboriginal women and girls.* Sydney: AMP Foundation.

Ecclestone, K. and Hayes, D. (2008). *The dangerous rise of therapeutic education: How teaching is becoming therapy.* London: Routledge.

Friesthler, B., Merritt, D.H. & LaScala, E.A. (2006). Understanding the ecology of child maltreatment: A review of the literature and directions for future research. *Child Maltreatment, 11*(3) 263–280.

Gable, S.L. & Haidt, J. (2005). What (and why) is positive psychology? *Review of General Psychology, 9*(2) 103–110.

Ipsos-MORI & Nairn, A. (2011). *Children's well-being in UK, Sweden and Spain: The role of inequality and materialism.* Retrieved 20 July 2014 from www.ipsos-mori.com/DownloadPublication/1441_sri-unicef-role-of-inequality-and-materialism-june-2011.pdf

Mosco, J. & O'Brien, K. (2012). Positive parent-child relationships. In S. Roffey (Ed.) *Positive relationships: Evidence-based practice across the world.* Dordrecht: Springer.

New South Wales Commission for Children and Young People (2007). *Ask the children: Overview of children's understandings of wellbeing.* Retrieved 14 July 2014 from http://apo.org.au/research/ask-children-overview-childrens-understandings-wellbeing

Noble, T., McGrath, H., Roffey, S. & Rowling, L. (2008). *Scoping study into approaches to student wellbeing.* Australian Catholic University and Erebus International. Retrieved 18 July 2016 from https://docs.education.gov.au/system/files/doc/other/scoping_study_into_approaches_to_student_wellbeing_final_report.pdf

Noddings, N. (1992). *The challenge to care in schools: An alternative approach to education.* New York: Teachers College Press.

Purdie, N., Dudgeon, P. & Walker, R. (2010). *Working together: Aboriginal and Torres Strait Islander mental health and wellbeing principles and practice.* Canberra: Australian Institute of Health and Welfare.

Roffey, S. (n.d.) *Respect4us: The practice and relevance of positive relationships.* Retrieved 11 August 2016 from www.respect4us.com/?p=sue.roffey

Roffey, S. (2011). *Changing behaviour in schools: Promoting positive relationships and wellbeing.* London: Sage.

Roffey, S. (2014). *Circle solutions for student wellbeing.* London: Sage.

Roffey, S. & McCarthy, F. (2013) Circle solutions: A philosophy and pedagogy for learning positive relationships. What promotes and inhibits sustainable outcomes? *International Journal of Emotional Education, 5*(1), 36–55.

Spratt, J., Shucksmith, J., Philip, K. & Watson, C. (2006). 'Part of who we are as a school should include responsibility for wellbeing': Links between the school environment, mental health and behaviour. *Pastoral Care, 24*(3), 14–21.

UNICEF (2007) Child poverty in perspective: An overview of child well-being in rich countries. Innocenti Report Card 7. Florence: UNICEF.

Werner, E.E. (2004) What can we learn about resilience from large scale longitudinal studies? In S. Goldstein and R.B. Brooks (Eds.) *Handbook of Resilience in Children.* New York: Kluwer Academic/Plenum Publishers.

Wolpert-Gawron, H. (2014) *Kids speak out on student engagement.* Retrieved 15 July 2014 from www.edutopia.org/blog/student-engagement-stories-heather-wolpert-gawron

Chapter 8.1 Out of school: Eliciting the child's voice in cases of extended non-attendance

Matt Baker

The research in context

When Isra Broadwin first identified a 'special form of truancy' involving fear of school (Broadwin, 1932), it is unlikely that he foresaw how little progress would be made in addressing this issue over the next eighty years. Extended non-attendance[1] ('school phobia' or 'school refusal') as it is now known affects one to two per cent of the UK school-age population, equivalent to some 10,000–20,000 children (Elliott, 1999; Kearney, 2008; ONS, 2013). Numerous interventions have been tried with this group, including psychodynamic, behavioural and cognitive-behavioural therapies and pharmacotherapy (Beidas et al., 2010; Miller, 2008). However, outcomes for all these appear mixed, with little evidence of any approach working consistently or more efficaciously than another (Bernstein et al., 1990; Knollman et al., 2010; Lauchlan, 2003). There are many possible reasons for this, the most obvious being that this is not an identifiable 'group'. To describe extended non-attenders as a 'group' is to define the issue by a symptom, that of non-attendance. Even a brief examination of the literature suggests that extended non-attendance results from many causes, including separation anxiety, social anxiety, depression, bullying, fear of academic failure or strict teachers or fear of leaving a vulnerable parent at home (Miller, 2008; Nuttall & Woods, 2013). Most commonly it results from an interactive mix of these and other factors (Gregory & Purcell, 2014; King & Bernstein, 2001), and hence needs to receive individual responses accordingly.

Different as the causes may be, the outcomes are all matters for concern. They include poor academic results and reduced social opportunities in the short term (Garry, 1996; Pellegrini, 2007; Taylor, 2012), with correlations being noted between extended non-attendance and subsequent poor adult mental health, criminality and substance misuse (McShane et al., 2004; Miller, 2008). A number of those affected end up somewhere in the criminal justice or addiction treatment system, which is where my interest in this group began.

Before training as a practitioner educational psychologist, I worked for some years as a substance misuse worker in what was a partly therapeutic and partly practical role, and was struck by the number of clients I met who had experienced ex-

---

[1] The term 'extended non-attendance' is used throughout in place of previous terms such as 'school refusal' or 'school phobia', reflecting an emerging convention within the recent literature (e.g. Gregory & Purcell, 2014; Pellegrini, 2007). This results from growing discomfort with the use of these other terms. 'School refusal', in particular, implies a choice on the part of the child not to attend, and when applied to children with genuine anxieties and other mental health difficulties is clearly unacceptable. If equivalent thinking was applied to adults with similar difficulties, it would result in us referring to those with depression and anxiety currently signed off work as 'work refusers', a usage that most would find unacceptable.

tended non-attendance. When I encountered the relevant psychological literature, I was puzzled by how confused it appeared. Given the disparate explanations of non-attendance and the clear individuality of cases, I was left asking why so little had been done to elicit the child's voice. Logically, I thought, the first step towards establishing effective intervention practice where previous attempts have shown such mixed outcomes needs to be an exploration of the lived experience of non-attendance. Only in this way can we begin to understand what individuals receiving the interventions feel works, does not work and why. I would still maintain that this conclusion was right, although I now know what I had then naively overlooked: persuading children who have effectively fallen (or, as they often feel, been pushed) out of the education system to talk about their experiences is hard and time consuming.

Which method?

Whatever methodology was to be used had to privilege the children's voices, placing detailed articulation of their experience at the heart of the project. The unit of analysis was, as a result, almost constrained to be semi-structured interviews, the 'conversation with a purpose ... which permits participants to tell their own stories' (Smith et al., 2009, p.57). The choice of phenomenology followed from the recognition that the most important element of the project was the exploration of lived experience, the process of unpicking and understanding the child's *phenomenon*, or self and experience as shaped and lived (Langdridge, 2007). The choice of Interpretative Phenomenological Analysis (IPA – Smith et al., 2009) followed, again naturally and logically, from the need to operationalise a methodology systematically across all cases. It also meant that the research was, if not perfectly replicable (qualitative methodologies involve too many subjective decisions and interpretations to claim perfect replicability), then at least clearly located and transparent in its process and assumptions.

This focus on the child's voice led to an initial paper, now accepted for publication (Baker & Bishop, in press), which presented an exploration of the lived experiences of four children. It also led to the finding that the other element missing from the evidence base was a detailed consideration of adult understandings (those of parents, teachers, etc.) of extended non-attendance, and their impact on the child's experience. Exploring this required a different and more unusual methodological approach, tailored towards examination of the impact of adult understandings on the child's phenomenon. The result was a blended approach, which sought to analyse adult accounts using Foulcauldian Discourse Analysis (FDA – e.g. Kendall & Wickham, 2003), and then explore the child's experience of being located within these dominant adult discourses. This approach drew on various influences, including Carla Willig's exploration of cancer diagnosis, which applied a similar methodology to examining the individual's life-world as impacted by the positions of others (Willig, 2011). In terms of articulating the child's voice the combination of the two methodologies allowed exploration of the child's opinions and experience, with a background understanding of how these were shaped, directed, limited or enabled by the adults in their lives.

Applications in practice

The first practical step was to define groups of participants. Child participants were defined as those who had been out of school for two terms or more, and whose parents/guardians *had not* been prosecuted (implying acceptance by the authorities of some genuine reason for non-attendance). All were of secondary age, in line with statistical data that suggests incidence of extended non-attendance peaks in line with transition to secondary school (Pellegrini, 2007; Nuttall & Woods, 2013). The groups of adults identified as important by the children in the initial study were parents, teachers, educational welfare officers and staff from the home education service, with the result that it was these adults who were recruited.

So far, so easy! However, advice from Isabel Gregory, one of the only other researchers to attempt a similar study (Gregory & Purcell, 2014), led me to conclude that recruitment via the usual channels (letters sent via agencies, etc) was unlikely to work – this was a group of children and parents who felt let down, often for understandable reasons, by many of the professionals they had encountered. As a result, recruitment was made via word of mouth and personal introductions through the Home Education and Educational Welfare services, a method that potentially skewed the sample, relying as it did on third parties, but which made the project possible.

Findings with illustrative quotes

Findings from the children's interviews at times made for difficult reading. Although participants differed markedly in their perception of the causes of their initial non-attendance, their subsequent support experiences were virtually identical, suggesting that little attention had been paid to individual circumstances. Themes common to most accounts included being disbelieved, struggling to access support, and feeling blamed and punished:

> [T]he school just thinks you're being naughty ... I didn't know who I could talk to. ('Cynthia' – subsequently diagnosed with anxiety and depression, and still out of school.)

> [T]hey told Mum to just take things away from me ... they refused to send work home because they thought, again, I was just being lazy. ('Malcolm' – now receiving ongoing support for ME)

> [T]hey [the school] wanted to start charging us for unauthorised absences ... It felt like the teacher was calling all the shots. Like, I didn't get a say. ('Graham' – receiving ongoing support for depression; hoping to go on to college this September)

> I have anxiety, I'm not naughty ... help for two or three days does not fix anxiety. ('Amelia' – receiving ongoing therapy; now at college)

Of the four participants, only one had seen a psychologist, despite clear psychological issues in all cases. All four had experienced initial interventions that consisted primarily of punitive responses to their absence, and then had to wait months for further support. Equally, despite their anger all four showed some understanding of why their support experience had been like this, with comments such as 'they've got too many students to deal with' (Cynthia) appearing in all accounts, suggesting a cumbersome system which overlooks individual needs and circumstances.

The cumulative and shaping effect on the participants' experience was clear, with those interviewed suggesting that they had learned to 'hide' emotions (Amelia) and 'block' conversations (Graham), and concluding that it was unsafe to talk to the professionals involved. Perhaps most worryingly what this implies is that local intervention practice as enacted in these cases did not draw on the evidence base, which suggests that responses should be swift, individual and based on a functional analysis of the purpose served for the child by their absence (Gregory & Purcell, 2014; Kearney & Silverman, 1990).

Care should be taken in commenting at this stage of the research on the content of the adult accounts, many of which have yet to be analysed, and some of which have yet to be collected. However, initial findings indicate differences in the understandings held by the various groups of adults interviewed. Given that these are the people whose beliefs structure the lived experience of the children whom they parent, educate or support, this is a matter of great concern. How a child is supposed to make sense of adult understandings of their non-attendance, when these range from viewing it as naughtiness requiring enforcement of the attendance through to regarding it as a mental health condition requiring pharmacotherapy, is a baffling question. The impact on the child's phenomenon is clear, if only in terms of the confusion this engenders and the emotional damage it causes.

Reflections on the method

In terms of the methodology, the approach used here is time consuming and labour intensive, but at the same time nuanced and powerful in the understandings it produces. Both phenomenology and discursive psychology share a social constructionist ontology (Martinez-Avila & Smiraglia, 2012), with commentators suggesting that the main difference between the two is that discursive psychology is more overtly constructionist in its understandings (Smith et al., 2009). They are compatible and appropriate ways of examining the phenomenon or *lifeworld* as experienced (Husserl & Heidegger, 1927), and the processes by which it is constructed.

The method was time consuming, in terms both of understanding the philosophical underpinnings on which the theory rests and of the actual analysis. Much of my summer was spent re-reading Sartre, Husserl and Foucault, and constructionist theory from Berger and Luckmann (1966) onwards. My phenomenological work involved both textual analysis, and the intellectual process of thinking myself inside the skin and the mind of another. This entailed attempting to initially bracket out my own self and interpretations, and seeking to enter fully into the children's lived experiences by exploring the places they described (school halls, classrooms, the paths and roads leading between them) whilst listening back to their descriptions. The ongoing discursive process entails a detailed textual analysis that seeks to contextualise how the speaker is positioned by the discursive resources at their disposal, and subsequently how this positions the non-attending children with whom they have involvements: even with practice, I have yet to devote less than two days to an interview.

As an overall research experience I'd do it all again, and feel that the process has numerous other applications. Only through rigour, and with transparency, can we genuinely hope to explore the meaning and texture of lived experience. By doing so, we are hopefully able to challenge and make significant improvements to what are sometimes quite blunt (if well meant) intervention practices, and ensure support is more responsive to children's voices and needs.

The research detailed here was undertaken as part of the researcher's doctoral training (DEdPsych) at the University of Southampton. Particular thanks are due to Dr Felicity Bishop and to Darren Suffolk for supervising and supporting this work.

References

Baker, M. & Bishop, F. (in press). Out of school: A phenomenological exploration of extended non-attendance. *Educational Psychology in Practice.*

Beidas, R., Crawley, S., Mychailyszyn, M. et al. (2010). Cognitive behavioural treatment of anxious youth with co-morbid school refusal: Clinical presentation and treatment response. *Psychological Topics, 19*(2), 255–271.

Berger, P., & Luckmann, T. (1966). *The social construction of reality.* Harmondsworth: Penguin.

Bernstein, G., Garfinkel, B. & Borchardt, C. (1990). Comparative studies of pharmacotherapy for school refusal. *Journal of the American Academy of Child and Adolescent Psychiatry, 29*(5), 773–781.

Broadwin, I. (1932). A contribution to the study of truancy. *American Journal of Orthopsychiatry, 2*(3), 253–259.

Elliott, J. (1999). Practitioner review: School refusal: Issues of conceptualisation, assessment and treatment. *Journal of Child Psychology and Psychiatry, 40,* 1001–1012.

Garry, E. (1996). *Truancy: First steps to a lifetime of problems.* Washington, DC: Office of Juvenile Justice and Delinquency Protection.

Gregory, I. & Purcell, A. (2014). Extended school non-attenders' views: Developing best practice. *Educational Psychology in Practice, 30*(1), 37–50.

Husserl, E. & Heidegger, M. (1927). Phenomenology – Draft B: The Encyclopaedia Britannica Article. R. Sheehan, trans. and revised. Retrieved 2 February 2015 from http://religiousstudies.stanford.edu/wp-content/uploads/PHENOMENOLOGY-ENCYCLOPAEDIA-BRITANNICA.pdf

Kearney, C. (2008). School absenteeism and school refusal behaviour in youth: An empirical analysis of absenteeism severity. *Journal of Child Psychology and Psychiatry, 48,* 53–61.

Kearney, C. & Silverman, W. (1990). A preliminary analysis of a functional model of assessment and intervention of school refusal behaviour. *Behaviour Modification, 149,* 340–365.

Kendall, G. & Wickham, G. (2003). *Using Foucault's Methods.* London: Sage.

King, N. & Bernstein, G. (2001). School refusal in children and adolescents: A review of the past ten years. *Journal of the American Academy of Child and Adolescent Psychiatry, 40*(2), 197–205.

Knollman, M., Knoll, S., Reissner, V. et al. (2010). School avoidance from the point of view of child and adolescent psychiatry. *Deutsches Arzteblatt International, 107*(4), 43–49.

Langdridge, D. (2007). *Phenomenological Psychology: Theory, research and method.* London: Prentice Hall.

Lauchlan, F. (2003). Responding to chronic non-attendance: A review of intervention approaches. *Educational Psychology in Practice, 19*(2), 133–146.

Martinez-Avila, D. & Smiraglia, R. (2012). *Revealing perception: Discourse analysis in a phenomenological framework.* Paper presented at the 23rd Annual SIG/CR Classification Research Workshop, Baltimore, MD. Retrieved 2 February 2015 from www.iskocus.org/NASKO2013proceedings/MartinezAvila_Smiraglia_Revealing_Perception.pdf

McShane, G., Walter, G. & Rey, J. (2004). Functional outcome of adolescents with 'school refusal'. *Clinical Child Psychology and Psychiatry, 9,* 53–60.

Miller, A. (2008). School phobia and school refusal. In N. Frederickson, A. Miller & T. Cline (Eds.), *Educational Psychology* (pp. 215–234). London: Hodder.

Nuttall, C. & Woods, K. (2013). Effective intervention for school refusal behaviour. *Educational Psychology in Practice, 29*(4), 347–366.

ONS (2013). *National population projections, 2012-based statistical bulletin.* Retrieved 2 February 2015 from www.ons.gov.uk/ons/dcp171778_334975.pdf

Pellegrini, D. (2007). School non-attendance: definitions, meanings, responses, interventions. *Educational Psychology in Practice, 23*(1), 63–77.

Smith, J., Flowers, P. & Larkin, M. (2009). *Interpretative phenomenological analysis.* London: Sage.

Taylor, C. (2012). *Improving attendance at school.* London: Department for Education.

Willig, C. (2011). Cancer diagnosis as discursive capture: Phenomenological repercussions of being positioned within dominant constructions of cancer. *Social Science and Medicine, 73,* 897–903.

Chapter 8.2 'Education, for me, it's the most important thing for everyone's life…because if I was not in education I would be alone': Hearing the voices of separated refugees on the topic of education

Claire Cox

Research in context

Separated Refugee Young People (SRYP) arrive in the UK having fled persecution and violence in their home countries, and are without the support of parents or carers. They have lost their homes, loved ones and culture as a result of recurring traumatic events. Typically aged between 14 and 16 years of age, SRYP make up a small percentage of children looked after (approximately six per cent, according to Barrie and Mendes (2011)) and often become care-leavers shortly after their arrival in the UK. In relation to their accompanied counterparts (those who arrive with family), as well as native looked-after child counterparts (who are typically English-speaking and British-born), SRYP have a distinct set of experiences, needs and strengths. Their educational experiences, prior to taking flight, are often wide and varied. Some young people have never learned within an educational context and cannot read and write in their home language, while others may have consistently attended education settings before the need to flee arose. Once acknowledged by a receiving UK local authority, the experiences of support and care for these young people are disparate, with provision in some cases meeting the holistic needs of SRYP and in others affording only the bare minimum. Although the research into this field is sparse and of variable quality, authors have noted the group's 'hunger for education, and a capacity and stubborn willingness to succeed despite the odds' (Kohli & Mather, 2003, p. 210).

Rationale

Within the broad field of psychology, Martin-Baro (1996) proposed that 'liberation psychology' approaches are the ethical obligation of all psychologists, particularly when working with traumatised groups or individuals. He suggested that psychologists should seek feedback and views from marginalised groups, rather than simply honouring the dominant culture's response to psychological intervention. In order to promote liberating approaches to psychological intervention, the educational psychologist (EP) role has been placed within a 'community psychology' framework strongly supported by literature and practice (e.g. McKay, 2006). Based on values and beliefs about nurturing the welfare of people, removing institutional barriers and redressing power imbalances in society, community psychology verifies the need to elicit views and participation from stakeholders across multiple systemic levels. Within EP training and practice, these frameworks are learned and implemented in many ways, including the use of consultation in schools and other education settings. The research project described here aimed to maintain and extend the principles of such frameworks in order to offer opportunities for SRYP to describe their experiences and potentially to shape future interventions for this multiply oppressed subgroup of children and young people. Within the field of educational psychology in particular, the project set out to raise awareness of this distinctly marginalised population, whose strengths and needs had barely been documented within EP literature.

Research methods

The current account portrays the voices of six male SRYP on the topic of education in the UK. The project was approached from a broadly social constructionist position, in which the aim was to yield rich, complex data in the form of SRYP's voices, as opposed to producing linear categorisations of their experiences. Once ethical approval had been gained, it was necessary to gain approval from the relevant Director of Children's Services in order to proceed with recruitment. Schools, colleges and relevant local charities were then approached with information leaflets for professionals and young people in order to reach potential participants within a London borough. As the researcher, I spent time in relevant organisations, such as local youth groups and residential settings for refugees, in order to build up trust with the young people and offer explanations of the project and my intentions in person. Across several months, six male SRYP came forward to take part. At this point they were reminded of their right to close the interview at any stage and confidentiality guidelines were explained again, before they were asked to sign a formal consent document. To allow for questions to be shaped by participants' individual responses within the session, semi-structured interviews were carried out (Kvale, 1996). In the context of potential fear and resistance to participation, due to negative and traumatic experiences of interrogation at the Home Office, this naturalistic approach enabled rapport and trust to be built between researcher and participant at various stages. It also allowed participants to share as much or as little information as they wished. Interviews were recorded using a digital audio recorder, and later transcribed and analysed using a hybrid inductive-deductive, manifest/ latent approach to thematic analysis (Fereday & Muir-Cochrane, 2006). Thematic analysis is considered an appropriate method when participants may have limited English, and can be used flexibly to meet the aims of research questions. Thematic analysis was carried out in a systematic, rigorous manner, as per the process set out by Braun and Clarke (2006) and Joffe (2012).

Findings

The following subheadings are illustrated largely by direct quotations from the interviews, followed by my own interpretations of SRYP's views. In particular, the captions below have been selected to strengthen the discourse that exists in the literature that education serves this population in a multifaceted and beneficial sense.

The piece aims to celebrate the positive impact of education on multiple aspects of participants' inner and outer worlds by direct quotations from interviewees.

Giving hope for the future

[I]f you keep studying and studying, it's good, one day you're gonna be someone, you're gonna have your own business maybe, you're gonna have your own chair and table at work. (Jeton)

[S]o my advice, I can't count for everyone, would be just do their best because they will then have future and if they do education they will have a job, and if they have a job, they will be able to have a family and to support that family, and to support themselves. (Yasin)

For me, education has given me a good life, it's why I'm so happy, I love my job because it is like a study and I love it. (Ibrahim)

When speaking about education in the UK, the young people made reference to the hope it enabled them to feel for their futures. In the context of many kinds of traumatic loss at multiple levels, including material, emotional and social, participation in education provided a platform from which they could reach for a better life. This seemed to influence a flexible view of their social and economic status over time, with aspirations to become independent and successful adults as a result of their efforts at college. All participants indicated implicitly that involvement in education enabled them to develop a sense of ambition, responsibility for their own futures and a strong determination to succeed. As the researcher, I was struck by the sense of agency which education allowed the young people to feel over their lives, particularly in the context of great uncertainty and ambiguity about other aspects of their experience.

Bringing social and emotional support

[T]his...is gonna sound like a bit nerdy but I just feel like very happy at college always, you know I just feel happy because more people around me more people that are friends, that I talk to, for me I'm like a very friendly person so I just get like very friendly with anybody. (Akhtar)

[I]t is almost a distraction, a form of distraction because I still like, everybody loves their mum and their family and I was really missing them actually...yeah reading books, studying, really distracted me. (Yasin)

I like to go in class with my friends, to enjoy, to know everything, to know new things, sometimes I like to speak with my friends in class to help chill out. (Belal)

[E]ducation, for me, it's the most important thing for everyone's life...because if I was not in education I would be alone. (Ibrahim)

I have some friends as well, and teachers were really friendly, they just give me emotional support, they provide me with mentor so I can talk to someone, and they knew that I was really motivated, so they put me with like volunteer work. They asked me to do this so it will help me enjoy life here and you will learn more things and that's good for you as well. (Yasin)

The experiences of being supported emotionally, socially and practically by peers and adults, as well as the feeling of connection to others, had a profound effect on many aspects of SRYP's lives. Participants shared details of both internal and external adversities such as intrusive thoughts, sadness and loneliness, as well as the continued traumas caused by living a liminal existence between countries and the uncertainty of deportation. The feelings of belonging, evoked by their association with education settings, teachers, mentors and peers, enabled young people to feel more resilient and able to cope with such adversities. A key aspect of this support was the nature of relationships that were developed with adults around them. Most participants described a relationship with an adult who brought a balance of nurturing and respectful qualities, together with a capacity to give practical support, guidance and advice. In addition, education gave a necessary focus to the lives of some participants, which allowed them to escape temporarily from their traumatic memories of the past.

A place to feel a sense of personal and academic achievement

[T]he best memory that I had, I was elected as student of the year the first year I was in college and I got an award, and that really was the best…because my support worker was there, social worker was there, teacher was there and I was sitting there and I just thought, well they are my family here…they were so happy for me and they were cheering and shouting and when they called my name they were crazy! Especially my teacher. (Yasin)

[W]hen teacher tell me 'well done' I mean I feel proud and I feel, that feeling inside and you just, you like that feeling to happen again and you just learn again and try again that push you a little bit. I don't know, I just love college.

…when I went in college at the beginning, I didn't really know nothing…I was scared or something I didn't really know how to answer and stuff, but now I can't stop the answering! (Jeton)

[T]he teacher was the best because the teacher was really helpful yeah she helped me…now I can see my reading writing improve a bit better. (Nabil)

Young people were encouraged by the progress and developments they were able to observe in themselves as a result of working hard and accessing appropriate support. Experiences of success provided an abundant source of positive emotions, which linked with participants' demonstrable feelings of capacity and agency over their educational lives. In turn, it seemed that their experiences in education settings were shaping their identities as learners, as well as functional, capable individuals. As these young people felt powerless in other areas of their lives, the opportunity to develop new narratives about themselves seemed to have a profound effect on their wellbeing. The celebration of achievement by important adults, as described by Yasin above, paved the way for positive memories to be created. All participants, in particular, noted the importance of learning the English language as a gateway to social integration, and an understanding of British culture, as well as academic and economic success.

Areas for development

While the purpose of this section is to substantiate views that education can activate a plethora of positive outcomes for SRYP, the views gathered in the project described above also alluded to some areas for improvement. Participants unanimously emphasised the importance of language learning, alongside learning key aspects of British youth culture, in determining their opportunities to develop social connections and, ultimately, to 'fit in'.

> [I]t's like a dream to learn English, to be a good speaker like English person. (Jeton)

> [S]o now I'm just improving my knowledge across uh the culture, because they talk about lots of things, about football, or I've watched some films or I've watched a series, for example, but normally I don't know anything, the actors, the people. They talk about 'blah blah blah blah' and I'm like 'what on earth you are talking about, it doesn't mean anything' ... yeah so I just keep studying and I just stay in my room, I don't go out, I didn't have chance to make friends. (Yasin)

The extreme loneliness reported by SRYP during interviews might be alleviated through the development of peer mentoring or buddy systems within education settings. The fundamental role of language (including slang and colloquialisms) in facilitating social connection was noted.

Reflections on the method

The use of qualitative research methods, grounded in social constructionist ways of thinking, allowed me to gather the personal and individual views of this small group of SRYP. A number of large, quantitative studies demonstrate robust research procedures within that paradigm, as well as the possibility of transferring findings to the wider population in some circumstances (for example Hodes et al., 2008; Hollins et al., 2003). On the other hand, due to the legislative and bureaucratic systems affecting this highly vulnerable group, as well as the huge time constraints posed by qualitative approaches, the currently described project elicited the voices of only six SRYP. In addition, the challenge of accessing the population for research purposes led to a limited spread of demographics amongst participants, so the transferability of findings was not possible. Consistent with my epistemological position, I suggest that quantitative studies into the needs or wellbeing of SRYP might subjugate their voices by imposing pre-determined and culturally inappropriate measures on participants who originate from a range of cultures and backgrounds (for example Hodes et al., 2008; Hollins et al., 2003). The use of surveys and questionnaires, designed by researchers of the dominant culture, could arguably constrain the voices of these already oppressed young people, thus opposing the premise of community psychology or liberation approaches. Conversely, the use of semi-structured interviews, as in the study described here, enables a more naturalistic environment to be created in which individual views can be shared in the context of participants' own culture and understanding. In addition, I would suggest that research participants in this particular study found the research interview to be a helpful and affirming experience in which their achievements could be celebrated.

Hearing the voices of these six SRYP has enabled me to gain insight into the many positive roles that education can serve as a complex and shifting catalyst for a number of constructive developments for this population.

Conclusions

The profile of children in care is currently on the rise, with the requirement for all local authorities to appoint a headteacher of a virtual school, for example, as stated in the Children and Families Act 2014. SRYP make up a significant minority of this population, and in many ways present with a distinct set of needs and strengths. Through the use of qualitative research methods and collaborative problem-solving approaches, educational psychologists could play a vital role in facilitating policy development and change for this group at a school and organisational level. EPs are well placed to elicit the views of this remarkable and distinct population in order to create conditions in which their strong determination can be constructively chan-neled. The clear and resounding voice of this small group suggested that education can provide them with the emotional, social and academic support and opportuni-ties necessary for positive self-development and protection from the harmful effects of extreme adversities in their lives. In my opinion, these multiple positive effects should be widely shared, and the good practice of teaching staff celebrated, in order to promote and develop further success in the future.

References

Barrie, L., & Mendes, P. (2011). The experiences of unaccompanied asylum-seeking children in and leaving the out-of-home care system in the UK and Australia: A critical review of the literature. *International Social Work, 54*, 485–503. doi:10.1177/0020872810389318

Braun, V. & Clarke, V. (2006). Using thematic analysis in psychology. *Qualitative Research in Psychology, 3*, 77–101.

Department for Education (DfE). (2014) *The Children and Families Act.* London: DfE.

Fereday, J. & Muir-Cochrane, E. (2006).Demonstrating rigor using thematic analysis: A hybrid approach of inductive and deductive coding and theme development. *International Journal of Qualitative Methods, 5*, 1–11.

Hodes, M., Jagdev, D., Chandra, N. & Cunniff, A. (2008). Risk and resilience for psychological distress amongst unaccompanied asylum seeking adolescents. *Journal of Child Psychology and Psychiatry, 49*(7), 723–32.

Hollins, K., Heydari, H. & Leavey, G. (2003). *Refugee adolescents without parents: A survey of psychological and social difficulties amongst unaccompanied refugee minors in Haringey.* London: Barnet, Enfield and Haringey Mental Health NHS Trust.

Joffe, H. (2012). Thematic analysis. In D. Harper & A. Thomson (Eds.) *Qualitative research methods in mental health and psychotherapy: A guide for students and practitioners.* London: Wiley.

Kohli, R. & Mather, R. (2003). Promoting psychosocial well being in unaccompanied asylum seeking young people in the United Kingdom. *Child and Family Social Work, 8*(3), 201–212.

Kvale, S. (1996). *InterViews: An introduction to qualitative research interviewing.* Thousand Oaks, CA: Sage.

McKay, T. (2006). The educational psychologist as community psychologist: Holistic child psychology across home, school and community. *Educational and Child Psychology, 23*, 7–15.

Martin-Baro, I. (1996). *Writings for a liberation psychology.* New York: Harvard University Press.

Chapter 8.3 Obtaining the views of children with profound and multiple learning difficulties

Emma Harding

Why is it important that we ascertain the views of children and young people with complex needs?

> Children and young people everywhere – across all regions and sections of society – want their views, experiences and suggestions listened to. It remains true that the hardest voices to reach are the ones that we most need to hear. (DfES, 2001, p.3)

Obtaining the views of children, including those with Special Educational Needs and Disabilities (SEND), and involving them in decisions concerning their life and learning has become an increasingly accepted and fundamental phenomenon. Enabling children and young people to make a positive contribution is high on the list of government priorities. The new SEND Code of Practice (DfE, 2014) highlights the importance – indeed the statutory duty – of ensuring that children and young people are involved in discussions and decisions about both their individual support and local provision, to be achieved through the use of person-centred approaches with a focus on outcomes co-produced with the child and family.

Whitehurst (2006) points out that 'children with profound and complex learning difficulties pose challenges to inclusion' (p.56). Markedly many studies in this area focus on the views, attitudes and changing perceptions of pupils with SEND who are able to communicate using spoken language, who have higher levels of cognitive functioning and more developed social, communication and interaction skills. Less research has focused on children who have more complex needs, such as those with Profound and Multiple Learning Difficulties (PMLD), therefore leaving their voices relatively silenced.

The attitudes of society towards disability are perhaps a barrier that limits professionals' ability to ascertain the views of children with more complex needs. Knight and Oliver (2007) propose that a more traditional perception by the public of disabled children as being passive, vulnerable and in need of protection makes advocating for these children challenging. Furthermore, methodological and ethical issues are also a problem, and Whitehurst (2006) states:

> The importance of the voice of the child has now been recognised and supported by both international and national legislation. However, the ways in which we elicit these views, the ethics surrounding them, their validity and reliability, remain problematic. (Whitehurst, 2006, p.56).

How can EPs access the views of children with PMLD?

Norwich and Kelly (2006) point out that educational psychologists (EPs) have led the way in assessing children's perspectives, in conducting studies of the impact of participation on motivation and behaviour and in advocating for participation. Furthermore, the Educational Psychology Services Report of the Working Group (DfES, 2000) suggests that EPs are well placed to ensure that children's views are both elicited in a neutral way and included in plans being drawn up for them.

Clark and Moss (2006) state:

> It is important to understand listening to be a process that is not limited to the spoken word. The phrase 'voice of the child' may suggest the transmission of ideas only through words, but listening to young children, including pre-verbal children, needs to be a process which is open to the many creative ways young children use to express their views and experiences. (p.5)

According to Holman (2004), communicating with people with higher support needs takes time and skill. Furthermore, Whitehurst (2006) suggests that eliciting the views of children with SEND demands extra consideration and that both strategies and tools to undertake such a task are limited.

Rationale and summary of review

It is timely to investigate how EPs can better access the views of all children and young people at a point where recent SEND legislation has made this a key focus. The usefulness of an exploration and critique of some of the available literature in this area is threefold. It raises awareness regarding the inclusion of pupils with more complex needs; assists EPs and professionals in consulting with these children; and therefore enables more effective and inclusive work.

When searching the associated literature only a very small number of articles were found to focus exclusively on children with PMLD. After reading through these papers, the following overarching research question became apparent: to what extent is it possible to ascertain the views of children with profound and multiple learning difficulties? A key theme within this broad research question incorporated an exploration of the methods and tools that may be effective in ascertaining the views of children with PMLD. This short review attempts to summarise and discuss a selection of the available literature that explores how best the views of children with PMLD can be accessed. This chapter also briefly describes an example of how one educational psychology service (EPS) has developed practice in person-centered (PC) approaches in order to promote the involvement of children and young people.

Methodological guidelines

A 2004 article by Lewis provides a number of research-based 'pointers' concerning methods that are relevant to 'chronologically or developmentally young children'. Examples of these include permitting or encouraging 'don't know' responses; countering the child's assumption that the adult knows the answer to prevent suggestibility; using statements rather than questions; using an appropriate level of generality in questions; avoiding repeating questions, yes/no alternatives and successive prompts; being aware of the impact of referents and pronouns and aiming for uninterrupted narrative. Importantly, Lewis points out that 'we lack evidence concerning the authenticity, credibility and reliability of particular methods for exploring the views of children with learning difficulties' (Lewis, 2004, p.4). In her article she highlights the importance of using multiple approaches so that the limitations of one are offset by the strengths of another. This is a notion which much of the literature sourced in this area supports.

Lewis and Porter (2004) emphasise some further issues that need to be considered, proposing a set of guidelines for critical self-evaluation by those who are engaged in collecting views from children with learning disabilities. The authors state that the group of children to whom they are referring in this paper might be described in educational terms as having 'severe or profound learning difficulties'. Methodological issues highlighted include those concerned with sampling, design, communication and methods. In terms of sampling the authors point out that because people with learning difficulties are a diverse group and have a high incidence of additional disabilities, including multiple impairments, there are few assumptions that can be made reliably about the characteristics of the whole population. They also point out that researchers should not assume that the addition of alternative modes of communication will be sufficient to make the experience meaningful to all potential participants and suggest that developing appropriate communication skills is one of the greatest challenges for the researcher.

Lewis and Porter (2004) suggest that the researcher can best validate their interpretation of the child's response through the use of additional methods which may serve to confirm or clarify their analysis. In support, Dockrell (2004) suggests that using multiple sources of data collection or triangulation to construct accurate interpretations when interviewing children with specific and general learning difficulties should be considered. This notion of using multiple methods to increase validity is in line with the views put forward in other articles (Knight et al., 2006; Lewis, 2004; Ware, 2004; Whitehurst, 2006).

This work serves to highlight that although ascertaining the views of children with PMLD can be seen as a basic right, at the same time the extent to which methodological issues may limit the ability to ascertain a reliable and valid view must also be acknowledged.

Tools and methods that may be effective in ascertaining the voice of the child with more complex needs

The Participation in Education Project (Watson et al., 2006) entailed a national survey of 'relevant' primary schools in England and was designed to identify current national practices for involving children with little or no verbal communication in their decision-making. Almost all schools reported that they used a range of strategies, equipment or information and communication technology (ICT) to support children with little or no verbal communication. These were categorised by the researchers as including signing, symbols, equipment, programmes, strategies, software programmes and low-tech equipment.

Knight and colleagues (2006) for the Department for Education and Skills carried out a review which involved an examination of consultations and methods used to ascertain the views of children and young people with learning disabilities about the support they receive from social services. This review is based on a comprehensive electronic and paper literature review and discussions with key experts. Similar to my experience, the authors found a relatively small number of studies that have focused on the views of children with learning and other disabilities. In this review no single method is advocated, but a range of consultation and research tools are identified that may enable children with a range of disabilities, including those who do not communicate through speech, to express their views and experiences. Knight et al. assert that recognition of the differences between children with SEND suggests that small-scale interpretative approaches are likely to be of particular value. They suggest that it is useful to equip practitioners with a range of tools which may be adapted to support communication, to spend time getting to know the child's preferred way of communication and to speak to people who know them well. They also imply that consultation is an ongoing process, rather than a one-off event.

The following methods and strategies are outlined as being useful in gathering the views and experiences of children with learning disabilities about the services they receive:
- Using everyday communication, such as sign language and high-technology communication aids;
- the In My Shoes method (Calam et al., 2000);
- the Talking Mats method (Murphy, 1998);
- the Mosaic Approach (Clark and Moss, 2006);
- consultative groups; and
- Facilitated Communication.

An example of the use of person-centered approaches in one EPS

Sanderson (2000) conveys the idea that person-centred (PC) approaches are based on learning through shared action, about finding creative solutions rather than fitting people into boxes and about problem solving and working together over time to create change in the child's life, in the community and in school. A recent study by Hayes (2004) reports the use of a visual, child-centred annual review process, which originated from an adaptation of the Making Action Plans (MAPs) PC approach developed by Forest et al. (1996). This study indicates that this method is a valuable tool, citing the preparation of the pupil before the review and the facilitation of the review as important factors linked to its success.

An EPS in the north-west of England recently introduced a new service delivery model in order to incorporate the promotion of PC approaches, in line with legislative direction which required local authorities (LAs) to convert existing Statements of SEND into Education, Health and Care (EHC) plans. Recent statutory guidance indicates that this process should incorporate PC approaches with a focus on co-produced outcomes with the child and family. This development began in September 2014 and initially involved creating a small expert team of four EPs who had knowledge of PC approaches and an interest in their development, and who also had dedicated time to work in this area. The primary aim of the EPs in this project was to focus on developing the capacity of staff in all schools across the LA. More specifically, this group took responsibility for rolling out a training programme across the LA which was offered to all key staff and was well attended. This programme involved exploring the principles of PC working; informing staff how to organise and run a PC meeting; cultivating opportunities for staff to share their best practice; and producing an action plan for next steps in developing practice and school systems. The remit of this EP team also included providing more tailored and context-specific support for individual staff within their settings and schools through giving information, modelling good practice, raising awareness and building confidence. This involved supporting schools to gather the most appropriate information, working with and empowering key people and/or the child and their family in preparing for the PC meeting and to express their views, finding the best methods for the child to communicate, signposting, contributing to the meetings where appropriate and supporting facilitation of the child's plan.

Although this project is in its initial stages formative evaluation highlights a number of facilitating factors which will be useful in informing this emerging practice. A major assisting factor is an openness to PC approaches across the school. This is largely dependent upon current practices and processes used within schools around SEND and how in line with PC approaches these are. Another positive factor is when key staff have confidence to use PC tools. The existing relationships between key staff in schools and the child and family is another factor that has a positive influence upon the adoption of PC approaches. Schools that ensure that there is time available for the necessary processes such as gathering the views of families and children also appear to be better able to incorporate PC approaches.

Implications for EP practice

The articles reviewed highlight the fact that ascertaining the views of children with more severe and complex needs, such as those with PMLD, is a difficult task which involves the consideration of a number of methodological issues. Work in this complex area appears to be in its initial and investigative stages and there is an apparent need for more research to establish effective and reliable ways to enable the views of children with PMLD to be heard, particularly with regard to the recent legislative emphasis on using PC approaches.

It appears that one way to ascertain the views of children with PMLD is to gather information from a variety of sources. One of these sources may include an attempt to directly gather accounts from the children themselves, using their preferred way of communicating, in an environment in which they feel comfortable and with people who understand them best (Whitehurst, 2006). A number of tools are available to facilitate this communication. Inferences from this collected information can then be made and this information can be triangulated or validated with people who know the child well, with a view to building up a holistic picture of the ways in which these children might think and feel about certain settings or situations. Whether this can actually be defined as a view, or whether it is just an expression of like and dislike is open to scrutiny; the need to acknowledge the fact that inferences of communicative behaviour may be inaccurate in reflecting the child's views is essential.

Several common ideas can be identified in the literature: the need for the professional to spend time learning about the child's preferred way of communicating; the requirement to acknowledge methodological and ethical issues and the level of inference involved in the techniques used; and the importance of interacting with those who are close to the child in order to build up a holistic picture of the child's communication behaviours. Due to the differences within the population of children with PMLD it appears that finding a single, common way of ascertaining the views of this group may not be possible, and that each situation will need to be approached differently with a view to tailoring the method to suit the child's own needs. Norwich and Eaton (2014) point out that there is a difference between calling a process PC and actually making it so, highlighting that for something to be 'authentically' (p.6) PC, the approach needs to be adapted in response to the young person and their family's needs. According to Detheridge (2000), small-scale interpretative approaches are likely to be most suitable. It is essential to be realistic about the level of involvement that some children may have in decisions about their life and learning; acknowledging limitations to participation is imperative. However, this is not an excuse for not attempting to involve children and young people. Their contribution, even if it is at a more micro level, is better than silence.

The role of the EP

EPs are well placed to become involved in ascertaining the views of children with PMLD regarding their education, and good EP practice should involve endeavoring to include these children in the design and implementation of their provision. EPs may become involved with children's participation at a number of levels (Norwich and Kelly, 2006). At an individual level EPs may work directly with the child, carry out ongoing observations of children in different settings and work with staff, professionals and those close to the child to understand the child's communication behaviours. At a more systemic level EPs may be influential in changing attitudes and promoting the fact that the voices of children with more complex needs can and should be heard. EPs might provide training and information about PC approaches and resources that can be used to facilitate communication to staff. They are well placed to work with other agencies to build capacity in this area and to share ideas. Importantly EPs are in a position to carry out and support research in schools with children, staff and other professionals in order to provide a more solid evidence base in this under-researched area.

References

Calam, R., Cox, A., Glasgow, D. et al. (2000). Assessment and therapy with children: Can computers help? *Child Clinical Psychology and Psychiatry, 5*, 329–343.

Clark, A. & Moss, P. (2006). *Listening to young children: The Mosaic approach.* London: National Children's Bureau.

Detheridge, T. (2000). Research involving children with severe learning difficulties. In A. Lewis & G. Lindsay (Eds.) (2000) *Researching children's perspectives* (pp.112–121). Buckingham: Open University Press.

DfE (2014). *SEND Code of Practice: 0–25 years.* London: Author.

DfES (2000). *Educational Psychology Services: Current role, good practice and future directions. Report of the Working Group.* London: Author.

DfES (2001). Learning to listen. London: Author.

Dockrell, J.E. (2004). How can studies of memory and language enhance the authenticity, validity and reliability of interviews? *British Journal of Learning Disabilities, 32*, 161–165.

Forest, M., Pearpoint, J. & O'Brien, J. (1996). MAPS: educators, parents, young people and their friends planning together. *Educational Psychology in Practice, 11*(4), 35–40.

Hayes, J. (2004). Visual annual reviews: How to include pupils with learning difficulties in their educational reviews. *Support for Learning, 19*(4), 175–180.

Holman, A. (2004). In Conversation. *British Journal of Learning Disabilities, 32*, 159–160.

Knight, A., Clark, A., Petrie, P. and Statham, J. (2006). *The views of children and young people with learning disabilities about the support they receive from Social Services: A review of consultations and methods. Report of a review prepared for the DfES.* London: Thomas Coram Research Unit.

Knight, A. & Oliver, C. (2007). Advocacy for disabled children and young people: Benefits and dilemmas. *Child and Family Social Work, 12*, 417–425.

Lewis, A. (2004). 'And when did you last see your father?' Exploring the views of children with learning difficulties/disabilities. *British Journal of Special Education, 31*, 4–10.

Lewis, A. & Porter, J. (2004). Interviewing children and young people with learning disabilities: Guidelines for researchers and multi-professional practice. B*ritish Journal of Learning Disabilities, 32*, 191–197.

Murphy, J. (1998). Talking mats: Speech and language research in practice. *Speech and Language Therapy in Practice*, Autumn, 11–14.

Norwich, B. & Eaton, A. (2014). The new special educational needs (SEN) legislation in England and implications for services for children and young people with social, emotional and behavioural difficulties. *Emotional and Behavioural Difficulties, 20*(2), 1–16.

Norwich, B. & Kelly, N. (2006). Evaluating children's participation in SEN procedures: Lessons for educational psychologists. *Educational Psychology in Pracice, 22*, 255–271.

Sanderson, H. (2000). *Person-centred planning: Key features and approaches.* London: Joseph Rowntree Foundation.

Ware, J. (2004). Ascertaining the views of people with profound and multiple learning disabilities. *British Journal of Learning Disabilities, 32*, 175–179.

Watson, D., Tarleton, B. & Feiler, A. (2006). *Participation in education: Full report on the findings from research on the involvement of children with little or no verbal communication.* Bristol: University of Bristol Esmée Fairbairn Foundation.

Whitehurst, T. (2006). Liberating silent voices: Perspectives of children with profound and complex learning needs on inclusion. *British Journal of Learning Disabilities, 35*, 55–61.

Chapter 8.4 Using IPA to investigate the experiences of young men growing up in a rural community: Reflections on identity and aspirations

Rachel Hayton

As a psychologist working with young people in a rural community I was keen to explore how young men in this community made sense of their world, which was so completely different to the world portrayed through mass media.

Literature surrounding rural life highlights the dissonance between perceptions of rural life and the reality of living in rural communities (Glendinning et al., 2003). Whilst there seems to be universal acceptance that rural communities are positive environments for bringing up younger children those very factors that make them good for this age-group make them less positive for older children and adolescents (Glendinning et al., 2003). Other writers (Cartmel and Furlong, 2000; Little, 2003; Shucksmith, 2000; Shucksmith et al., 1996) identify factors such as low social capital, high visibility, isolation, low availability of age-appropriate social opportunities, poor local employment prospects, highly constructed views of gender and transport difficulties as contributing to the negative experience of growing up in rural communities.

This piece of research sought to elicit the views of five male students aged from 14 to 18 in relation to their notions of who they were at the time of the study and how they saw themselves in the future. This was an area of interest to me when thinking about issues relating to a perception that some young people in rural communities have lower work and educational aspirations than their urban peers. Bajema and colleagues (2002) commented that the 'aspiration level of youth in rural communities is more vulnerable to the social influences of a community' (Bajema et al., 2002).

I was also keen to look at 'attachment to place' (Green and White, 2007; Giuliani, 2003; Hayton, 2009a, 2009b; Tuan, 1974) as a concept. I wanted to investigate whether attachment to a locality made it more difficult for young people to pursue their goals if that meant leaving the community. Using the students' selected images, listening to their interpretations and listening to them making sense of their world gave me an insight into the hopes and aspirations that the participants held as well as an insight into how they had constructed their identities.

The research question was concerned with finding out what it was like to be a young man growing up in a rural community in Cumbria. The questions that the participants were trying to answer were 'Who am I?' and 'What do I want?'

Having established what I wanted to find out about I considered several methods before selecting Interpretative Phenomenological Analysis (IPA) (Smith and Osbourn, 2008) as the method of analysis for my study.

Rationale for using IPA

In psychology and the social sciences IPA is a relatively recent method of analysis. The assumptions of IPA include the notion that 'People are "self-interpreting" beings' (Taylor, 1985, cited in Shaw, 2008) and that making sense of one's life, through interpretative enquiry, is central to one's experience as a person.

IPA was developed as a research method by Jonathan Smith in the 1990s and seeks to gain first-person accounts of specific thoughts, experiences and feelings. Data collected is idiographic in that it focuses or sheds light on the specific. Idiographic research makes no claim to make generalisable predictions but rather works at an individual level and can then make specific claims about that particular individual. Data is usually collected through semi-structured interviews although other means of data collection are also possible, such as journals or diaries. Sample sizes are usually small and homogeneous; a case-study approach is used. In the analysis phase of the research there should be a balance between inductive (bottom-up processes, or those generated by the data) and deductive processes. Reaching an understanding through joint working between the participant and researcher is an important feature of IPA. The scope of the analysis includes descriptions of the data, provides a narrative and offers an interpretation of the findings.

Eatough and Smith (2006) state that IPA 'shares…a concern with unravelling the relationship between what people think (cognition), say (account) and do (behaviour),' (p. 486). Smith claims that IPA is most effective when exploring areas of 'hot cognition' (Smith, 2008). Hot cognition is a fresh understanding or realisation about a situation or experience. Since my research question sought to explore the participants' sense-making of their world particularly, did not seek to make generalisable claims for the population and was concerned with considering each participant as a case study, I chose IPA as my method of analysis.

In order to generate data suitable to be analysed using IPA, I constructed a research question that required the participants to reflect on an aspect of their life that engages them in much thought. I asked the participants to reflect on what it is like for them being a young person growing up in Cumbria.

Overview

IPA offers a psychological perspective for exploring with participants how they make sense of their life world and how they interpret the meaning of their situations and circumstances. Rather than looking at the social contexts that encapsulate the phenomena being studied, IPA offers an opportunity to look at the essence of the phenomena identified by the participants. This method offers a collaborative approach to research into young people's experiences and gives them an opportunity to consider their lifeworld.

Through reflecting on their lived experiences participants and the researcher are able to identify themes that are relevant for them as an individual. The research is phenomenological, in that it requires the participants to reflect on their own situation and the phenomena that arise from it. It is ethnographic to some extent, as it focuses on a specific part of the population that is defined by its geography. Through analysis and interpretation of the collected findings this enables a rich, rounded understanding to be developed.

After considering many alternative methods for data collection a visual research method was used. To generate data, the participants were given disposable cameras and instructed to take photographs that illustrated their lives and aspirations. Use of the camera gave participants an opportunity to step outside themselves for a while and consider their lives from a different point of view. It was important to use disposable cameras in order to facilitate discussion when sorting through the images participants wanted to discard or keep. This helped to scaffold conversations for the participants and generated their constructs to some extent. A case-study approach was used to look at the lived experiences of the five young men. Common themes arose between participants, although there was no intention to compare between participants: each participant was reflecting on their understanding of their individual lived experiences.

Using the photo-elicitation technique (Capello, 2005; Clark-Ibañez, 2004; Hayton, 2009a, 2009b) and interviewing the participants individually on their photographs, a range of initial themes emerged. For some participants there were more themes than others. Although research was carried out with five participants, participants A and B were part of a pilot study. I have chosen to illustrate my findings through the data generated by participant C.

Participant C had just completed his A-levels and was awaiting his results before hopefully going off to university in Manchester. He had already planned to move to Manchester regardless of his results and did not know whether he would be studying at the university or working. Participant C had clusters of themes emerging from his interview around agency, creativity, rural living, the Protestant ethic and self-doubt.

Using IPA I identified initial themes (see Box 1), clustered the themes (see Box 2) and then further analysed Participant C's comments relating to a superordinate theme of momentum (see Box 3) and its opposite, inertia (see Box 4).

Box 1: Initial themes for Participant C

I have my own agenda

It's me against other people

To fulfil myself I have to leave

I love ideas

My own and other people's ideas

Sometimes I doubt myself

What's it all about?

Search for meaning

I want to tell you what I think

I'm creative and it's very important to me

I'm a mad social animal

I live in a really beautiful place

My thirst for knowledge is the thing that drives me on (Watt, 1983)

Fears of debt and illness

Protestant ethic

How I live at the moment I'm really happy, it's brilliant

Earn through doing something I love

Ambition

Altruism

Attachment

Exasperation and bewilderment at peers' attitudes

Box 2: Clusters of themes emerging from interview with Participant C

Agency, self-determination, independence
    I have my own agenda
    What's it all about? Search for meaning
    Thirst for knowledge
    Earn through doing something I love
    Exasperation, bewilderment with peers' attitudes
    It's me against other people
    I'm a mad social animal
Creativity and self expression
    I value ideas, my own and other people's
    I'm creative and it's really important to me.
    I want to tell you what I think
Rural living
    I live in a really beautiful place
    How I live at the moment I'm really happy, it's brilliant
Protestant ethic
    Ambition
    Altruism
    Motivation, do my best, live a full life
Self-doubt, anxiety
    Fears of debt, illness
    Sometimes I doubt myself

Themes could be bracketed together around notions of agency, self-determination and independence, creativity and self-expression and the 'Protestant ethic' (Weber, 1905). Other clusters of themes included expressions of self-doubt and anxiety and items relating to location.

Participant C's interview was very dense, with themes sometimes conflicting. Deeper analysis of the themes that emerged from the interview with Participant C revealed feelings of momentum and inertia, the exploration and acceptance of self and optimism for the future.

The overall feel of the interview with Participant C was one of momentum. The feeling of momentum embraces some of the other themes that emerged from the interview such as self-improvement, the yearning for independence and the Protestant ethic.

Box 3: Comments illustrating Participant C's superordinate theme of momentum

'I'm moving on Saturday and I'm really looking forward to getting out and living... independently...'
'I think I'm ready to get out and be more independent...'
'The plan there is to get better, get published again in higher places'
'I just want to do well... get a first... quite like to do an MA... keep going'
'I'm really looking forward to the university experience and want to do very well'
'I like throwing myself into things...'
'... I want to do it now... I'm fired up to do it'
'I'm pretty driven to achieve them, very driven to achieve at university...'
'Changing my ideas and grabbing other people's ideas...'

The language that Participant C used to describe his experience was dynamic; phrases such as 'grabbed', 'throwing myself into', 'driven', 'fired up' and the use of comparative words – 'higher', 'better', 'do very well' – demonstrate the sense of momentum in his interpretation of his experiences and ambitions.

In contrast to the concept of momentum, feelings of inertia also emerged in the interview with Participant C. Describing one of his photographs, for instance, he portrayed himself as being 'slightly stuck'. When discussing his choice to leave the area the implication was that remaining behind would be an example of inertia.

Box 4: Comments relating to Participant C's theme of inertia

'It's about feeling, at the moment, slightly stuck'

'it's pretty hard to get things done when you live in the countryside, apart from on the internet...'

'I'll get a part-time job in Tesco's but once I've finished my job I don't want to get stuck there'

'...if I stayed at the university too long I'd have to become part of the digging up literary bits and bobs'

'...make sure I don't squander the time I have there'

'...it seems to be a sort of divide between the people who haven't got any interest in... outside of how it is...outside of general sort of life'

'...some of them have spent their first year just drinking and wish they hadn't already'

For all of the participants, experiences seemed to be of great importance in helping them focus on how they saw their futures. All the participants reflected on experiences that they had had, found enjoyable and wanted to repeat or explore in more detail. The participants were able to identify elements of an experience that had appealed to them and discriminate between what they did and did not want to repeat. When Participant E talked about the possibility of joining the army, which was an idea still very much at the experimental stage in his career planning, he was able to say that he did not want to be involved in frontline warfare, but was interested in the aspects of soldiering connected to computers and military intelligence. He was not interested in one aspect of the work but still able to identify elements of that work that appealed to him.

Participant C talked about his future ideas in terms of a more global scale, encompassing family life, personal fulfilment through writing, a desire to make sense of the world and a love of ideas, both his own and those of other people. These were all issues that he had talked about in some detail, from his experience of writing, publishing and performing poetry, through his evaluation of his parents' roles in his upbringing, to critically interacting with works of literature and philosophy and his analysis of his own desire to learn.

When thinking about higher education Participant D reflected on his experiences of being with his brother in Newcastle. He also talked about a cousin who has a media role with a professional football club; he had been to look around her place of work and talked to her about her work. He also has the experience of being involved in the school newspaper and thinks that that is something that he would like to take further as a career.

The pilot study participants, although slightly younger, likewise were building their aspirations based on their experiences. Participant B, a talented footballer and sportsman, reflected that this might be where his future lay. Interestingly, though, other areas of success, such as the early acquisition of his GCSE in English, had not led him to explore studying English further.

Both Participant A in the pilot study and participants D and E in the main study talked about spending a lot of their free time playing on computers, surfing the internet and watching television. Whilst these are common features in the lives of many young people, in rural areas it seems that these may become the main free time occupation for some young people. Regular, reliable transport, organised sports activities and accessible social opportunities are not widely available within rural communities. This leaves those young people growing up in rural communities dependent on adults for transport and thus dependent on adult approval of the activity in which they may want to take part.

It seems that, although experiences of school and education play an important part in a child's life, they are not the only source of experiential opportunity. All the participants talked about a range of experiences which they had reflected upon and which they could explore further.

Reflection on the methodology

The methods used were not without difficulties, particularly the method of analysis. On occasion it was difficult to stand alongside some of the participants and appreciate their view of their lifeworld. Instead of the research being about the participants, it became about me, the researcher. It would be very easy to put oneself as the researcher at the centre of the research. Instead of shedding light on the lived experience of the participants the method would, at times, seem to be focused more on the lifeworld of the researcher. As the researcher it was important for me to acknowledge my feelings through a reflexive diary and to reflect upon those feelings. I found that experiences and reflections that echoed my own were those I was more likely to accept. For example, I am conscious that I perceive there to exist an inertia and complacency associated with living in the countryside and so saw, and perhaps unconsciously sought, some recognition of those perceptions in some of the statements made by the participants, particularly participants C and D.

Because IPA makes no claims about offering an objective perspective it is perhaps an honest way of looking at data. The researcher acknowledges their position, recognises their prejudices and constructs and reflects on those as part of the process of analysis. Similarly, when two individuals interact, whatever the circumstances, there is a reaction at a personal level. This is recognised through IPA rather than going unacknowledged.

The use of film cameras and printed photographs was worthwhile and it was interesting to note, when the participants were given all their photographs and asked to sort them, where this technique was at its most potent. When the more modern technology of digital cameras was used the resulting discussion around the photographs produced was not as informative. This could have been for several reasons; for one, the participant who used the digital camera was not otherwise as reflective in discussing his lifeworld as the other participants. Equally, the photographs had been chosen and edited well before the interview; the participant had selected photographs for their technical merit, as photographs, rather than by reference to the meanings they represented.

This study used qualitative research methodology to ascertain from participants what the experience of growing up in the countryside was like for them. It sought to challenge some widely-held national and local government perceptions that rural communities are areas of low aspiration. Using IPA and a mixed data generation method (photo-elicitation and semi-structured interviewing), the study was designed to give control over what was raised and discussed to the participants. The work forged links between previously unrelated areas of research and attempted to make connections within an overarching framework concerning the rural community. It has added to the complex story told about young men growing up in rural communities. Links were made between aspiration, subjective wellbeing and positive youth development.

For young people who grow up in rural communities the landscape is the least of their worries. The landscape is constant and predictable in its seasonal changes, and the need to negotiate how to live within the landscape is learned at an early stage: the landscape is accepted as unchangeable. I realise that the key word when considering rural communities is not the word 'rural', but the word 'communities'. It is the communities that create difficulties for young people to be included, communities that have developed norms and expectations about young people and that young people then need to manage.

References

Bajema, D.H., Miller, W.W. & Williams, D.L. (2002). Aspirations of rural youth. *Journal of Agricultural Education, 43*(3), 61–71.

Capello, M. (2005). Photo interviews: Eliciting data through conversations with children. *Field Methods, 17*, 170–182.

Cartmell, F. & Furlong, A. (2000). *Youth unemployment in rural areas. Work and Opportunity Series Report JRF-18.* York: Joseph Rowntree Foundation.

Clark-Ibañez, M. (2004). Framing the social world with photo-elicitation interviews. *American Behavioral Scientist 47*(12), 1507–1527.

Eatough, V. & Smith, J.A. (2006) I was like a wild wild person: Understanding feelings of anger using interpretative phenomenological analysis. *British Journal of Psychology, 97*, 483–498.

Finlay, L. (2003). Through the looking glass: Intersubjectivity and hermeneutic reflection. In L. Finlay and B. Gough (Eds.) *Reflexivity: A practical guide for research in health and social sciences.* Oxford: Blackwell.

Giuliani, M.V. (2003). Theory of Attachment and Place Attachment. In M. Bonnes, T. Lee and M. Bonauito, *Psychological Theories for Environmental Issues* (pp.137–170). Aldershot: Ashgate.

Glendinning, A., Nutall, M., Hendry, L. et al. (2003). Rural communities and well-being: A good place to grow up? *The Sociological Review, 51*, 129–156.

Green, A.E. & White, R.J. (2007). *Attachment to place, social networks, mobility and prospects of young people.* York: Joseph Rowntree Foundation. http://www.jrf.org.uk/sites/files/jrf/2126-attachment-to-place.pdf Accessed 24 April 2009.

Hayton, R.A. (2009a). *Who am I and what do I want? Using interpretative phenomenological analysis to investigate the experiences of young men growing up in a rural community: Reflections on identity and aspirations.* Unpublished PhD thesis, Newcastle University.

Hayton, R.A. (2009b). Young people growing up in rural communities: Opportunities for educational psychologists to work with emerging adults. *Educational & Child Psychology 26*(1), 60–66.

Little, J. (2003). Riding the rural love train: Heterosexuality and the rural community. *Sociologia Ruralis, 43*, 401–417.

Midgley, J. & Bradshaw, R. (2006). *Should I stay or should I go? Rural youth transitions.* Newcastle upon Tyne: IPPR North and Commission for Rural Communities.

Mulveen, R. & Hepworth, J. (2006) An interpretative phenomenological analysis of participation in a pro-anorexia internet site and its relationship with disordered eating. *Journal of Health Psychology,* 11, 283–96.

Shucksmith, M. (2000). *Exclusive Countryside? Social inclusion and regeneration in rural Britain.* York: Joseph Rowntree Foundation.

Shucksmith, M. (2004). Young people and social exclusion in rural areas. *Sociologia Ruralis, 44,* 43–59.

Shucksmith, M., Chapman, P. & Clark, G. (1996). *Rural Scotland today: The best of both worlds?* Aldershot: Avebury.

Smith, J.A. (1994). Reconstructing selves: An analysis of discrepancies between women's contemporaneous and retrospective accounts of the transition to motherhood. *British Journal of Psychology 85,* 271–392.

Smith, J.A. (1995). Qualitative methods, identity and transition to motherhood. *The Psychologist 8,* 122–125

Smith, J.A. (1996). Beyond the divide between cognition and discourse. *Psychology & Health, 11,* 261–271.

Smith, J.A. (1999). Identity development during the transition to motherhood: An interpretative phenomenological analysis. *Journal of Reproductive and Infant Psychology, 17,* 281–300.

Smith, J.A. and Osborn, M (2008). Interpretative phenomenological analysis (2nd. edn.). In J.A. Smith (Ed.) *Qualitative psychology: A practical guide to research methods.* London: Sage.

Taylor, C. (1985). *Human Agency and Language. Philosophical papers Vol. 1: Human Agency and language.* Cambridge: Cambridge University Press.

Tuan, Y-F. (1974). T*opophilia: A study of environmental perceptions, attitudes and values.* Englewood Cliffs, NJ: Prentice Hall.

Willig, C. (2008). *Introducing qualitative research in psychology.* Maidenhead: Open University Press.

Chapter 8.5 A jolly good sort: The influence of Q Methodology on practice that aims to interpret and represent voice

Martin Hughes

'Educational psychologists cannot just ask the child for their view of their situation, and expect them to tell us.' (Hobbs et al., 2000, p.110)

Introduction

My aim here is to discuss some recent and ongoing work in relation to understanding children's and young people's views using card sorts. After briefly discussing Q methodology, some examples drawing on recent work with primary- and secondary-aged pupils is described so as to demonstrate how their voices have been incorporated into intervention work and written reports.

Q methodology

In my recent research I have used Q with young people who have worked as young researchers (Hughes, 2012, 2014), explored the viewpoints of pupils in Year 6 (the final year of primary education) regarding transition to secondary school and followed up the same pupils once they have made the transition. A study then that sought the views of young people regarding *what they think* transition is going to be like and what it *actually was like* from their perspective.

Here, before focusing on my work as a practitioner using card sorting, I shall provide an introductory explanation of Q. I have indicated elsewhere (Hughes, in press) what Q has to offer the researcher-practitioner and made a case for why Q contributes to a critical educational psychology, namely, that it explores a first-person perspective; is an ethical methodology that challenges a one-size-fits-all solution; attempts to hear a range of voices, including those at the margins; and respects participants' viewpoints by avoiding or reducing the imposition of the researcher's view of the world on the people being researched. There is space here to give only a brief description of the methodology; those interested can find out more about Q by consulting the references (e.g. Watts and Stenner, 2012).

Q methodology was developed by William Stephenson as a method to capture the subjective or 'first-person' viewpoints of a single participant or, more usually, a group of participants. In Q, an early stage usually involves generating a set of statements, achieved by considering what has already been written about the topic and by asking others for their views about the topic in question, often from interviews or focus groups. In my Q-related work, the sentences for my Q-sets are often rooted in statements that I have collected from young people in one way or another. For instance, following a literature review of transition, I worked with sixth-form psychology students to develop a Q-set that contained statements that might all be said by young people, by drawing on the literature and adding to this with items 'donated' by young people themselves.

Participant data is then gathered in the form of Q sorts, where (typically) statements are ranked using a grid, using a scale that relates to participants' likes and dislikes, from 'agree' to 'disagree', for instance. The completed Q sorts are then factor analysed to reveal factors or shared viewpoints. This analysis involves comparing a Q sort with each and every other Q sort, often by using a dedicated package such as PQMethod (Schmolck, 2001). This process of comparison identifies sorting patterns that are similar enough to support the conclusion that the participants sorting the items into the pattern share in common a particular viewpoint. Thus, the approach is qualitative *and* quantitative: factors are interpreted having been derived from a statistical analysis.

Interpreting voice using card sorting

Children's voices are frequently under-represented and so much of the literature relating to young people is written from adult perspectives. Q methodology is increasingly being employed to explore a range of issues relevant to education (more recent studies from the last ten years include Bracken and Fischel, 2006; Bradley and Miller, 2010; Combes et al., 2004; Deignan, 2013; Gale, 2011; La Paro et al., 2009; Madoc-Jones and Gajdamaschko, 2005/2006; Ramlo, 2006/2007; and Yang, 2011); children as young as five have been involved as participants (see Ellingsen et al., 2014). The doctoral work of trainee EPs at Sheffield University (Crosby, 2015; Frearson, 2013; Massey, 2010; Plummer, 2012; Stollery, 2013; Wint, 2013) has added to this trend and I have worked with young people extensively and used Q in a number of research studies.

My focus is very much on hearing the voice of children and young people and my work described in this chapter tries to show how this is done by using 'pre-prepared' statements that the young people sort. My belief is that it is the sorting (a fairly novel and engaging activity) that enables voice to be raised in a way that is relatively devoid of adult 'interference' or power and entirely respectful of using the pattern of statements placed by the young person for interpretative purposes. I think that the card sorting process is much less 'influenced' by the researcher/practitioner than is the use of, for example, a semi-structured interview, where the young person has virtually no control over what is discussed, with the questions being decided by an adult in advance.

The influence of Q on my practice as an educational psychologist (EP) and my approach to card sorting tasks has been described elsewhere (see Hughes and Booth, 2009), in the context of a case where card sorting was used to explore what young people think about their behaviour. Relying less on a conventional interview, it seemed a useful 'hands-on' approach to working with young people who experienced difficulty putting their thoughts into words, or when they seemed uncomfortable talking to an adult.

To recap, Q and card-sorting involve the participant, in this case a child or young person, looking at a number of items on cards, in order to decide how they regard them, often according to a dimension such as most agree/most disagree, most like me/most unlike me. The items are often sentences or short phrases and can be single words, but could equally be pictures, objects or film clips. One is bounded only by the limits to creativity and what is practically determined by the size of the area in which the sort can be conducted.

The sorting is achieved by placing the cards onto a grid. I have different interlocking plastic pieces that I usually invite the young person to help me to make into the shape that will hold all of the cards, one space for each card (see Figure 8.1).

Figure 8.5.1: Typical arrangement when a young person is sorting cards using a grid

Once we've made the grid, showing the cards, I often say something like, 'these are all sentences that someone of your age might say about their behaviour (or school, or parents…). I'd like you to read them and decide how much you agree with each one. Make a pile here of the ones that you agree with, here for the ones that you disagree with and the ones that you are unsure of, put in the middle.' Some young people are able to do this in a few minutes, whilst others require longer or my help in order to read the sentences and/or understand them. Once the three piles of cards have been established, I explain that they need to decide which three cards in the agree pile they most agree with, in order to place them in the column on the far right of the grid. This is repeated for the disagree pile and so on until each cell of the grid has a card placed on it.

When the young person has placed all of the cards I ask them if there are any that they would like to change. I then invite them to comment on any that they have placed at either end of the grid (or anywhere else for that matter). If I notice something that catches my interest I might point this out or ask them about it. I make notes as we talk, writing down any comments in relation to each of the items.

Once we've finished, I usually ask if there were any cards 'missing' – *'is there anything else that you would have liked to have had a card for?'* If the young person thinks of something I write it on a spare card and invite them to place it in their preferred position. I ask them if they have told me anything that they would rather I kept to myself. At the start of the session, having explained that what we talk about is confidential, unless I think they are at risk of being harmed in anyway, they are usually able to understand my question once we've finished and just occasionally might ask that I don't tell anyone that they like the girl in the class that they talked about, or that they think that their teacher is mean sometimes. I might explain that I'd like to talk with some of the adults about what we've done (their parents, teacher, Teaching Assistant…) and I often say that I'll write to them. If I do this I often copy in their teacher, which is a good way of economising on a written report! Two examples follow.

Steph: A report for statutory advice
The assessment for Steph was started during the school summer holidays. Steph lived in the area that I served but did not attend the local school, instead attending a primary school in a neighbouring local authority. I knew nothing about Steph, but managed to collect some information from the EP who had worked with Steph's school. With a short deadline I had little time to complete my report and was only able to speak with the special educational needs co-ordinator once the school opened again in September. After several attempts, Steph's mother and I arranged a convenient time for me to visit their home. Steph lived with her mother and sister. Steph's mother and I talked in the kitchen whilst I could hear Steph playing noisily on a games console in the room next door. Time was short and it was clear on this occasion that I was not going to get very far with working with Steph individually, so Steph's mother and I agreed that she would try to complete the card sort with Steph once I'd left their home and I left the statements on cards with her (see Appendix 8.5.1).

I explained the shape of the grid and also left some instructions for them both to follow. Steph's mother sent me the completed sort as shown in Figure 8.2.1.

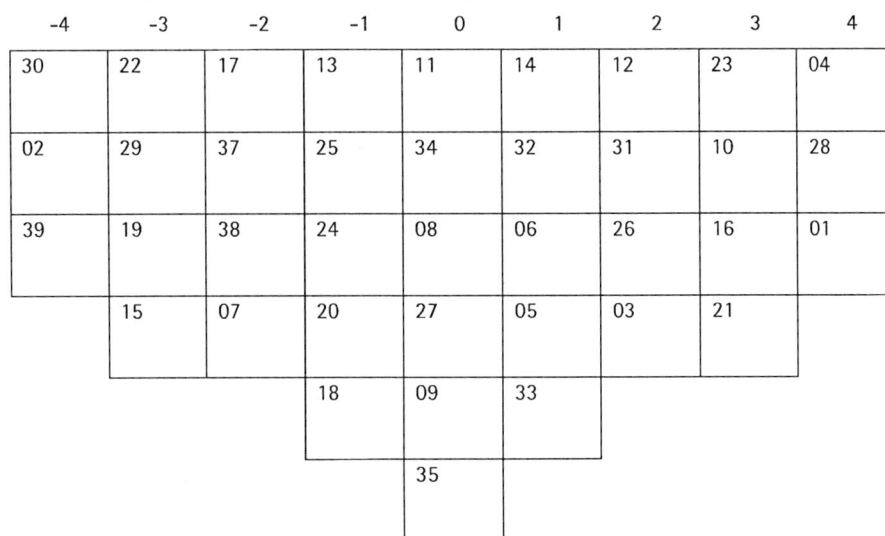

-4	-3	-2	-1	0	1	2	3	4
30	22	17	13	11	14	12	23	04
02	29	37	25	34	32	31	10	28
39	19	38	24	08	06	26	16	01
	15	07	20	27	05	03	21	
			18	09	33			
				35				

Figure 8.5.2: Steph's completed card sort

In my report I explained that the following passage retains the statements as presented to Steph, so that Steph's voice might have a more 'authentic' representation. The position of where Steph placed a statement is shown in brackets. For instance item 4, *'Don't always put an adult with me, allow me to do and learn things for myself' (4, 4)* means that Steph agreed with this statement, placing it on the right of the grid in the '4' column. Disagreement with this item would have been shown as *(4, -4)*.

Don't always put an adult with me: allow me to do and learn things for myself (4, 4). I don't want to be provided with someone who I can look up to and learn from (19, -3) – their respect (27, 0) and me feeling trusted (35, 0) is more important than this as well as helping me to really feel that I can rely on them (31, 2). Don't give me lots to do so I am always active (36, -4). Providing visual cues (e.g. pictures) to help me to understand is not particularly important to me (17, -2).

You don't need to work hard to communicate with my family (15, -3) and encouraging me to take responsibility for myself and my possessions is less important (29, -3).

You can take time to find out my opinion about decisions that affect me (3, 2) but I'm less interested in you helping me to set goals that I can aim for in the future (7, -2). I do not want people to help me to think about what I'd like to do when I leave school (30, -4).

Help me to explore and try new things (21, 3), recognise when I have done well (23, 4) and do not criticise me or tell me off in front of other people (37, -2). Talking to me about my mistakes in a way that helps me to improve is also less helpful (24, -1) – focus on the things that I can do really well rather than those which I find difficult (11, 0).

Help me to learn ways that I can cope if I'm in a difficult situation (26, 2) and help me to feel that I belong in the school (10, 3). Supporting me in learning new skills which help me to communicate with other people (25, -1) or making it easy to communicate (18, -1) is less important, but I'd like you to help me to make friends in school (16, 3).

It's really important that you do not talk to me like I'm stupid (1, 4) and I would really prefer it if people don't 'look at me when they are talking to me' (2, -4). Don't make too much of an issue of my difficulties, as I don't want to be seen to be different (28, 4) – don't compare me to other people (32, 1). Understand that sometimes I don't want to talk about how I'm feeling (38, -2) and that I may not want you to talk to me about any difficulties that you think I have (20, -1). Although there might be times when you can help me to feel happy (33, 1), I'm much less interested in you understanding what my problems are (8, 0) or you teaching me ways that I can make myself feel better (22, -3).

Kim: An example of a behavioural intervention

Here is an example of some work with Kim, a pupil in Y8 who had a number of behavioural issues that presented challenges for the teachers. Kim and I looked at the statements together which were then sorted using the grid. The grid went from

-4 (most disagree) to +4 (most agree). I wrote to Kim with my understanding of the view which the card sort represented, based on how the statements had been placed, as follows:

> You disagree that recently you've got worse (-4), agreeing that you get into less hassle now (+4) and that although it's hard work, you feel like you are getting somewhere (+4). You are not happy with your behaviour (-3), recognise that you are disruptive (-2) and disagree that you are OK as you are (-2). You feel that your behaviour gets you into a lot of trouble (+2) and you don't like this (+3). Staying at St Swithin's is important to you – you are worried about getting kicked out (+4). You are aiming to keep out of trouble (+2) and aiming for good reports (+3). There are times when you are polite to teachers (+1) and overall you think that you get on better with the teachers now (+1). It's been hard to change your behaviour but you think it's been worth it (+1). You know some ways to change and they are helping (+1) – some of the things that you do keep you out of trouble (+1). However, you don't always feel that you know enough to keep out of trouble (-1) or that when something is about to go wrong you can figure out what to do (-1).

Kim finished the summer term knowing that staff were aware that they shared similar concerns and of Kim's resolve to try and keep out of trouble. The last I heard, permanent exclusion had been avoided and talk of a move to a special school had reduced.

Conclusions

Elsewhere (Hughes, in press) I have discussed the notion of 'getting' children and young people in practice. By this I mean an approach that develops and illuminates a 'first-person perspective' which 'gets' people, imagining what it might be like to be them. I hope that this has been illustrated by describing my development of Q-inspired card sorting.

The process involves doing things *with* rather than to or for children and young people; providing an appropriate vehicle for them to convey their beliefs, and avoids or at least reduces adults' tendency to keep 'the upper hand' (see Harding and Atkinson, 2009). My aim is to 'get' children and young people, to develop a first-person perspective so as to imagine what it might be to be like them. In contrast perhaps to the belief that 'what these children need is a jolly good talking to', I find that card sorting helps me to listen in a particular way that facilitates my trying to make sense of what I am hearing.

References

Bracken, S.S. & Fischel, J.E. (2006). Assessment of preschool classroom practices: Application of Q-sort methodology. *Early Childhood Research Quarterly, 21*(4), 417–430.

Bradley, J. & Miller, A. (2010). Widening participation in higher education: Constructions of 'going to university'. *Educational Psychology in Practice, 26*(4), 401–413.

Combes, H., Hardy, G. & Buchan, L. (2004). Using Q-methodology to involve people with intellectual disability in evaluating person-centred planning. *Journal of Applied Research in Intellectual Disabilities, 17*(3), 149–159.

Crosby, R. (2015) *Teachers managing work demands and maintaining a sense of wellbeing: A Q methodology study to investigate the views of primary and secondary school teachers.* Unpublished thesis, University of Sheffield.

Deignan, T. (2013). Using diverse system perspectives to develop policy and practice in an answerable way – the case of dyslexia support in higher education. In V. Farnsworth & Y. Solomon (Eds.), *Reframing educational research* (pp.119–138). London: Routledge.

Ellingsen, I.T., Thorsen, A.A. & Størksen, I. (2014). Revealing children's experiences and emotions through Q methodology. *Child Development Research, 2014*(2), 1–9.

Frearson, A.E. (2013). *A Q-methodological study to explore Muslim girls' viewpoints around how a secondary school setting can promote and support their inclusion.* Unpublished thesis, University of Sheffield.

Gale, E. (2011). Exploring perspectives on cochlear implants and language acquisition within the deaf community. *Journal of Deaf Studies and Deaf Education, 16,* 121–139. doi: 10.1093/deafed/enq044

Harding, E. & Atkinson, C. (2009). How EPs record the voice of the child. *Educational Psychology in Practice, 25*(2), 125–137.

Hobbs, C., Todd, L. & Taylor, J. (2000). Consulting with children and young people: Enabling educational psychologists to work collaboratively. *Education and Child Psychology, 17*(4), 107–115.

Hughes, M. (2012) *Researching behaviour: A Q methodological exploration of the position pf the young person as researcher.* Unpublished doctoral thesis, University of Sheffield.

Hughes, M. (2014) What might adults learn from working with young researchers? In J. Westwood, C. Larkins, D. Moxon et al. (Eds.) *Participation, citizenship and intergenerational relations in children and young people's lives: Children and adults in conversation.* London: Palgrave Macmillan.

Hughes, M. (in press). Joining the Q: What Q methodology has to offer the researcher practitioner. In A. Williams, T. Billington & D. Goodley (Eds.) *Critical Educational Psychology.* Oxford: Wiley Blackwell.

Hughes, M. and Booth, V. (2009) Assessing pupil motivation for change: Using card sorting methodology. In E. McNamara (ed.) *Motivational interviewing: Theory, practice and applications with children and young people* (pp.127–144). Ainsdale: Positive Behaviour Management.

La Paro, K.M., Siepak, K. & Scott-Little, C. (2009). Assessing beliefs of preservice early childhood education teachers using Q-sort methodology. *Journal of Early Childhood Teacher Education, 30*(1), 22–36.

Madoc-Jones, G. and Gajdamaschko, N. (2005/2006). Theoretical incompatibilities in teachers' self-understandings of educational practice: An examination using Q methodology. *Operant Subjectivity, 29*(1/2), 58–80.

Massey, R. (2010). *A Q-methodological study to investigate adults' role in supporting the social and emotional well being of children and young people who are deaf.* Unpublished thesis, University of Sheffield.

Plummer, C. (2012). *Who cares? An exploration, using Q methodology, of young carer and professionals' viewpoints.* Unpublished research thesis, University of Sheffield.

Ramlo, S.E. (2006/2007). Student views of learning in a first semester college physics course: A study using Q methodology. *Operant Subjectivity, 30,* 52–63.

Schmolck, P. (2001). PQMethod software. Retrieved 18 July 2016 from http://schmolck.userweb. mwn.de/qmethod/

Stollery, R.L. (2013). *A Q methodological study of the support valued by students with English as an additional language.* Unpublished thesis, University of Sheffield.

Watts, S. & Stenner, P. (2012). *Doing Q methodological research: Theory, method and interpretation.* London: Sage.

Wint, F.E. (2013). *'Am I bothered?' Using Q methodology to explore what bothers young people on Facebook.* Unpublished research thesis, University of Sheffield.

Yang, Y. (2011). *A Q factor analysis of college undergraduate students' study behaviors.* Unpublished doctoral thesis, Florida International University.

Appendix 8.5.1: Statements used with Steph (adapted from Massey, 2010)

01	not talk to me like I'm stupid	02	look at me when they are talking to me
03	take time to find out my opinion about decisions that affect me	04	not always put an adult with me, allow me to do and learn things for myself
05	always check that I understand something, not just assuming that I do	06	believe that I am able to do well
07	help me to set goals that I can aim for in the future	08	understand what my problems are
09	make me part of decisions about my learning	10	help me to feel that I belong in the school
11	focus on the things that I can do really well rather than those which I find difficult	12	help me to see that they like me
13	not make me feel that I stand out from the other pupils	14	encourage me to solve my own problems
15	work hard to communicate with my family	16	help me to make friends in school
17	provide visual cues (e.g. pictures) to help me to understand	18	make it easy for me to communicate with them
19	provide me with someone who I can look up to and learn from	20	talk to me about any difficulties that they think I have
21	help me to explore and try new things	22	teach me ways that I can make myself feel better
23	recognise when I have done well	24	talk to me about my mistakes in a way that helps me to improve
25	support me in learning new skills which help me to communicate with other people	26	help me to learn ways that I can cope if I'm in a difficult situation
27	show me respect	28	not make too much of an issue of my difficulties, as I don't want to be seen to be different
29	encourage me to take responsibility for myself and my possessions	30	help me to think about what I'd like to do when I leave school

31	help me to really feel that I can rely on them	32	not compare me to other people
33	help me to feel happy	34	use clear facial expressions which make it easy for me to understand how they are feeling
35	help me to feel that I am trusted	36	give me lots to do so I am always active
37	not criticise me or tell me off in front of other people	38	understand that sometimes I don't want to talk about how I'm feeling

Chapter 8.6 Exploring the friendship experiences of young adolescents with a visual impairment

Sandra Meehan

Research in context

It is thought that vision plays a key role in the development of relationships. Brazelton and Cramer (1991) suggest that vision is developmentally significant in the attachment of parent and baby, and see babies' inherent interest in faces as a means of learning about their carers and the world around them. Furthermore, as the child develops, learning through visual means continues through modelling and mimicking, which may be hampered for a child with a visual impairment (VI). A reduced ability to use non-verbal communication may impact upon social skills development (Sacks and Wolffe, 1998) and Wolffe (Sackes and Woolfe, 2006) proposes that adolescents with VI may not make the shift from family life to social life as quickly as their sighted peers because of personal or parental concerns over orientation and mobility issues. Children and young people with a VI, then, may experience challenges in their relationships and friendships. Friendships are thought to provide children and young people with emotional and cognitive resources and provide a context in which to practise and develop social skills (Hartup, 1992). High-quality friendships are seen as key for psychological health and wellbeing (Hartup, 1992), signifying that this is an important area of study.

A review of the literature focusing on the social experiences of adolescents with a VI raises concerns about experiences of isolation, loneliness and difference (Gray, 2010); difficulty explaining the nature of their visual impairment to peers (Rosenblum, 1998); difficulty engaging in particular activities within the school setting (George & Duquette, 2006; Gray, 2009; Lifshitz et al., 2007); and engaging with peers outside school less regularly than their sighted peers (Kroksmark & Nordell, 2001). However, these studies indicate that in particular contexts, and with appropriate support, young people can make and maintain successful friendships (George & Duquette, 2006; Rosenblum, 1998, 2000). In this review, there was a paucity of research available in the UK. The study under discussion sought to add to this research base.

Method and rationale

The discussion presented here forms part of a wider mixed-methods study undertaken as part of a doctoral research thesis between the spring of 2011 and summer of 2012. The study used both interpretative phenomenological analysis (IPA) and repertory grids (see Kelly 1955/1991) to explore the experiences and understanding of friendship among Year 7 students with a VI. Year 7 students were chosen for practical purposes (a cohort of VI Year 7 students were identified within the local authority) as well as to reflect an interest in the developmental nature of friendship (Berndt, 1982; Hartup, 1992) and the significance of transition to secondary school in the social lives of young adolescents (Simmons et al., 1987; Tobbell, 2003). IPA was utilised as a qualitative methodology due to its focus on exploring the personal lived experiences of participants (Reid et al., 2005), enabling a particular phenomenon to be explored in detail and depth. Repertory grids were also used in a quantitative phase of the study to explore how participants construed friendship as a result of their experiences. The current discussion will focus on the results obtained from the qualitative phase of this study to demonstrate the depth and detail of information gained by using an IPA approach. As part of this process, semi-structured interviews were undertaken with participants to explore their experiences of friendship. The interview schedule was developed in line with Smith (1995) and aimed to guide, but not dictate, the interview process. The interviews were recorded, transcribed and analysed; adhering closely to guidance provided by Smith and colleagues (2009).

Method
The participants in this study were four Year 7 students, three of whom attended mainstream secondary schools (Bart, Robyn and Tom[1]) and one who attended a mainstream secondary school with a VI unit (Mark). All participants' VI ranged from moderate to severe (6/18 to 6/60 Snellen/Kay; where 6/6 represents normal visual acuity). Robyn, Mark and Tom were born with a VI while Bart's VI was progressive and developed later in childhood.

Findings
The sense of belonging as a key theme emerged from analysis of all four interviews. Each participant presented a story that was in some way unique to them and their context; the four views are presented individually below.

Bart
Bart reflected on the way in which his confidence and sense of place increased once he started to make some new friends in secondary school:

> When I came here it's like I didn't know anyone and I felt small and in my primary school, I was like, started to know the people better so […], I got to feel bigger […] as I like made new friends [in this school] I started to feel a bit more on, a bit more like confident, like wherever I turned there was one of my friends and I was like 'hello!'

Bart was proactive in engaging with others in order to make friends. He demonstrated awareness that this would help him to 'feel bigger' and find his place in secondary school:

> It's like em… (pause) like I find it easy to talk to people. I mean let's say on my first day here, I was really confident to go up to people and you know say 'hello, what's your name?!'

---

[1] Pseudonyms were used to protect participants' anonymity. A full discussion of ethical considerations can be obtained from the researcher upon request.

For Bart, spending time with friends was an important aspect of feeling included with his experience of groups. He reflected on feeling excluded from his friendship group outside school:

> Well, I don't know (...) It's like because they go out with their other friends and like to the park or something and I feel like I want to go but I can't.

He also described similar experiences within school:

> ...em well I can see them in class but I just can't talk to them in class because I have to sit with a helper and then yeah in a separate place, yeah.

Bart reflected that the capacity of his friends to understand his VI was crucial to his ability to take part in games.

> Sometimes when I play with my friends they might help me, for example, em (...) like sometimes when we play they are more aware that I can't see and then they just like tell me when the ball is coming or something. Yeah. Then there are other times when they just like want to win and yeah.

Robyn

Robyn expressed a strong desire to belong to a friendship group. For Robyn, friends were 'like family', and she appeared preoccupied by the prospect of losing friends:

> Like say if you've been with one person for your whole entire life and then you go to college and then they're not in the same college as you and you're in university and they're not in the same university as you so I'm really worried about that...

The need for friends to understand the experience of having a VI was as important for Robyn as it was for Bart. She expressed a desire to meet somebody with a VI the same as hers:

> ...we'd probably be best friends as well and we'd always go out and go, we'd take our glasses off and go 'oh isn't everything like fuzzy and everything doubled' and they would say 'yeah yeah it is, do you get this feeling whenever, do you ever, does it some-times sting in one eye when you put your eye drops in?' stuff like that.

Robyn explained her desire to belong to the 'cool' group in school and she de-scribed how she tried to 'impress them [...] and be like nice and cool with them'; however, this effort had met with limited success:

> I've done nothing wrong and all they care about is coolness and everything, that's all that they care about, being cool and being really popular.

When talking about lunch times at school, Robyn expressed a sense of isolation and helplessness:

Nothing. Stand outside and now that the library is closed down I just don't do nothing, I just stand and do nothing.

Robyn felt that with the right support from school, her friendship experiences could be more positive. Her idea of support was arranging a trip so that she could spend more time with her peers so that they could get to know her better.

Robyn spent some time reflecting on the changing nature of her friendships now that she had started secondary school:

I'd like always have like four or three friends and we always used to play games and stuff like that and now when everybody's here all they can do is gossip and they don't like playing these childish games because they think 'I'm old enough now, I'm going to gossip'. [...] And em so it's like, it's like all rumours and gossip and I hate it.

Mark

Mark explained that for him, friendship is 'just having someone that will be with you for the time you are at school'. In his interview, Mark made considerable reference to conflict in his peer relationships, which appeared to undermine his sense of belonging. He described friendships going 'wrong' and arguments breaking out. He explained that some of his friends are sometimes 'a bit willing to see something happen' and 'stir it up'. Indeed, Mark also spoke about feeling 'attacked' in school, which he felt was a result of his VI. Indeed, Mark's interview was dominated by feelings of being targeted by his peers in school for this reason:

They have a dig at me because of something, because of my eyes or something, and that's how arguments start to break out.

He communicated a sense of helplessness in relation to being targeted in this way, which furthered the feeling of victimisation:

Try and ignore people? But then that doesn't help if you're getting it all the time.

Perhaps as a result of this, he suggested that having supportive friendships is vital in school life:

To me, em... (pause) being friends with someone that actually like sticks up for you throughout life.

Mark's comments suggested a lack of confidence in the support structures school have in place; he believed that giving 'punishments' does not make a difference:

Cuz it's their decisions that they make to like, it's their reactions they choose to make. Cuz you could give them all the punishments in the world and they could still carry on.

Mark showed some preoccupation in comparing himself to his peers who did not have a VI which resulted in him feeling different. Throughout the interview, he continually referred to his peers without a VI as 'normal':

> Well it's kind of difficult for me to do these kinds of things and em I can do pretty much anything a normal person can do but not as easy and em I find it a lot harder in life to do what a normal person can do ... I don't know. I reckon it's because it's not really normal, like. Not everyone's like me so. It's kind of different in a way.

It was difficult for him to feel that friends really understood what it is like to have a VI:

> My friends don't understand because they don't know the experience of what it's like, they don't understand what I go through.

Tom

Tom appeared to communicate his sense of belonging in his friendships by explaining how he has friends in many different places:

> I already have four friends, four main friends and there are other friends scattered around like some in 'x' school, some are in 'y' school, one is in 'z' school and 'b' school and 'c' school.

He explained that because some friends transferred with him to secondary school, he did not think that he needed to worry about making new friends following his transition. Indeed, Tom demonstrated some passivity in initiating contact with peers more generally and explained that he might see friends after school but only 'when my Mum invites them'. Similarly when asked what might attract Tom to a friend, his response suggested that this was dependent on the other person making contact with him: 'Like, they start talking to you, like they ask to be your friend.'

Tom reported being part of a group of friends but he appeared to take a passive role in the group:

> Eh (...) we talk about, well most of my friends talk about some game but I just listen because I don't know anything about the game.

Additionally, although Tom said he would have preferred to play with friends, he did not feel that he could ask them to play because they are too 'grown up' now. Tom spoke animatedly about some of the make up games he and a friend used to play in primary school, but in discussing how he spends his time with friends in secondary school, he appeared less enthusiastic, reporting, 'We don't really play [...] we go outside and talk'. He reflected that this was 'probably because they've grown out of games and stuff'.

Tom reflected that his VI means that it takes him longer to do things than other people. For instance, he spends most of his time in the evenings completing homework because his VI makes it harder for him to access the work: '...it takes me longer than everyone else'. For Tom, this meant that seeing friends after school was often not possible.

Reflections on the use of IPA

Although a common theme for all participants, their sense and experience of belonging is clearly expressed in individually unique ways. Using an IPA approach provided the researcher with the flexibility to explore and present particular, individual lived experiences creatively, and therefore encouraged valuing the unique position and voice of each young person. Using an IPA approach in this study promoted the appreciation of difference and the requirement for educational psychologists to remain curious and open-minded about young people's experiences. For the young people in this study, the experience of telling their stories was transformative for their own understanding, showing that an IPA approach can empower those whose voice may not otherwise be heard.

References

Berndt, T.J. (1982). The features and effects of friendship in early adolescence. *Child Development, 53*(6), 1447–1460.

Brazleton, T.B. & Cramer, B.G. (1991). *The earliest relationship: Parents, infants and the drama of early attachment.* London: Karnac Books.

George, A.L. & Duquette, C. (2006). The psychosocial experiences of a student with low vision. *Journal of Visual Impairment and Blindness, 100*(3), 152–163.

Gray, C. (2009). A qualitatively different experience: Mainstreaming pupils with a visual impairment in Northern Ireland. *European Journal of Special Needs Education, 24*(2), 169–182.

Gray, C. (2010). Visual impairment: The educational experiences of young people in Northern Ireland. *Educational and Child Psychology, 27*(2), 68–78.

Hartup, W.W. (1992). *Having friends, making friends, and keeping friends: Relationships as educational contexts.* Eric Digest. Retrieved 2 January 2012 from http://ericeece.org/pubs/digests/1992/hartup92.html

Kelly, G. (1955/1991). *The psychology of personal constructs.* London: Routledge.

Kroksmark, U. & Nordell, K. (2001). Adolescence: The age of opportunities and obstacles for students with low vision in Sweden. *Journal of Visual Impairment and Blindness, 95*(4), 213–225.

Lifshitz, H., Hen, I. & Weisse, I. (2007). Self-concept, adjustment to blindness, and quality of friendship among adolescents with visual impairments. *Journal of Visual Impairment and Blindness, 101*(2), 96–107.

Reid, K., Flowers, P. & Larkin, M. (2005). Interpretative phenomenological analysis: An overview and methodological review. *The Psychologist, 18*, 20–23.

Rosenblum, L.P. (1998). Best friendships of adolescents with visual impairments: A descriptive study. *Journal of Visual Impairment and Blindness, 92*(9), 593–608.

Rosenblum, L.P. (2000). Perceptions of the impact of visual impairment on the lives of adolescents. *Journal of Visual Impairment and Blindness, 94*(7), 434–445.

Sacks, S.Z. & Wolffe, K.E. (1998). Lifestyles of adolescents with visual impairments: An ethnographic analysis. *Journal of Visual Impairment and Blindness, 92*(1), 7–17.

Sacks, S.Z & Wolffe, K.E. (2006). *Teaching social skills to students with visual impairments: From theory to practice.* New York: AFB Press.

Simmons, R.G., Burgeson, R., Carlton-Ford, S. & Blyth, D.A. (1987). The impact of cumulative change in early adolescence. *Child Development, 58*(5), 1220–1234.

Smith, J.A. (1995b). Semi-structured interviewing and qualitative analysis. In: J.A.Smith, R. Harre & L. Van Langenhove. (Eds.) *Rethinking methods in psychology* (pp.162–177). London: Sage.

Smith, J.A., Flowers, P. & Larkin, M. (2009). Interpretative phenomenological analysis: Theory, method and research. London: Sage.

Tobbell, J. (2003). Students' experiences of the transition from primary to secondary school. *Educational and Child Psychology, 20*(4), 4–14.

Chapter 8.7 Doing qualitative research differently: How using a psychosocial approach provided an opportunity for investigating self-harm in schools

Jane Reichardt

Social scientists have long debated the use of qualitative approaches as a means of understanding the real-world experiences of research subjects. Surveys and interviews can provide useful ways of accessing views. However, questions about veracity and significance of results remain a challenge for qualitative researchers, in particular when research questions ask about ambiguous, complex and contradictory topics.

Hollway and Jefferson (2000) proposed taking a psychosocial approach; bringing the subtlety of everyday knowing about the complexity of real life into the research arena. This approach takes the view that individuals are the product of both their unique psyche and shared social world. Psychosocial research is a relatively new emerging paradigm within psychology and growing within education (Bibby, 2011). It has been influenced by a diverse range of interdisciplinary backgrounds, including psychoanalysis, sociology and ethnography.

This paper aims to provide a reflective account of the use of a psychosocial methodology within educational psychology research. The focus of the study was to explore the school experiences of young people who have self-harmed. Opportunities and challenges associated with the use of a psychosocial method are considered.

The research in context: Why self-harm?
A study into public attitudes towards self-harm found that it was the topic of most concern to young people, professionals and parents (Cello Group & Young Minds, 2012). The study reported that teachers and GPs believe self-harm is increasing and they may only be seeing 'the tip of the iceberg'. The BBC reported that teachers' unions claim schools are struggling to deal with rising numbers of students self-harming (2015).

The 2006 National Inquiry into self-harm found much self-harming behaviour is carried out secretively and used as a means of managing emotional pain. This inquiry found that many young people do not seek professional intervention. Hawton and colleagues (2002) had four years previously surveyed approximately 6000 fifteen and sixteen year olds: 6.9 per cent reported an act of self-harm in the previous year (roughly two pupils per average class of thirty). Of those, only 12 per cent reported to hospital. They concluded that self-harm in this age-group is largely a community-based issue.

The present study aims to find out from young people who have self-harmed about their experiences of school; relationships with peers and adults; how they experienced and engaged with help; and how they managed difficult times. It also intended to consider how school staff and professionals might support these vulnerable young people.

The method: Why psychosocial?

The focus of this study was on exploring young people's experiences of school. 'Doing Qualitative Research Differently' (DQRD) (Hollway & Jefferson, 2000; reissued 2012) provided a framework and methodology to capture the voices and experience of research participants.

Drawing on ideas established in clinical psychoanalysis, DQRD acknowledges that unconscious defences against emotional anxiety (Klein, 1988a, 1988b) are active within and between individuals. Interpreting possible defences to inform data analysis can illuminate areas of potential emotional resonance.

The psychosocial method was useful for this topic because it brings with it a deeper analysis and new ways of thinking about the secretive and hidden nature of the behaviour and associated complexities of obtaining help within the school setting.

Application in practice

Five young people (four female, one male) aged fifteen to seventeen years old were recruited from the child and adolescent mental health service (CAMHS) in which they were receiving treatment. Four were white British; one white other. All participants gave informed consent to join the study; parents of those under sixteen also provided consent, following British Psychological Society (BPS) guidelines (2010). None had Statements of Special Educational Needs (SEN); all attended school (though they had not always done so in the past) and spoke English fluently. Participants were receiving treatment following referral for self-harming behaviours from a specialist adolescent CAMHS in outer London, and were assessed by clinicians as low risk. Robust and rigorous procedures for safeguarding were granted ethical approval by the Research and Governance department of the relevant NHS Trust.

Interviews were conducted on two occasions following the Free Association Narrative Interview (FANI) technique developed by Hollway and Jefferson (2000). Open questions elicited responses associated with participants' experiences, for example, 'tell me about your experiences of school'. The second interview revisited themes and obtained reflections on the process. Questions explored good and more difficult experiences; first time self-harming; coping; feeling supported/ helped; noticing changes in themselves; experiences of bullying. A final question asked 'how can schools can help?'

Researcher's field notes were recorded before, between and after interviews. Detailed reflections about the experiences included emotional responses noticed in participants and researcher. This recognised the possible defences active in both researcher and subject.

The interview method used active listening skills (e.g. non-verbal attention, reflecting back, clarifying comments and summarising), taking a clinical style. In this way the researcher's attunement to the narratives of the participant provided the participant with an experience of feeling heard, valued and understood, offering containment and allowing further stories to emerge[1] (Bion, 1962). Interpretations were not made during the interview but reserved for data analysis.

Following the interviews, audio recordings were transcribed and anonymised. Transcripts and field notes were analysed using Braun and Clark's (2006) approach to thematic analysis. Attending to hesitations, associations, contradictions and rationalisations provided a means of noticing areas of potential emotional significance. Understanding psychoanalytic ideas (e.g. containment, splitting, rationalising, denial, projection, transference and counter-transference) provided opportunities to attend to areas where these unconscious processes may have been active (Lemma, 2003; Stapley, 2006).

Findings with illustrative quotes

The findings were clustered into three overarching themes: (1) pursuing the narrative of identity; (2) pain and the mind–body dichotomy; and (3) relationship to help. These themes considered the challenges of the adolescent process of self-discovery; managing emotional pain and interacting with help. The following examples have been selected to demonstrate the unique contribution of the psychosocial approach.

Pursuing the narrative of identity

The contradiction between the benefits of belonging to and difficulties in engaging with groups emerged as a point of internal challenge:

> We were security blanket for each other kind of thing ... If you were friends with someone who didn't really talk to anyone, who was quiet, then you were like a freak for talking to them. Like a freak for talking to the freak. (Penelope[2])

When other young people were found to be self-harming, a strong sense of identifying with their experience was present. It could be, though, that this prevented individual differences from being recognised and underlying difficulties addressed.

> A few days later she said 'I need to show you something. I've been doing this for a few weeks now and I didn't want to tell you because I didn't think you'd understand. I've seen that you do the same, I understand how you feel and you understand how I feel'. Um, and it was so heartbreaking really. I didn't want anyone else to have to go through and it really did upset me.... I just knew how she felt and I took such pity on her. (Claire)

Pain and the mind–body dichotomy

Sam's experience of being bullied was a particularly painful one. The physical scarring left on his body could be interpreted as metaphorical; a physical representation of emotional pain.

---

[1] Containment (Bion, 1962) relates to a pattern of interaction between caregiver and baby, where the infant needs the caregiver to think about and make sense of their emotional experience.
[2] Pseudonyms have been used throughout.

Sam:	I got attacked by 20 kids. And each one of them took a turn to beat the hell out of me.
Interviewer:	That must have been very frightening.
Sam:	Yeah... Just slightly.
Interviewer:	And what happened?
Sam:	What happened? Everything happened then. And then I went home and everyone, everyone was fine but I just went back home and I went upstairs and there was a razor on the side and I just gave up, I picked it up, took it into my room, broke it in half and used it to cut myself.
Interviewer:	You were very distressed at that point.
Sam:	Yeah. I've got some permanent scars now because people think they were funny. All my arms are messed up. My hands still got a lighter burn on it [shows arms and hand scars]. And now I get taken the pee out of because people think I've got a third nipple [shows a scar on his upper chest]. Because someone put a fag out on my chest.

At one point in the interview, Sam expressed an association between his experience of loss of relationships to the use of self-harm to manage painful feelings:

Sam:	Just this week I had my girlfriend tell me she hated me, I had Ms B. leave who was one of the three teachers who really understood me. And my great great nan just died.
Interviewer:	How are you coping with those losses?
Sam:	I'm alright I guess... I have found something out though. Sea salt heals wounds.
Interviewer:	Sea salt heals wounds.
Sam:	Yeah. E.g. it seals my wounds up [shows cuts on his arms].
Interviewer:	It's helped to heal your physical wounds.
Sam:	Yeah.
Interviewer:	Maybe not so much your emotional ones.
Sam:	No they're always gonna be there, just gotta deal with them.

Relationship to help

Ambivalence was present in participants' narratives about accessing help. This emerged as contradiction, rationalisation and expressions of hopelessness. Claire's statement exemplifies her ambivalent feelings, although it could also be interpreted to indicate the painful experience she was going through and an underlying wish for help.

> Like teachers, I can't expect them to be able to help me coz they're not professional human beings and especially if they're not trained to help people in that way. And nothing they can say is gonna help change things. They can be encouraging and give like kind words and be supportive and maybe help me calm down in that moment but then I think what's the point in actually talking to them about it because it's not going to solve anything for me. (Claire)

Receiving help from peers was a point of complexity, exemplifying a wish to be helped and understood alongside a risk of feeling further alienated.

> When they first find out it's something new to them, especially if they haven't experienced anything like that before. And they want to help because obviously, well, they know how bad it is, how bad it can be. And then they just sort of realise that helping them is a lot more than it seems to be and they just, they don't want to help anymore because they don't realise what they're getting themselves into. And they just end up getting sick and tired of you. (Rebecca)

When Rebecca was unable to follow advice from peers, she noticed herself becoming more isolated. She explained succinctly what she found to be helpful.

> Understanding and listening is a key part. And to be honest, I wouldn't really mind if they didn't give me advice as long as they listened. Cos I just really want someone to listen and understand. (Rebecca)

Finally, one example of using the researcher's field notes as a way of interpreting the data came following an interview with Claire. She talked about a sense of guilt and responsibility towards a friend who had started self-harming after her.

> I think I've influenced her because she still now has that attitude. She says, 'what's the point, I don't care'. And it's really, really upsetting because I think I put that into her head... It really upsets me because I feel that's my fault... She could have come to that herself, to develop those feelings, but I feel so guilty that I caused that. (Claire)

My experience following this interview was different from others.

> I have a huge headache and am worried about what she is left with. She expressed that some of my questions had raised feelings in her that she hadn't connected before, such as bullying and her feelings of responsibility towards her peers who also self-harm. (Researcher's field notes)

I wondered if this feeling could be a counter-transference[3] response to Claire's strong feelings. Just as Claire felt responsible for her friend's self-harming, this feeling had been activated in me and I felt concerned and responsible for her. For that moment, I had lost touch with alternative evidence of the benefits of being heard, having someone make connections and links and validating her experience.

Extrapolating this idea into the school system, I have since wondered how school staff might experience working with young people expressing strong and distressing feelings. It is possible that unconscious processes of denial and avoidance within school networks may protect school staff from feeling overwhelmed by feelings such as these, as documented by Menzies (1960) in her paper on social defences against anxiety. Educational psychologists may benefit from using these ideas to support staff working with this vulnerable group.

---

[3] Youell (2006) defines counter-transference as the way we recognise and think about our feelings in response to a patient.

Reflections on the method: Opportunities and challenges

DQRD and the FANI method provided a therapeutic style of interviewing within a research context. This enabled a deeper, richer picture of young people's experiences to emerge and their distinctive voices to be heard. It attended both to the surface meanings of their responses as well as to potential unconscious communications. In addition, engaging with complexity, contradiction and ambivalence allowed for broadening understanding. Reflecting on the subjectivity of the research encounter, in particular regarding the counter-transference experienced, allowed a different dimension of the analysis and interpretation to emerge.

Various challenges and debates confront the psychosocial researcher. Having a robust rationale and reasoning for using the method can contribute to the construction of a valid and transparent approach. Some of the challenges of using this approach are considered here as questions.

How can a researcher using psychosocial methods assure an in-depth and valid analysis?

Using Braun and Clark's (2006) six-step approach to thematic analysis provided a thorough framework for data analysis. This included immersion in the data, coding sections and eventually constructing a meaningful thematic map. An audit trail demonstrating how the data was analysed ensured transparency. However, alternative ways of analysing the data may also be possible.

Should psychoanalytic ideas remain the remit of a clinical encounter?

Hollway and Jefferson (2000) argue that interpersonal dynamics, feelings and emotions occur everyday within and between people; analysing them is of relevance to the research encounter, particularly interviews. Using psychoanalytic ideas within research can 'thicken or enrich understanding' (Frosh and Baraitser, 2008).

Is it possible to protect against 'wild analysis'?

Hollway and Jefferson (2000) argue that in order to protect against the potential threat of 'wild analysis' (Freud's phrase, meaning overstretched or implausible interpretation, 1910), interpretations of the data must stick closely to the material, holding true to the narratives. Emergent themes can be tested against the data. Using the researcher's emotional response to the data and a second interview provides an opportunity for triangulation and exploring potential themes.

Could talking about difficult issues inadvertently exacerbate the problem?

Several studies into the use of screening tools with depression have concluded that talking about suicide and self-harm with a non-judgmental adult neither increased feelings that life is not worth living (Crawford et al., 2011) nor increased distress or suicidality among adolescents (Gould et al., 2005). However, it was important to attend to participants' experience of the interviews (both during and afterwards) as part of the researcher's duty of care.

How can a relatively inexperienced researcher be supported to mobilise this approach?

Structures that supported this study included regular supervision, access to reflective space such as conferences, and peer support. Using open, exploratory questions and reserving interpretation for outside the interview encounter ensured the process was undertaken within a zone of professional competence. Ethical procedures designed to reduce potential for any harm to participants and prioritise the duty of care were paramount.

Conclusion

The use of the psychosocial approach to qualitative research in educational psychology is in its infancy. The method provides ample opportunity for researchers interested in obtaining a rich picture of the experiences of people within social systems, such as schools. Reflecting on the use of novel means of obtaining data and approaches to data analysis should be encouraged. Support networks where material can be brought and reflections shared may be beneficial. Myriad opportunities are present to obtain the voices of vulnerable groups and apply this understanding to supporting young people and school staff.

References

BBC (2015). Schools 'struggling to cope' with students self-harming. *BBC News*. Retrieved 18 July 2016 from www.bbc.co.uk/newsbeat/30695657

Bibby, T. (2011). *Education – An 'impossible profession'? Psychoanalytic explorations of learning and classrooms*. Abingdon: Routledge.

Bion, W. (1962). *Learning from experience*. London: Heinemann.

Braun, V. & Clarke, V. (2006). Using thematic analysis in psychology. *Qualitative Research in Psychology, 3*(2), 77–101.

British Psychological Society (2010). *Code of human research ethics*. Leicester: Author.

Cello Group and Young Minds (2012). *Talking self-harm*. London: Author.

Crawford, M.J., Thana, L., Methuen, C. et al. (2011). Impact of screening for risk of suicide: Randomised controlled trial. *The British Journal of Psychiatry, 198*, 379–384.

Freud, S. (1910). *'Wild psychoanalysis': Five lectures on psychoanalysis, Leonardo da Vinci and other works. The standard edition of the complete psychological works of Sigmund Freud, Vol 11*. London: Hogarth Press.

Frosh, S. & Baraitser, L. (2008). Psychoanalysis and psychosocial studies. *Psychoanalysis, Culture and Society, 13*(4), 346–365.

Gould, M.S., Marrocco, F.A., Kleinman, M. et al. (2005). Evaluating iatrogenic risk of youth suicide screening programes: A randomized controlled trial. *Journal of the American Medical Association, 293*, 1635–1643.

Hawton, K., Rodham, K., Evans, E. & Weatherall, R. (2002). Deliberate self-harm in adolescents: Self-report survey in schools in England. *BMJ: British Medical Journal, 325*, 1207–1211.

Hollway, W. & Jefferson, T. (2000). *Doing qualitative research differently: Free association, narrative and the interview method*. London: Sage.

Klein, M. (1988a). *Love, guilt and reparation: And other works, 1921–1945 (Vol. 1)*. London: Virago.

Klein, M. (1988b). *Envy and gratitude: And other works, 1946–1963*. London: Virago.

Lemma, A. (2003). *Introduction to the practice of psychoanalytic psychotherapy*. London: John Wiley & Sons, Ltd.

Menzies, I. (1960). *A case study in the functioning of social systems as a defence against anxiety*. London: Tavistock.

Stapley, L. (2006). *Individuals, groups, and organisations beneath the surface*. London: Karnac Books.

Youell, B. (2006). *The learning relationship: Psychoanalytic thinking in education*. London: Karnac Books.

Chapter 8.8 Distinctive experiences of children in the early years evaluating their provision

Anita Soni

The research in context

The 2006 Childcare Act gave increasing recognition to young children's rights, going beyond protection, provision and prevention to include rights to participate, voice opinions and influence decisions in matters relating to their lives. However, whilst it is recognised that children are competent to understand, reflect on and offer views about their experience, this does not always easily include the very young. The government's recommendation is evident in the following quotes:

> For services to be successful and have a positive impact on young children's lives, the voices of young children themselves need to be listened to and actively taken into account. Undertaking consultations with young children as the primary users of early years services, can inform not only front-line practitioners and managers of their needs but also reveal barriers to development which can inform more strategic planning to improve outcomes and opportunities for all young children. (HMI, 2008, p.2)

> In discharging their duties under this section an English Local Authority must have regard to such information about the views of young children as is available and relevant. (Childcare Act 2006, Section 3(5))

The official publication *Early Years Foundation Stage Guidance* (EYFS) (DCSF, 2008a) set out the need for practitioners to listen to children within areas of learning such as personal, social and emotional development (PSED) and communication, language and literacy (CLL). However, this stance was weakened by its omission from the statutory guidance for the EYFS.

The current incarnation of the EYFS also recognises the importance of children's rights, as is evident from the reference to the United Nations Convention on the Rights of the Child (UNCRC, 1989) on the front cover of the non-statutory guidance document *Development Matters for the EYFS*:

> Children have a right, spelled out in the United Nations Convention on the Rights of the Child, to provision which enables them to develop their personalities, talents and abilities irrespective of ethnicity, culture or religion, home language, family background, learning difficulties, disabilities or gender. (Early Education, 2012, p.1)

However, Rix and Parry (2014) have argued that there are conflicting messages within the current EYFS, as the right identified in *Development Matters* is not a right within the UNCRC, but a mix of Articles 2 and 29, and Brooker (2014) argues that it positions the child as 'material for future successful learning and earning' (p. 13). In contrast to this, the Mosaic approach is a participative approach and highlights the need to focus on children in the here and now and therefore to elicit their views focusing on the present.

Overview of the Mosaic approach

The Mosaic approach (Clark and Moss, 2001, 2011) is a participatory methodology that seeks to enable children to reflect on their experiences using a range of different research methods. It has been used with young children in the maintained, independent, voluntary and private sector to gain their perspectives on the quality of the provision they attend. A number of tools are used within the Mosaic approach that seek to enable children to explore their experiences of attending early years provision, and these are based on communication methods that children choose to use with their family and friends. Clark and Moss (2011) highlight that the Mosaic approach is a framework for listening to young children that is multi-method, participatory, reflexive, adaptable, focused on children's lived experiences, and embedded in early years practice.

There are three stages within the approach:
1. Children and adults gathering documentation;
2. Piecing together the information for dialogue, reflection and interpretation; and
3. Planning for change and continuity

A number of methods are identified in the Mosaic approach, but Clark and Moss (2011) emphasise that these do not form a complete list and can be developed or supplemented. The methods identified include:

- Observations of children focusing on the question 'what is it like to be here?' This includes noting what children enjoy and like to play with based on practitioners' observations of children.
- Child conferencing, which is based on interviewing children about their experiences at nursery, including asking about the people, places, activities and role of adults, and about the best day at nursery. It is important to ask children within this about what or whom they don't like as well as what or whom they do like.
- Children can be asked to photograph events or people they themselves find important and events or people important in the setting to younger children. These can be used to support child conferencing. Child-led tours can be supported by cameras or an audio recorder, allowing children to talk more freely about the setting, or can be structured by use of a prop such as a teddy or by the use of questions.
- Mapping of the setting can be a way children can show the places they find important spaces. Taking photographs may well be simpler and easier for them than drawing maps.
- Role play using 'small world' figures can be used to elicit children's views of the early years setting.
- Parents' perspectives are an important dimension that can add to children's own views but should not dominate what has been gained from children first-hand. In the Mosaic approach, the same questions and areas that are discussed in child conferencing are used.

- Practitioners' impressions of children's likes, dislikes, friendships and so on provide another perspective.

This list includes a number of participatory visual methods and materials generated and provided by the child that can later be used for discussion. Clark and Moss (2011) observe that these methods have become more popular for qualitative research in education and social sciences. Dahl and Aubrey (2005) suggest that to gain children's views effectively and ethically, traditional 'question–answer' approaches should be avoided, and propose instead a variety of practicable methods, and a range of tools, such as toys, drawings and photographs, for eliciting children's views and ideas. Mooney and Blackburn (2003) found that tours, photographs and tape recorders worked most successfully with the younger children in their study.

Application of the Mosaic approach in an early years setting

The method's application is described using the three stages identified by Clark and Moss (2011).

Stage 1: Gathering documentation

At an initial meeting, practitioners were introduced to the Mosaic approach, which was suggested as a way of involving children in evaluating the quality of the setting. The following research questions were identified with the eight practitioners at the early years setting (a private nursery in the West Midlands, attended by approximately fifty children) where the research was undertaken:

- What activities/aspects are enjoyed and valued by the children?
- What activities/aspects are not enjoyed and valued by the children?
- What might be changed in order to improve the provision for the children?

These questions were discussed with the practitioners working at the nursery, who then explored simpler versions of the questions. This stage was important to help the practitioners become active stakeholders in the process. The simplified questions were as follows:

- What, who or where does x like at nursery? Why?
- What, who or where does x not like at nursery? Why?
- What would x wish for as a change to the nursery? If Debbie (a notional practitioner) had extra money, like £50, what should she get with that?

Practitioners identified six children aged between two and four years to participate in the research. Each child's Key Person (DCSF, 2008b) was identified as the most appropriate adult to work with the child, as this was an initial trial for this approach. The practitioners identified children on whom they wanted to focus to gain their views: reasons for the choice of the child varied, some practitioners identifying children who have an additional need, some who were reticent and some who attended infrequently. The practitioners wanted to use this additional opportunity to get to know the child, so chose not to select the most confident and talkative children, whose views would tend to be better known. Practitioners encouraged and validated each other's choices: each had a clear rationale as to why they were interested in capturing that particular child's perspective.

Different methods for eliciting children's views were discussed with the practitioners, including observations, use of cameras, child-led tours, parental perspective and child conferencing. The practitioners were aware that there was a need for flexibility, to follow the child's lead and select the approach that was most appropriate for the maturity, ability and interest of the child. The Key Person focused on the three questions listed above, explicating and elaborating them to make sure the children clearly understood what was being asked. Children were allowed to choose whether to participate or not (British Educational Research Association, 2004), use a teddy and/or camera as they preferred and leave the research as and when they wanted.

Practitioners raised important issues about the stability of children's views and it was agreed to gather the child's views over the period of a month. It was also agreed that it was important to check the views with each child on a later date/s and consider whether a view came from multiple sources or not. This aspect of the research was developed in Stage 2, wherein practitioners shared their initial observations, photographs and interview data to triangulate and support initial views. It was agreed that if the child's view was ascertained from a range of sources and on multiple occasions, then it was likely to be more strongly held.

Stage 2: Piecing together the information for dialogue, reflection and interpretation
The practitioners met for an hour and initially presented what the child had shared from their perspective. The practitioners presented this in a range of ways – some had used a simple scrapbook and others had put together a poster.

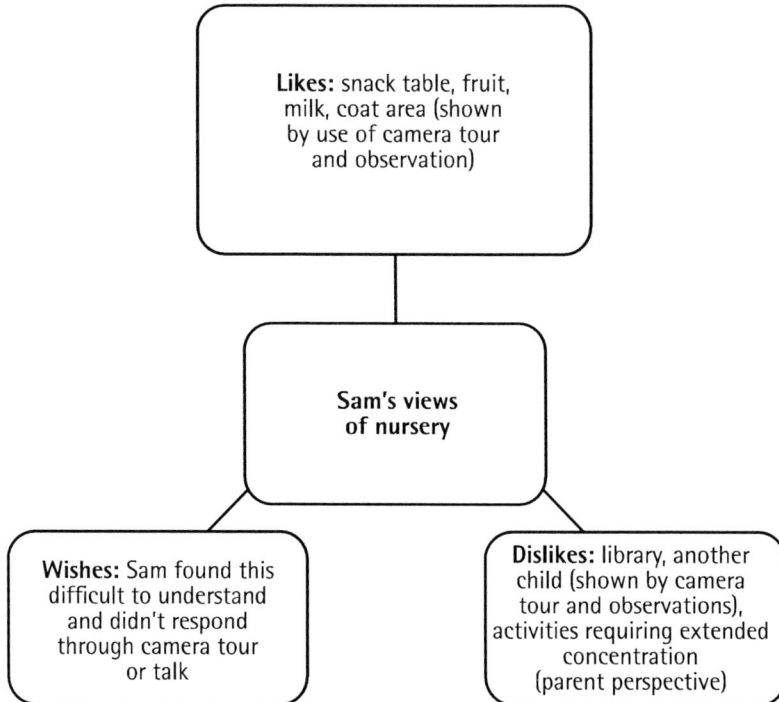

Figure 8.8.1: Example of information gathered in Stage 1

The process of sharing and collating children's views was useful as other practitioners triangulated and gave additional examples. This was a valuable process in which practitioners were able to compare their individual reports on the same children, pooling their experience. The children's views were written on sticky notes (see tables 8.8.1 and 8.8.2) and collated under the three research questions to produce a collective view of the nursery, its strengths and weaknesses and what the children's perspectives indicated that they would like to be different.

Table 8.8.1: Children's likes as a group, based on sticky-note findings

Theme	What the children identified
Vehicles	Cars (3) Buses Train track Diggers
Construction	Construction (2) Construction area (2)
Craft	Craft Scissors Large painting Junk modelling Gluing and sticking
Small world/role play	Dressing up (3) Pirate ship (2) Dinosaurs (2) Restaurant Role Play
Media characters	Buzz Lightyear (3) Frozen Star Wars
Food/meals	Chicken Dinners Ham cobs Fish fingers Snack area
People	Friends Becky (practitioner) James (practitioner)
Physical	Dance (2) Throwing and catching Playing games
Technology	Computers (2) Using the camera
Quiet space	Book corner
Water tray	Water tray
Coat	Coat

Table 8.8.2: Children's wishes and dislikes

Wishes	Chance to perform for Mum Scooter/bike Rocket station Buzz Lightyear Taking things home
Dislikes	Other children

Stage 3: Planning for change and continuity

The collated results were discussed and mapped into an action plan for the nursery, through discussion with the practitioners and managers (see Table 8.8.3). As Clark and Moss (2011) emphasise, it was important to recognise and value the desire of many of the children to continue in the same way. However, there were themes within the data and these were used to launch discussion about how practice and resources could further be developed. There were also other unintended outcomes from the project, such as the increased confidence of practitioners in their knowledge of particular children or sense of developing a stronger bond with them. Some raised issues of fairness; some believed this approach was needed with a wider range of children; some thought children may have felt under too much scrutiny. It was agreed that the approach would be a regular feature of the setting's practice and would be used alongside other evaluative tools such as the Ofsted self-evaluation schedule (Ofsted, 2013) and questionnaire feedback from parents.

Table 8.8.3: Action plan for continuity and change

What?	How?
Develop the variety of vehicles that are available for children to play with	Buy wooden cars where the tops can be swapped Buy small-world vehicles such as tractors, diggers, buses, planes, boats, and branded toy cars, remote control cars, car mat and garage Extend the construction materials for building cars and transport Making paper aeroplanes and developing cardboard play to make trains and buses Enhance water play by having boats
Develop small world play	Make/buy a dolls house Purchase pets for children to play with Purchase some Disney characters such as those in Frozen, Rapunzel, Toy Story and princesses Bring-a-doll/figure week
Develop expressive arts	Take paint outside e.g. splatter painting Painting outside Develop the children's use of a stage to show their dancing, drumming, singing etc. Develop a child-centred talent show for parents to come along to

Table 8.8.3 (continued)

What?	How?
Develop a quiet area	Review the book corner and create a quiet space that is cosier, smaller and more visible to the children using soft furnishings, cushions
Review the use of ICT	Develop staff confidence with the material available to use on the computers and the space for ICT
Develop outdoor play	All staff to take out indoor play to use outdoors

Reflections on the approach

The practitioners involved were excited by this piece of work, and it offered a useful contrast with other evaluations conducted in early years settings by quality assurance schemes such as the Early Childhood Environment Rating Scale (ECERs) (Harms et al., 2004) which are typically adult-led and give few opportunities for children's participation. The approach also offered an alternative or addition to the traditional self-evaluation as advocated by Ofsted (2013). However, the research was recognised as limited to a single event, and there was clearly greater value in being part of a regular evaluation cycle, and a need to evaluate the impact of the changes, and to embed this as part of the nursery's ongoing approach. The experience had developed practitioners' confidence and knowledge of the children they worked with, and helped them consider how the setting may be experienced by the children.

While it offers a useful way to evaluate early years settings, this relatively simple approach can be adapted and used by EPs. The approach would include ways in which the views of young children can be sought, albeit over time, and at times through the child's Key Person, a practitioner who knows the child well. It can be applied to older children. It can also be used with children with Special Educational Needs, since it builds upon the child's chosen communication methods with family and friends. It does, however, require an investment of time and the desire to work alongside the key people in the child's life.

References

British Educational Research Association (2011). *Ethical Guidelines for Educational Research.* Retrieved 27 April 2011 from www.bera.ac.uk/wp-content/uploads/2014/02/BERA-Ethical-Guidelines-2011.pdf

Brooker, L. (2014). An overview of early education in England. In J. Moyles, J. Payler & J. Georgeson (Eds.) *Early years foundations: Critical issues* (pp.6–16). Maidenhead: Open University Press/McGraw Hill.

Clark, A. & Moss, P. (2001). *Listening to young children: The Mosaic approach.* London: National Children's Bureau.

Clark, A. & Moss, P. (2011). *Listening to young children: The Mosaic approach* (2nd edn.). London: National Children's Bureau.

Dahl, S. & Aubrey, C. (2005). *Children's views: What the children of Bright Eyes Nursery think about the play and learning opportunities available in their setting.* Childhood Research Unit, Institute of Education, University of Warwick. Retrieved on 1 March 2011 from www.ness.bbk.ac.uk/support/local-evaluation-findings/documents/1312.pdf

DCSF (2008a). *Practice guidance for the Early Years Foundation Stage.* Nottingham: Author.

DCSF (2008b). *Statutory framework for the Early Years Foundation Stage.* Nottingham: Author.

Early Education (2012). *Development Matters in the Early Years Foundation Stage (EYFS).* London: Early Education/Department for Education.

Harms, T. Clifford, R. & Cryer, D. (2004). *Early Childhood Environment Rating Scale.* New York: Teachers College Press.

HM Government (2008). *Raising standards, improving outcomes: Statutory guidance on the Childcare Act 2006 Early Years Outcomes Duty.* Retrieved on 22 July 2014 from http://dera.ioe.ac.uk/6889/5/Raising%20Standards%20-%20Improving%20Outcomes%20-%2003%20Dec.pdf

Mooney, A. & Blackburn, T. (2003). *Children's views on childcare quality. Nottingham: DfES Publications.* Retrieved on 1 March 2011 from www.education.gov.uk/publications/eOrderingDownload/RR482.pdf

Ofsted (2013). *Early Years self-evaluation form.* Retrieved on 27 July 2014 from www.ofsted.gov.uk/resources/early-years-online-self-evaluation-form-sef-and-guidance-for-providers-delivering-early-years-foundation-stage

Rix, J. & Parry, J. (2014) Without foundation: The EYFS Framework and its creation of needs. In J. Moyles, J. Payler & J. Georgeson (Eds.) *Early years foundations: Critical issues* (pp.203–214). Maidenhead: Open University Press/McGraw Hill.

Chapter 8.9 Giving children of prisoners a voice

Fiona Weidberg

Why listen? The context of the research.

Children have a right to have their voices and opinions heard, including in research (Lundy et al., 2011). Bradbury and Taylor (2015) advocate creating a space to listen to children and support the shift from researchers focusing 'on' children to concentrating on working 'with' or 'for' children. From a social constructionist perspective, children are social agents and therefore do not need to be interviewed indirectly, as long as appropriate methods are used (Einarsdóttir, 2007). This was the view I took when carrying out my doctoral research into children with a parent in prison, a population within the literature frequently described as hidden or invisible (e.g. Rosenberg, 2009), despite there being an estimated 200,000 children of prisoners in the UK (Ministry of Justice, 2012). An estimated seven per cent of children will experience parental imprisonment during their school years, not including reconstituted families and step-children (Gill, 2009).

The rationale for my research was to focus on the young people's wellbeing (rather than being interested in decreasing parental recidivism rates) and to concentrate directly on the young people's views (in contrast to gaining these views indirectly through parents, carers or observation). I carried out a small-scale piece of qualitative research with five young people aged 8–13 years old, interviewing each young person on two separate occasions.

Gaining access to vulnerable groups of children is difficult because of the need for two gatekeepers: professionals and parents (Tisdall et al., 2008). I found recruitment the most difficult part of the whole research process. I used revelatory case sampling, where potential participants are approached because they are the first-known members of a specific group (Cohen et al., 2011). After eight months of contacting professionals and organisations, I gained my first participant. Eventually, I found two participants via a charity-run support group, one via a SENCO, and two more through another charity in a different part of the country. However, this sampling procedure had the advantage of including young people who varied in the amount of contact they had with their fathers (from semi-regular contact to contact being prohibited, including calls and letters). This emerged as an important factor during analysis. Separate information and consent sheets were designed for parents/carers, children and young people. At the start of each interview I went through both the information and consent sheets with the participants to check their understanding and give them an opportunity to raise any questions. I fed back each young person's results in an individualised letter to them and encouraged them to call or email me if they wanted to discuss any part of this.

How to listen: A description of some of the techniques used in the interviews

Long and colleagues (2012) recommend using creative techniques to enable young people to be the experts in their own lives by encouraging engagement and providing opportunities to talk about their worlds. My chosen methodology was interpretative phenomenological analysis (IPA), which aims to explore ways in which people make sense of their personal and social worlds (Charmaz, 2003). IPA has the advantage of allowing the researcher to be flexible within the semi-structured interviews, meaning that I could use many tools and adapt each interview to the young person's interests and needs. Arksey and Knight (1999) suggested using a variety of activities in research with younger children and Clark (2005) highlighted the importance of making the process enjoyable and flexible so that children can choose how they want to express themselves.

I wanted to encourage open conversations. Many of the techniques I used were based on Personal Construct Psychology (PCP) (Beaver, 1996), which enables children to express their views without adults imposing their beliefs or expectations. PCP materials are often presented visually, giving young people the choice to communicate non-verbally if and when they wish. PCP fits with IPA's ethos of letting individuals lead (Willig & Stainton-Rogers, 2008) and encouraging them to explore their own theories and views. When interviewing young people about a parent in prison, I was conscious of the level of stigma they may feel and quickly realised that most of these young people had difficulties in knowing who to trust (e.g. whether or not to tell friends or teachers). The PCP activities allowed me to use indirect questioning initially and to follow the young person's lead about what they wanted to tell me. This had the advantage of creating a safe environment where the young people seemed to feel comfortable and wanted to open up.

I started off by using 'Kinetic family drawing' (Beaver, 1996) as an activity to build rapport and start to find out about their relationships with various family members. I also used a 'Drawing the ideal self' technique (Moran, 2001), which includes asking the young person to draw the person they would not like to be, followed by a picture of a person they consider as ideal. I found this a useful tool to explore the ways the children view their own situations, and when used in this research it revealed how much they valued their imprisoned father's opinion of them. Figure 8.9.1 illustrates an example of the third part of this activity, where we discussed the two drawings, others' opinions and how to move towards your ideal self.

I found the 'Portrait gallery' tool (Beaver, 1996) useful in my interviews. This involves discussing four emotions, listing three events/people/objects that make them feel each one, then describing how they believe others view them. This process did not directly ask about their parents in prison but the subject came up for each participant, showing that the young people were sufficiently comfortable talking about their different experiences and describing emotions linked to these experiences without being influenced by any prejudices or presumptions. Figures 8.9.2 and 8.9.3 give two examples (some information has been removed to retain anonymity; highlights were added later for clarity).

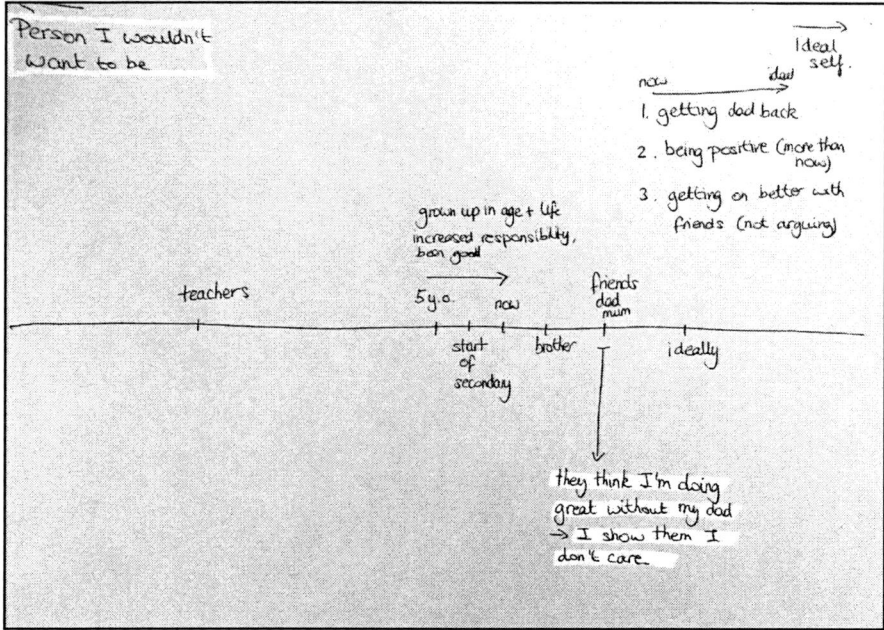

Figure 8.9.1: Ideal self, part 3

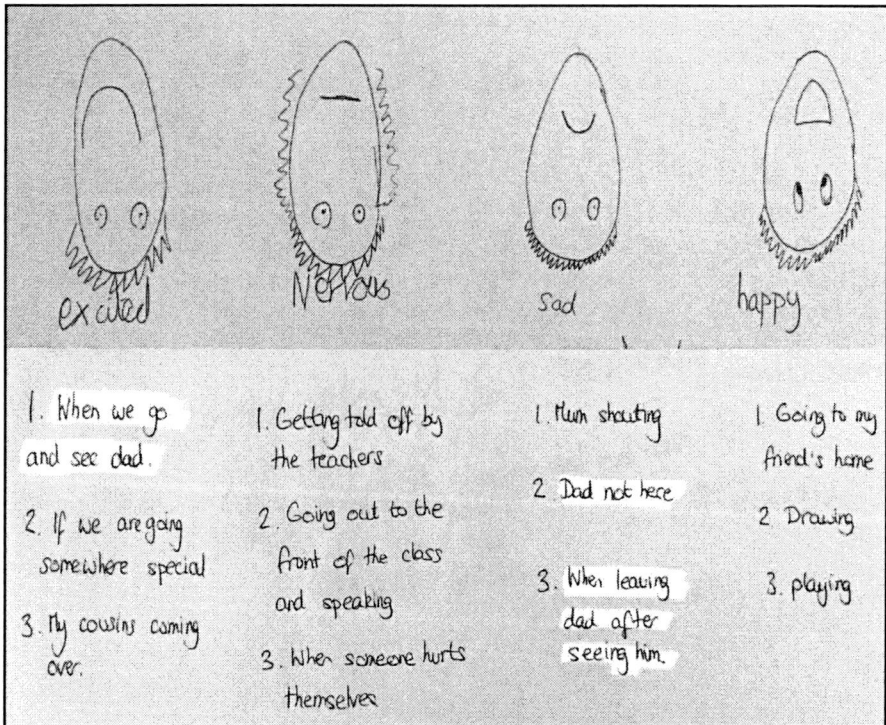

Figure 8.9.2: Family portrait gallery (I)

Figure 8.9.3: Family portrait gallery (II)

I also used Daniel and Wassell's (2002) 'Domains of resilience' model as a visual aid and talking tool to start a discussion about what each young person thought helped them cope. This allowed us to discuss different subjects in more detail, including participants' talents and interests, friendships, education and secure bases.

At the end of each set of interviews I asked the young people how I could improve the process for the next person; all said that they had really enjoyed talking to me. Particularly encouraging was one young person who had spent much of the first interview explaining how she did not enjoy discussing feelings, who then told me how much she had enjoyed talking about her feelings with me.

The interviews were then transcribed and analysed using the guidelines for my chosen methodology: IPA (Smith et al., 2009). IPA analysis requires a detailed analysis for each individual case before looking at shared meaning across cases.

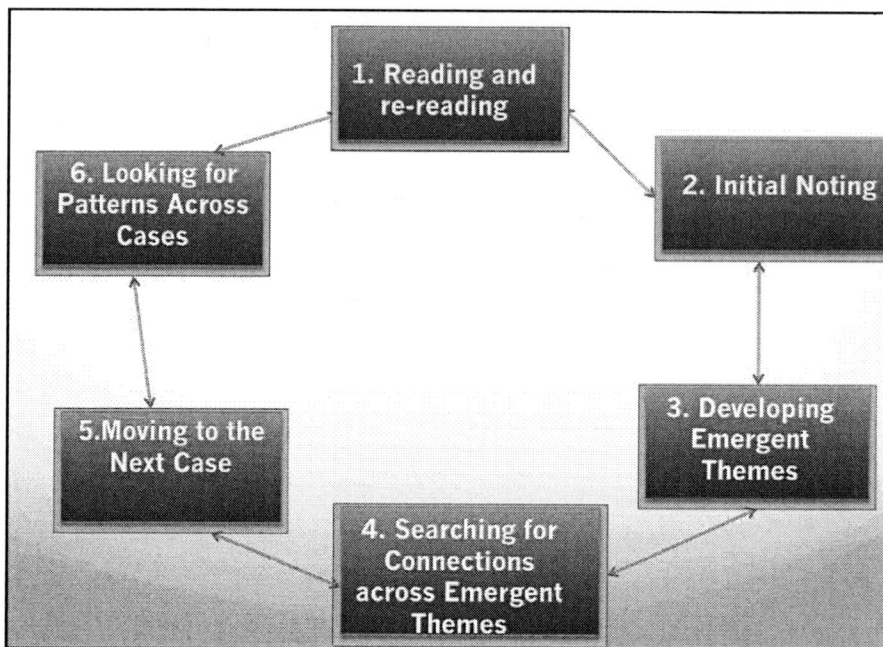

Figure 8.9.4: Smith et al.'s (2009) six-step guide to IPA

Although IPA is more frequently used for qualitative research with adults, it can also be used with children and young people. However, the key to having a rich analysis is having good data, which requires gaining the young people's trust sufficiently to allow them to open up to the researcher. The PCP activities allowed the young people to feel listened to and express their opinions.

Example findings with illustrative quotes

The tools described above and the use of two interviews to develop rapport led to the emergence of interesting themes during analysis. These themes fit best under three headings (master themes): coping mechanisms, anxieties and trust. I will briefly describe examples of superordinate themes from each of these master themes, illustrating them with quotes to show how these young people were able to open up about a sensitive topic that is surrounded by stigma.

Coping mechanisms

One important superordinate theme was the supportive relationship the young people had with their mothers, for those who lived with them:

> I think the relationship between me and my mum has actually helped. Cos like I know that she's there if I need to talk to her.

The young people interviewed also explained their own individual coping mechanisms, which included adapting and normalising, blocking feelings, distraction and avoidance strategies and a strong sense of independence:

I've got used to it now, so it was OK. I just like pretended it wasn't happening. So like blanked it out. And that's what I do with most things. My mum says it's wrong to blank things out.

Contact was an essential coping mechanism for several of the young people as it gave them something to look forward to:

I don't really care [...] because I see him. It's not like I'm never going to see him again. I see him and visit.

Anxieties
Contact was also a source of anxiety. This was sometimes due to the complexities of organising visits, or to their infrequency; others had difficulties saying goodbye or were not able to visit or make contact of any kind:

Not being able to see dad, I think that's like the most important thing to me, so, [...] it's like really hard. ... We can't exactly stay in contact with dad, so yeah...that's the reason we are in this mess.

I don't really like changes. I really hate changes. And I hate saying goodbye. When I go and visit him, it's like great when I see him, when I go, but then I realise you have to say 'bye' after, so it's kind of like, you know...I don't like leaving him.

Another source of anxiety and frustration was not being heard or listened to by the justice or education systems, in part because they did not always want to risk telling teachers or because their teachers made assumptions about the cause of any upsets. This added to the young people feeling that they had no control over their own lives and were dependent on others' behaviour.

Trust
Trust was complicated for these young people as they had to choose whom they could turn to for support. This contributed to many of their anxieties and vulnerabilities, including problems with believing the explanations about their parent's whereabouts:

We was like in the house, when they came into the house and they like handcuffed him and took him away. And I didn't know why because my mum wouldn't tell me.

The young people in this study tended to hide their fathers' imprisonment from their friends and classmates, even when one young person discovered a classmate also had a parent in prison.

I said how do you get home and he said, cos his mum and dad are both in prison. [...] cos he's new so I don't trust him.

The young people described the stigma surrounding their parent's imprisonment, and the fear of being bullied or teased by peers or of suffering threats from the community. However, these particular young people, unlike some described in the literature, did not feel any direct shame about their fathers and explained how much they trusted them, enjoyed their company and often wanted to have a job or hobby like those of their fathers, seeing them as role models. This was a very interesting finding as it contradicted some of the previous research in the area that found children felt shame towards their imprisoned parent (e.g. Brown et al., 2001).

Part of the complexity with the interviews and analysis was the emergence of trust as such an important theme, given that I had to gain the participants' trust before they could explain this to me. For example, one young person started off by explaining that the only reason she had not told her friends as follows: 'Just haven't found the time. [...] No it's not that I don't trust them.' However, in the second interview, the young person explained: '[It's] just in case we fall out, I don't know if I trust them enough that I'd go round telling other people, just in case we fall out. So I'd rather keep my distance and not tell them.' This highlighted the importance of carrying out two interviews and focusing on building rapport to enable the young people to trust me and to talk openly about experiences and feelings.

Reflections on the methods and techniques used to access young people's voice

I believe the key to the success of these interviews was linked to my focus on building rapport and trust, being flexible and adapting each interview to meet the young person's needs. When interviewing children, Smith (2004) recommends that the researcher take a stronger role than with adult interviews, and for the researcher to use their experiences as a practitioner to adapt data-collection methods. Some young people included in my study were able to clearly verbalise their experience and express their opinions, while others were confused about their situations, taking slightly longer to open up and trust me. The PCP activities could easily be adapted to focus on drawing, writing or talking. Visual symbols of emotions were a very useful talking tool to help one young person increase their own understanding of their feelings. I always followed the young person's lead. If they preferred to draw or doodle when talking to me then I would encourage this. I even played noughts and crosses whilst talking to one young person who seemed to find it easier to talk about her experiences when not all of the attention was on her. One young person developed her own creative way of feeling comfortable enough to open up to me. During our second interview, she asked me to pretend to put her to sleep. Despite my initial confusion, I decided to follow her lead. I soon realised that whilst she was in this pretend state of sleep she suddenly felt comfortable talking openly and honestly about her feelings and experiences, whilst before she had been one of the hardest to engage as she was easily distracted. This is not something I could have predicted nor is it something I am likely to be able to use again during any research or individual work, but it did highlight the importance of being flexible and following the child's lead.

The advantage of semi-structured interviews is the scope to adapt the interview schedule and vary the order of questions and activities by following the young person's lead. It is very unlikely that direct questioning alone, without the PCP activities, would have allowed the young people to open up about topics such as trust and stigma. The five young people mentioned enjoying the experience and appreciated having the opportunity to be heard. Even with the intense time pressures and workloads of the EP profession, I believe it is still essential to remain flexible and follow the child's lead to start with so that they can feel comfortable enough to trust us and show their strengths and qualities. I consider this to be the key ingredient when working with pupils in situations where other professionals are convinced that young people will not engage in any activity or assessment.

References

Arksey, H. & Knight, P. (1999). *Interviewing for social scientists: An introductory resource with examples.* London: Sage.

Beaver, R. (1996). *Educational psychology casework: A practice guide.* London: Jessica Kingsley Publishers.

Bradbury-Jones, C. & Taylor, J. (2015). Engaging with children as co-researchers: Challenges, counter-challenges and solutions. *International Journal of Social Research Methodology, 18*(2), 161–173.

Brown, K., Dibb, L., Shenton, F. & Elson, E. (2001). *No-one's ever asked me: Young people with a prisoner in the family.* London: Federation of Prisoners' Families Support Groups.

Charmaz, K. (2003). Grounded theory. In J.A. Smith (Ed.) *Qualitative psychology: A practical guide to research methods* (pp.81–110). London: Sage.

Clark, A. (2005). Listening to and involving young children: A review of research and practice. *Early Child Development and Care, 175*(6), 489–505.

Daniel, B. & Wassell, S. (2002). *Adolescence: Assessing and promoting resilience in vulnerable children.* Jessica Kingsley Publishers.

Einarsdóttir, J. (2007). Research with children: Methodological and ethical challenges. *European Early Childhood Education Research Journal, 15*(2), 197–211.

Gill, O. (2009). *Every night you cry: Case studies of 15 Bristol families with a parent in prison.* Bristol: Barnardo's South West.

Long, L., McPhillips, T., Shevlin, M. & Smith, R. (2012). Utilising creative methodologies to elicit the views of young learners with additional needs in literacy. *British Journal of Learning Support, 27*(1), 20–28.

Lundy, L., McEvoy, L. & Byrne, B. (2011). Working with young children as co-researchers: An approach informed by the United Nations Convention on the Rights of the Child. *Early Education and Development, 22*(5), 714–736.

Ministry of Justice (2012). Prisoners' childhood and family backgrounds. London: Author. Retrieved on 18 July 2016 from www.gov.uk/government/uploads/system/uploads/attachment_data/file/278837/prisoners-childhood-family-backgrounds.pdf

Moran, H. (2001). Who do you think you are? Drawing the ideal self: A technique to explore a child's sense of self. *Clinical Child Psychology and Psychiatry, 6*(4), 599–604.

Rosenberg, J. (2009) Children need dads too: Children with fathers in prison. Human Rights & Refugees Publications. Geneva and New York: Quaker United Nations Office.

Smith, J.A. (2004). Reflecting on the development of interpretative phenomenological analysis and its contribution to qualitative research in psychology. *Qualitative Research in Psychology, 1*(1), 39–54.

Smith, J.A., Flowers, P. & Larkin, M. (2009). *Interpretative phenomenological analysis: theory, method and research.* Los Angeles: Sage.

Willig, C. & Stainton-Rogers, W. (2008). *Handbook of qualitative methods in psychology.* London: Sage.

Chapter 8.10 The stories young people with social, emotional and behavioural difficulties (SEBD) tell about their futures

Charlie Tellis-James & Mark Fox

Positive psychology: A strengths-based and future-focused approach

Much of the work carried out with young people with Social and Emotional Behavioural Difficulties (SEBD) identifies risk factors and documents negative outcomes. More recently researchers such as Spiteri (2009) and O'Riordan (2011) have started to explore possibilities of help for such young people. Most research still encourages them to look back, for example on earlier school experiences. There is, however, a small body of research that has sought these young people's view on their futures (Kloep et al., 2010; Mainwaring and Hallam, 2010; Solomon and Rogers 2001). Shifting the focus from the past to the present and future allows a person to 'look at his identity through a different lens, no longer seeing himself as a victim of unfortunate circumstances' (Spiteri, 2009, p.245).

Within positive psychology there is a significant body of literature evidencing the importance of focusing on the future. The application of positive psychology to young people with SEBD may at first appear unusual, given that it is usually concerned with flourishing lives rather than those in need of help (Boniwell, 2008). However its focus on strengths, growth and potential stands in direct opposition to the preoccupation with risk and deficits that has characterised much research with young people with SEBD. Furthermore, the stance that positive psychology takes towards negative experiences is particularly relevant; rather than ignoring the presence of negative experiences in young people's lives, positive psychology accepts that they are part of life and can actually build qualities (Boniwell, 2008).

The narrative interview: Helping young people with SEBD to tell their stories

Narrative psychology is a wide area in psychology and the current research drew on one particular part: narrative analysis. Narrative psychology is based on the premise that people tell stories about their lives, real or imaginary, exceptional or ordinary (Bruner, 1986). It is concerned with self and identity, and proposes that we live through the stories that we tell about ourselves and that others tell about us (Murray, 2008). Furthermore, individuals know or discover themselves, as well as reveal themselves, in the stories that they tell (Lieblich et al., 1998). Therefore if individual narratives are foregrounded and given authentic expression, then a wider understanding of young people who struggle can be developed (Cefai & Cooper, 2009). Narrative researchers suggest that telling their 'story' helps people make sense of

their experiences, especially when they have had difficult life transitions and traumas (Riessman, 1993).

We drew on narrative methodology (Hiles and Cermak, 2008) to seek the 'stories' that young people with SEBD tell about themselves in the future. This is a
social-constructionist worldview, accepting that each young person constructs their
future selves based upon their own subjective experience, each having their own
story to tell, resulting in multiple stories that are equally valid.

Eight secondary-aged pupils between 14 and 16 years old were interviewed. Five
of the young people were female and three were male; all were in receipt of specialist provision for SEBD. They were interviewed using an informant-style interview
(Powney & Watts, 1987), characterised by the identification of broad areas for discussion. The pupils formed an opportunity sample of secondary pupils accessing
specialist provision for SEBD available and willing to take part in the research. Each
pupil was introduced to the research aims, purpose and questions before giving
their informed consent, achieved via face-to-face meetings and written information
sheets. Parental/carer consent was obtained in the same way and the young people
received feedback in the form of letters at the end of the research.

During the interviews, the young people were encouraged to consider their futures first before discussing their past experiences, which were likely to be more sensitive. A life path approach, informed by O'Riordan (2011), was used to help them
to identify significant events in their lives and consider the transactional nature of
these experiences. The life path consists of a simple line drawing, dissected at various points to represent transitions e.g. starting primary school, starting secondary
school, finishing secondary school etc. Having considered their futures and identified significant memories/events in their past, the young people were encouraged
to identify strengths and resources that had helped them in the past. They also considered ways in which these might assist them in the future, with particular emphasis
on the qualities that they had built as a result of earlier negative experiences. The
life path proved invaluable when a young person found it difficult to identify the
strengths and resources in their life. At these times the life path was used in order
to encourage young people to consider past experiences and what had helped them
at the time. Drawing the life path was more than just a way of exploring the 'total
space', but also aided thinking, facilitated narratives and helped the young people
consider the 'exceptions' in their lives.

In terms of process the life path approach was more than just a useful way of
building rapport. It also reduced the pressure and overall intensity, or 'temper-
ature', of the interview, for example by allowing the young people to avoid eye
contact. It also went some way in addressing the power dynamics between the researcher and the young people, by positioning them as co-constructors.

Narrative analysis: Presenting stories authentically
Hiles and Cermak (2008) describe narrative analysis as the 'new kid on the block',
though they acknowledge that interest in 'stories' has a long history in the field of
psychology. Howitt (2010) describes the field of narrative analysis as existing in a
'current state of anarchy', noting that researchers tend to be left to draw on abstract
theoretical ideas rather than models of narrative analysis. The current research
drew on Hiles and Cermak's (2008) model of Narrative Oriented Inquiry (NOI),

which incorporates a number of different approaches to narrative analysis. The inclusive and pluralistic – rather than exhaustive and definitive – nature of this model allowed us to draw on those analyses most helpful in understanding the positive nature of the future-oriented stories.

The first step was to break the whole narratives down into separate and smaller story episodes. These were then reconstructed into two groups: the young person's past and future stories. This was followed by a categorical-content analysis to explore the young person's perceptions of the future, using positive psychology to identify themes of potential, growth, strengths and resources in the stories. This resulted in each young person having a re-constructed past and future narrative made up entirely of their words, as demonstrated in Kieran's future narrative below (emphasis added):

> …I'm going to go to college and do performing arts…theatre first then…film work… I love comedy…after I've done my acting……I want to start directing films…*I've got loads of back-up plans* [emphasis added]…if none of that happens with the acting I'll just go straight into my cooking…I learnt at college, I did a cookery course for a year with Sarah…it's my ideas all along…my imagination…never read a cookery book in my life…I want to own my own restaurant…borrowing money from a bank and then pay them back from all the money I make…I rap as well so I wanna get into my rapping, do music…and then I will write a book one day…cause I've had quite an interesting life…

> …still working, still keeping my hands scruffy, still doing business. Earning…as much money as I can, hopefully buy a big house…money ain't that important…more to me is having friends and family…money is always gonna be there, money comes and goes, money comes when you put your mind to it, money does this and that, but your life only comes once. You've got to take the opportunity to make sure you live life to the fullest, be who you wanna be and my ambitions are what I'm telling you now…money don't buy you happiness but money sure does help. So I want to get money to help me with my dreams…*I just want to have a nice life* [emphasis added]…

> …I feel it's a gift to be not that money motivated cause people can do nasty things for money…nasty, horrible, rotten things…but that's not me…if I didn't get all this, I wouldn't care to be honest, I would care but I wouldn't. I would be like 'Oh, there's my dreams gone right out the window' but I wouldn't really mind…I'd just carry on to lead the normal boring life…
> …I've got ADHD, I do things on impulse, and get in trouble for my behaviour. But I think that it's helped me think what am I going to do in life…think positive…think quicker…think deeply about things…plan my life without think negatively and getting down, thinking it's never going to happen…I'm not one of those people who thinks 'Shit this ain't never gonna happen so I'm gonna go out and rob someone', some people think like that…

> …all of this may not happen…these are just dreams…always boost, pushing me up… but I am gonna try my hardest to make it happen…using my imagination and my ability and my capability…look at Richard Branson…school will just become a memory, man…things only get better…

Positive psychology applied to young people with SEBD: A new, alternative understanding of this group

The young people in the current research identified a unique range of strengths and resources in their stories. Even more importantly, many also identified qualities built up as a direct result of early negative experiences. This included determination to secure a better life for themselves in the future as a result of growing up with little money; self-determination in the face of an unexpected pregnancy; determination to work hard having been at risk of permanent exclusion; self-belief having overcome undiagnosed dyslexia and ADHD and associated negative school experiences, and a strong sense of self-belief having experienced neglect and coped with a great deal of responsibility as a child.

Fundamentally, this research showed that young people with SEBD do have strengths and resources in their lives. Their ability to attribute positive meaning to what were, for many of them, exceedingly challenging circumstances is a credit to them. Our strength-based and future-focused approach helped us develop new understandings of this group of young people, shifting our focus from deficits to strengths, resources and the potential for growth.

Implications for practice

The narrative interview, comprising an informant style of interview and the life path tool, can be used with young people with SEBD to elicit their views. At the most basic level, it could facilitate these young people's thinking, allowing them to feel listened to and to validate their experiences. It can also go beyond this and help them to attach new meaning to their experiences. The narrative interview allows the young people to gain insight into their feelings and develop some sense of coherence in their lives. As 'Emma' commented: 'It would have been in my head already, just maybe not throughout my whole life. Thank-you for telling me that…[T]his has all been definite.'

The life path can also be used in a more therapeutic way. If we are the assembled stories that we tell about ourselves, then it is possible that we have the power to 'tell more empowering stories' (Hiles & Cermak, 2008, p.149). It is the process of 're-telling' that is key, as it is through this that we are able to inhabit and live out new alternative stories. In practice this means educational psychologists (EPs) encouraging young people with SEBD to 're-story' their lives, by encouraging them to identify the strengths and resources in their lives. This process has the potential to help young people view themselves in a more positive light, and to take a more optimistic view of what they can achieve in the future. By engaging in this process, EPs can shift their focus from the problem to the solution, which can alleviate feelings of helplessness and make young people feel as though they are more than their problem.

EPs are well placed to draw on narrative approaches and to carry out this strength-based and future-focused identity work with young people with SEBD. The focus of this work will vary from one young person to another; some will benefit from support to develop a coherent story of the past, whereas others may need encouragement to explore and consider their future. Some will need support to re-construct or 're-tell' their life stories, to embrace more empowering alternatives. In whatever form such intervention takes, it should aim to develop these young people's sense of agency over their lives. Ultimately, it is our retelling of these stories that is the story told here. We hope it offers an alternative and more empowering narrative of young people with SEBD, and will go some way in altering the way in which they are perceived in the future.

References

Boniwell, I. (2008). *Positive psychology in a nutshell* (2nd edn.). Maidenhead: Open University Press/ McGraw Hill.

Cefai, C. & Cooper, C. (2009). *Promoting emotional education: Engaging children and young people with social, emotional and behavioural difficulties.* London and Philadelphia: Jessica Kingsley Publishers.

Hiles, D. & Cermak, I. (2008). Narrative psychology. In C. Willig & W. Stainton-Rogers (Eds.) *The SAGE handbook of qualitative research in psychology* (pp.147–164). London: Sage.

Howitt, D. (2010). *Introduction to qualitative methods in psychology.* Essex: Pearson Education Limited.

Kloep, M., Hendry, L.B., Gardner, C. & Seage, C.H. (2010). Young people's views of their present and future selves in two deprived communities. *Journal of Community & Applied Social Psychology, 20*, 513–524.

Lieblich, A., Tuval-Mashiach, R. & Zibler, T. (1998). *Narrative research: Reading, analysis and interpretation.* London: Sage.

Mainwaring, D. & Hallam, S. (2010). 'Possible selves' of young people in a mainstream secondary school and a pupil referral unit: A comparison. *Emotional and Behavioural Difficulties, 15*(2), 153–169.

Murray, M. (2008). Narrative psychology. In J.A. Smith (Ed.) *Qualitative Psychology: A practical guide to research methods* (2nd edn.) (pp.111–132). London: Sage.

O'Riordan, Z. (2011). Living in the 'real world': The experiences and support of school-leavers with social, emotional and behavioural difficulties. *Emotional and Behavioural Difficulties, 16*(3), 303–316.

Powney, J. & Watts, M. (1987). *Intervening in educational research.* London: Routledge and Kegan Paul.

Riessman, C.K. (1993). *Narrative analysis. Qualitative Research Methods Series 30.* Thousand Oaks, CA: Sage.

Solomon, Y. & Rogers, C. (2001). Motivational patterns in disaffected school students: Insights from Pupil Referral Unit clients. *British Educational Research Journal, 27*(3), 331–345.

Spiteri, D. (2009). Forging an identity over the life-course. *Emotional and Behavioural Difficulties, 14*(3), 239–249.

Chapter 9 Engaging children and young people with technology

Imogen Howarth

Professionals face pressure as never before to engage with the views of children. They are legally required to seek, to record and to do something groundbreaking with this child-centred information. Whilst these objectives seem laudable and overdue, current research has shown that the process of gathering children's views might not be as straightforward as it first appears. The majority voice (for example Harding and Atkinson, 2009; Norwich and Kelly, 2006) finds that children are left out of decision making and that simply completing 'I like…' statements is far from adequate. So, how might technology play a role as educational psychologists (EPs) seek to be more person-centred? This chapter explores some first steps in motivating and engaging children through the use of multisensory technologies and promotes the repositioning of adults to empower children throughout this process.

Which directions might future engagement take?

Research is beginning to reflect a steady societal shift towards seeing children as insightful people, whose interesting perspectives should be welcomed as a key to co-constructing better solutions. How this improved level of engagement might take shape will be determined in part by the technologies and resources adopted, and by the extent to which professionals are able to redress some of the power differentials in adult–child dyads.

Mobile forms of assistive technologies that might motivate children to interact, and support them to share their views, are rapidly proliferating. A multitude of much-coveted, cheap and aesthetically beguiling smartphone apps now lure children's attention. Among these, there are many which professionals note can be adapted to address physical needs or to differentiate literacy levels. Any attempt to summarise, at one point in time, these continually evolving interfaces will inevitably serve only to offer a snapshot that will rapidly become obsolete. Instead, it is the author's intention to describe research that looked less at the 'what' and more at the 'how', emphasising that the *process* of seeking children's views and the role of the adult is just as important as the *outcome*.

Language matters, and so it is important to establish the meaning of 'children's views' in this context. Stafford and colleagues assert that 'consultation should be a genuine attempt to listen seriously to young people's views, and then act on them' (2003, p.365). Listening requires reciprocal expectations: children will not voice their opinions into a vacuum. Dickins (2011) reiterates that it is the interactive skill of listening which both acknowledges children's right to be listened to and validates the importance of their views. Accepting that children's views are constructed through the interactive process of being listened to, we here define children's views as *all communications from children offered in response to a given prompt:* communications that are listened to, understood and responded to.

Reality versus rhetoric

This section describes the research methodology and findings from a doctoral action research project that explored the ways in which children with communication difficulties (CD) could be enabled to express views on their experience of meeting educational professionals (Howarth, 2013). It elicited children's understandings of the process and outcomes of assessment, looking beyond mere descriptions of what they did or did not like.

ICAN[1] (2014) define CD as any combination of:

- difficulties articulating speech;
- struggling to say words/sentences;
- misunderstanding words and instructions heard; and
- difficulties knowing how to talk and listen in conversations.

Overlapping but also widening the indications of CD, the Royal College of Speech and Language Therapists (RCSLT) (2010) has categorised competencies which may pose difficulties:

- Articulation: effective expression through speaking, writing or non-verbal communication.
- Perception: recognising and understanding speech, text, body language and facial expressions.
- Listening skills: being able to listen carefully to what is being said.
- Recall: remembering information that has previously been given.
- Expression: expressing feelings and emotions in an acceptable manner.
- Interaction: relating to others in a socially acceptable manner and thereby promoting social integration.

It is of interest that the RCSLT includes the support of abilities in memory and interaction as integral to a notional picture of CD, and these latter characteristics and competencies are adopted here as a working definition of CD.

Government research specifies that CD as a primary need increased by 58 per cent between 2005 and 2010, but also co-occurs with other types of Special Educational Need (SEN) including autism, learning difficulties and physical impairment (Lindsay et al., 2011). UK figures for the prevalence of CD highlight this significant concern: Gascoigne (2012) estimates that seven to ten percent of all children have CD, with the figure rising higher in areas of greater social deprivation. ICAN (2014) contextualises this as equating to two or three pupils in every classroom.

Social constructionist ontology and epistemology

The ontological position taken within this research was social constructionism. In subscribing to this worldview, the researcher understands that the way in which the world and others are experienced is the product of dynamic and reciprocal social interactions. A tenet of social constructionism is therefore the belief that social processes, including language, are fundamental to everyday life and the creation of knowledge.

---

[1] ICAN is a national children's communication charity. ICAN's mission is to ensure that no child who struggles to communicate is left out or left behind. ICAN provides a wide range of information services that provide help and advice to parents and practitioners about speech, language and communication.

Epistemologically, social constructionism proposes that knowledge is constructed within one or more social groups (for example groups according to gender, age, families, pupils and educational psychologists). A person can simultaneously belong to and interact with a number of groups. Knowledge is described by social constructionists in relative and subjective terms. It is relative (inter-group), because each group seeks a consensus and justification for knowledge, and this differs from group to group. Knowledge is also subjective (intragroup) because each individual member of the group brings and shares their previous experiences. Consciously or unconsciously this impacts upon and shapes the understandings of knowledge within the group.

A communication difficulty (CD) is also a social construction, and the power imbalance confronting children with CD is profound. To help give the participants a voice the emancipatory approach chosen was rooted in the tenets of social constructionism and aimed to elicit children's views on the process and as an outcome. The research intended to increase understanding of the views of this marginalised group and to empower the participants. The design that flowed from the principles above was based on action research. It was selected after careful consideration of the manageability of the research topic and the participatory intent of the research purpose, and aimed at a flexibility of design. Fundamentally it is research which proceeds 'in a spiral of steps, each of which is composed of planning, action and the evaluation of the result of action' (Kemmis & McTaggert, 1990, p.8).

The conditions of the research did not permit power to be transferred wholly to the participants. Instead the researcher sought praxis – putting theory into action through reflective cycles – through mutual collaboration with participants at different stages.

Literature review

The research began with a systematic analysis of studies of the barriers to and alternative approaches that could enable children with CD to communicate their views. In particular, it considered children's understanding of the process of meeting an educational professional. This review of current literature on children's participation found a gap: children's views were rarely sought about their own participation in SEN procedures and how they felt about being involved (Howarth, 2013). This raised questions about the potential for misunderstandings on the part of the children at every stage of the meeting: their preparation; the purpose; everyone's roles; and the impact they could have during and after the meeting. Aston and Lambert (2010) express their fundamental concern that the views of young people with CD were not sought, leaving them unprepared and unpractised in voicing their opinions.

This lack of experience is echoed by Gersch (2001) and by Rabiee and colleagues (2005). If children do not expect to contribute and their efforts are not supported, they may come to believe that their role is not to question or offer views. They could become disempowered and further marginalised (Jelly et al., 2000).

The meaning that children with CD take from meeting professionals could be said to be altered by their expectations, their experience of the event, their relationships and communications, such as their level of understanding of what took place, how they related to those present, whether they felt competent and listened to, how much choice they were given and their sense of autonomy. Gersch et al. (1993) stress the need for EPs to explain their role clearly at the outset and to encourage children to ask lots of questions about this, perhaps with the aid of a leaflet.

The need for clear, child-friendly information remains. As Education, Health and Care Plans (EHCPs; DfE, 2014) begin to change the nature of children's contact with multidisciplinary professionals, it is essential that children are helped to understand the value of their participation in the process. EPs play a key part in cultivating the listening ethos that empowers each child to be heard: 'Listening and acting upon children's voices has historic prevalence in the professional practice of educational psychologists' (Day, 2010, p.54).

I found that, across the UK, research studies report methodologies and creative resources that have been devised to enhance children's engagement in expressing their views. However, there has been a paucity of participatory studies that focus on children with CD and also employ digital technologies. The literature focused either on children with very little language, in special schools, or children who are literate, have well-developed language skills and attend mainstream schools. This left a gap representing research with children with CD within mainstream settings, and it is this that my research addresses.

It was clear from the literature review that spoken and written language remained the predominant means of conveying information to such children. Children with CD are already facing the disadvantages of having fewer opportunities to express views, and so are likely to have reduced feelings of competence based on prior experiences (Stafford et al., 2003). Meeting an educational professional already establishes a situation that exposes power differentials and hinders children's autonomy (Lubel and Greaves, 2000), so if verbal communication is the preferred mode of communication, children's ability to relate to others will be impaired.

Researchers working with children with complex needs have used digital videos, photographs, Widgit Literacy Symbols[2] and images (Komulainen, 2007) and digital communication books (Mortimer, 2004). These are highly personalised and designed for individual use with children for such purposes as expressing likes and dislikes about their daily activities. I was unable to find any evidence of children with complex needs being asked directly about their views on the communication process or resources. Therefore my aim was to empower the children in this marginalised position by gathering their views and exploring ways to enable them to participate meaningfully in educational meetings.

Stages of the action research

Stage 1: To identify enabling and restraining factors when pupils talk about a meeting with an educational professional

I observed seven children with CD as they expressed their opinions on the preparations, process and outcomes of meeting with an educational professional, supported by an adult and using a text-based questionnaire. Then I interviewed the pupils to

---

[2] Widgit Literacy Symbols covers over 40,000 words which enables people to 'translate' text by combining it with symbols. They are a way to understand, learn and communicate which overcomes the barrier that text represents to many people of all ages and abilities.

facilitate and elicit their views on this meeting and to identify the enabling and restraining conditions in this process.

Each cycle of observations and interviews helped me to revise my approach and the questions I used. Content analysis of the videotaped observations and interviews were summarised as 'problems, positives and possibilities' (PPP). The information gathered was used to develop an EPs' checklist and semi-structured questions used in Stage 2.

Stage 2: To understand EPs' perceptions of pupils' involvement in the process and outcomes of educational assessments

The next stage was to bring the initial issues from the PPP analysis back to professionals to stimulate discussion about their experiences of pupils' involvement in assessment. They also evaluated the EP checklist. Five EPs participated in a focus group that I facilitated. Their discussion followed a semi-structured format and I videotaped the group so that notes on non-verbal communication could be included in the full transcription.

This provided rich data which I analysed thematically. The main and sub-themes from the focus group data were combined with the PPP to create a taxonomy of factors which appeared to enable or restrain children's expression of their views. The focus group discussed current practice and suggested changes to the process, including creating podcasts of EPs and communicating child-friendly explanations of outcomes. The EPs responded favourably to the checklist and PPP sheet, which took the dialogue in new directions.

Stage 3: To draw upon the ideas, research and resources from local authorities that enable pupils with communication difficulties to contribute to meetings with educational professionals

I contacted EPSs, Parent Partnership Services and charities across the UK to request examples of child-friendly explanations of assessment. Examples included children's focus groups, online questionnaires, information leaflets, DVDs, digital cameras, diaries, scrapbooks, verbal questions, role play, tours, child interviews, visual prompts, digital communication books and signed or symbol-supported questionnaires. Through a content analysis I was able to note the most enabling features of each example.

Interestingly, only one piece of research explicitly raised the issue of obtaining children's own assent in participating, as well as that of adults consenting on their behalf (Lewis, 2002). Most research again focussed on eliciting children's likes and dislikes concerning a product or outcome, and the participants' views did not have any observable impact. The explanations of educational assessments were disappointing. Rarely were they designed for children; few used engaging visual supports and simple language. Most made no reference to outcomes and did not mention who was visiting the child or why. They were typically paper-based, and of those available digitally, none could be personalised or were interactive.

From this plethora of methods and resources used to try and engage children of all ages, the most helpful ideas I could find were as follows:
- Online modes were superior to other self-completion modes in terms of data quality, anonymity and privacy, visual stimulation, appeal and cost.

- Older children in particular were helped by the use of scaling questions and a progress bar.
- The very youngest children could give feedback on their experiences of using the web-based questions, navigation and process.
- Clarity of instructions was vital. When younger respondents did not understand what was meant they simply skipped the question. Younger children preferred the presence of a familiar adult for comfort, reassurance or support.
- Using a cartoon-style format was a particular strength
- Preparation was all the more important for pupils with additional support needs, to have experience of how, when and why they could give their views.
- A mixture of visual prompts, photographs and some oral and written questions appears to be more likely to appeal to a range of children, and is especially supportive for children with CD.
- Finding a balance between the use of questions and more creative visual methods may enhance the perceived value of the process and outcomes of gathering children's views, in the eyes of key adults around them as well as from the children themselves.
- There is a need for a mixture of tools to be available to the child: to cue them in; to reduce, simplify and repeat language; and to use visual supports to allow the child to describe their views rather than only answer direct questions.

Now back to the technology...

I used the findings of Stages 1–3 to inform collectively the development of a Pupil Information Leaflet (PIL) and to begin the iterative process of gathering children's views on the use of a prototype tablet app. I was interested in their level of understanding, the authenticity of their response, their enjoyment of the process and any and all ideas that they felt able to share, through pictures, speech, drawing, multiple choice, sliding scales and their verbal and non-verbal communication. Each child's views made a difference, and I made continual adjustments to the interface and to the whole process to reflect their ideas.

Eventually this led to the development of a tool, named MiView (see Figure 9.1), that attempted to address as many of the aforementioned points as possible.

The MiView app was my modification of the free app iSurvey. It was designed as a child-friendly, multimedia and engaging way to help pupils talk about their assessment and their experience of meeting with educational professionals. Taking forward the children's ideas, MiView had:

- multiple choice questions, using the children's own pictures (or their choice of my collection of line-drawn pictures) on an uncluttered background;
- a very simple interface, with the ability to go back and review answers;
- options to make a choice or leave out a question;
- speech output (screen reading);
- some open questions in a choice of formats (speech, drawing, video, text); and
- personalised responses and flow (initial answers influence what appears on subsequent screens).

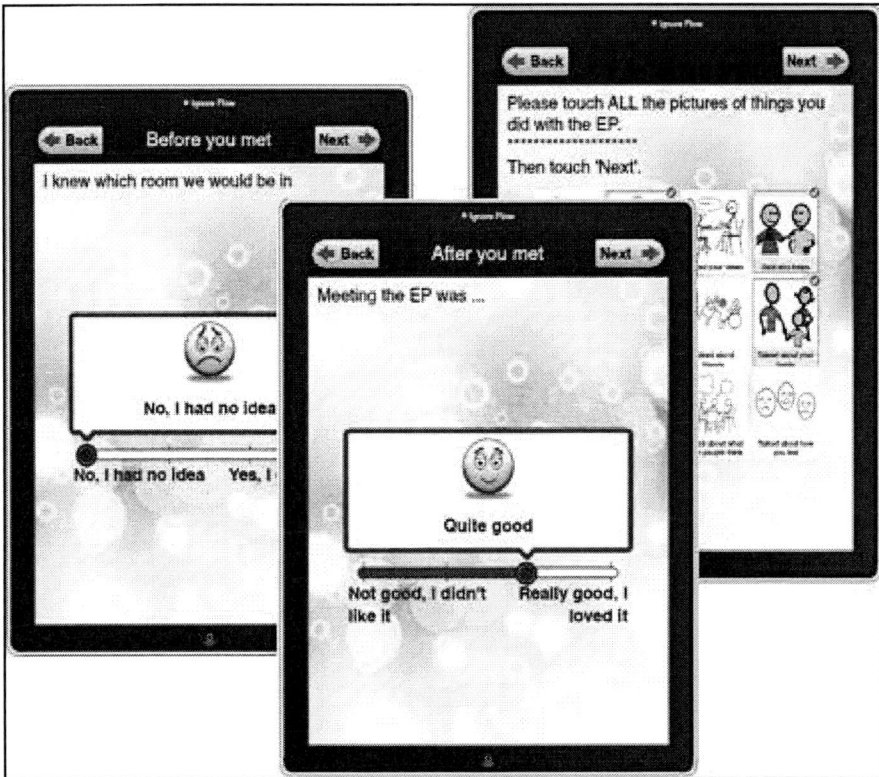

Figure 9.1: Screens from MiView

Stage 4: To identify enabling and restraining factors when pupils express their views on the preparations, process and outcomes of meeting with an educational psychologist, supported with PIL and MiView

The purpose of this fourth stage was to explore whether a modified approach to eliciting children's views would give them a greater understanding of their involvement in meeting with an educational professional. The child and their parents received the Pupil Information Leaflet (PIL) before meeting with the EP. This was to give them accurate information about the process in advance. When the pupil met with the EP they were again shown this information. MiView was used as a conduit to support pupils to express opinions on meeting an EP for assessment.

I observed 13 children with CD, supported by adults, using MiView. Immediately afterwards I discussed with them their views on this conduit to identify the enabling and restraining factors within this process. Again this was video recorded and the observations and interviews were fully transcribed, coded in NVivo and thematically analysed.

169

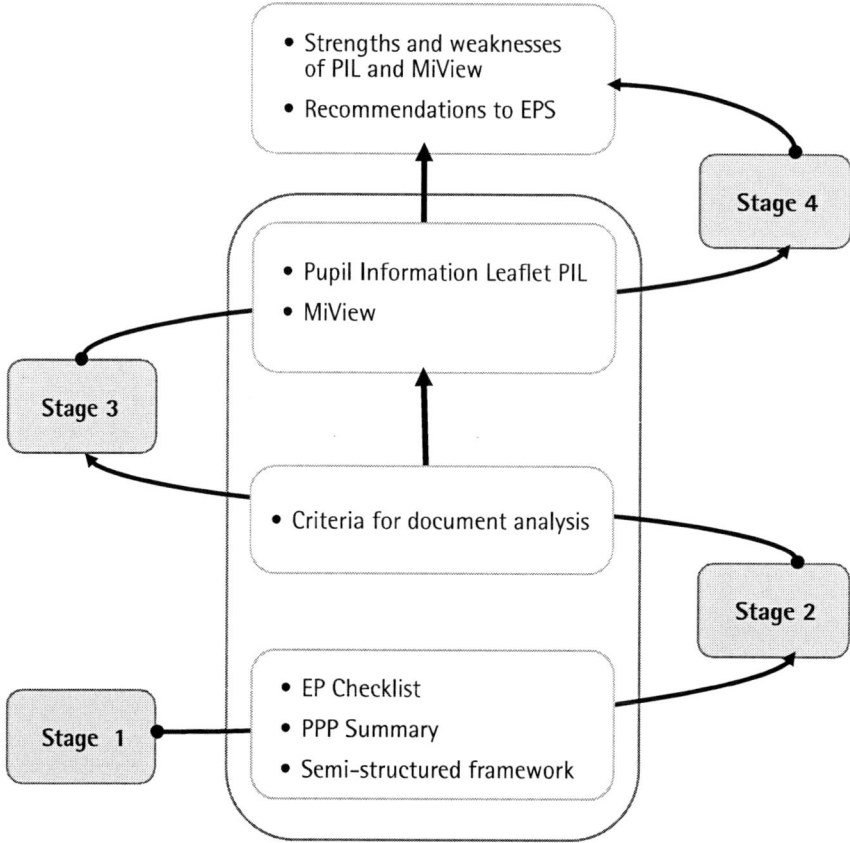

Figure 9.2: Overview of the research stages

During my observations of children's responses to MiView, it was encouraging to see the probable benefits of such a resource demonstrated. It could achieve a consistency and familiarity that current methods of giving pupils just text or blank boxes to fill in do not. The iPad app has the potential to summarise, repeat, give targeted praise (speech or specific sounds and tunes), give visual and verbal cues (including signing), encourage drawing on screen, bring in photos, and have each pupil shape this whole process and experience in exactly the right way for them.

What technology would not replace is the need for a supportive adult, to help with navigation, or explanation, or cueing and recall, or the hundreds of attuned responses that were observed during this action research. Also, it would be necessary to divide the questions so that some were asked before the child actually met an educational professional. This would address the issues faced by children with difficulties in suppressing current knowledge to comment on a previous state of mind. Those questions relevant to ask after their meeting would be best given later the same day or the next, to maximise pupils' recall of the event.

The key findings can be summarised thus:

- All pupils reported that it was helpful to have talked through the meeting with the school Special Educational Needs Co-ordinator (SENCO) (or similar role) beforehand, using a child-friendly, visually supportive leaflet that they could take home. A photograph supplied in advance of the professional/s with whom they were meeting was always welcomed.

If questions were misunderstood, pupils were able to understand with repetition, rephrasing and time to process.

If the child had expressive or receptive difficulties or needed more processing time, allowing them to pass on questions, or return to questions later on was reported as particularly helpful.

If there was confusion over particular professionals and their respective roles, pupils reported that recalling the room and layout aided their memory of the event. They asked for photographs to be used more often to help them remember meetings with different people.

If a child did not want to engage, it was more useful to stop and then consider the time of day, what they were missing to attend the meeting and how daunted or nervous they might feel at having to give their view. Engagement improved when the duration and expectation of the task was clearly explained to pupils and it helped to give a combination of visual indication of progress and verbal reassurance.

Children unsure of what would happen next liked to be reminded of the next steps and asked for greater explanation of the terms and concepts. Children were often unsure as to whether they were going to see a particular professional again, and if so when.

Taking the best ideas forward

Current research has shown that small changes which help prepare children and provide simple and accurate information to families are perceived as very helpful and empowering. Giving the children greater knowledge of what the professional process is all about, and how they can contribute and influence outcomes could elicit more authentic views and therefore maximise the benefits of assessment.

To maximise the opportunities for children's future engagement, children themselves need to be involved in the process and need to see tangible outcomes of their efforts: they must feel listened to and valued. This requires a shift in attitudes and practice, and all in the time allotted to meet with children on multiple occasions. Children need preparation in expressing their thoughts and current best practice highlights some key guidance for all professionals concerning the integration of technology into seeking children's views:

- Introduce yourself and your service first, perhaps with a podcast, photos and other printed or digital information that is accurate and can be processed slowly.
- Explain how you are there for the child: increase their sense of agency.
- During your meeting, take photos of the room and layout, and any resources used or people present, to help the child with their recall later on.
- Involve the child in many different ways, particularly drawing, recording their speech and using scaled, multiple-choice and open questions.
- Use their answers to shape the conversation and invite them to ask questions as much as possible, to ensure their understanding and empowerment.
- Use a format that can be completed over two or more short sessions. Digital questions can be read aloud and repeated as many times as a child likes.

Some children might prefer to wear headphones to aid independence and concentration.

- Leave further information for the child and their family at the end of your meeting. An app could print out a simple plan with pictures in situ. Verbal information needs backing up with visual prompts and to be kept where the pupil can access it.
- Embrace and adapt the mobile technologies that can be used in listening to children. Hand-held devices allow children to participate in the best way for them – little and often, with choice and over time. They are a powerful resource, a readily available, playful, motivating conduit that helps to differentiate for children with additional needs and, above all, to engage.

Summary

The purpose of this chapter was to highlight some of the issues for professionals seeking to engage with, and accessibly record, the views of children with communication difficulties. Technology, whilst not replacing the need for nuanced adult support, can play a powerful role in helping children to understand, comment upon and ultimately shape what is happening. Listening to their authentic views is paramount for finding collaborative ways forward, where children feel valued and motivated to achieve.

The children I met gave some very specific pointers in terms of how the assessment process could be changed in order to help them be better prepared, more relaxed, empowered and autonomous. They want technology to be integral to this process, helping them to repeat questions at their own pace, to prompt, to record and to recall in an accessible and engaging way. Getting technology right for children with communication difficulties means making genuine improvements in listening, understanding and responding to the views of children of all abilities. So, what are we waiting for?

References

Aston, H. and Lambert, N. (2010). Young people's views about their involvement in decision-making. *Educational Psychology in Practice, 26*(1), 41–51.

Day, S. (2010). Listening to young children: An investigation of children's day care experiences in Children's Centres. *Educational and Child Psychology, 27*(4), 45–55.

Department for Education (2014). *Special educational needs and disability code of practice: 0–25 years.* London: Stationery Office.

Dickins, M. (2011). *Listening to young disabled children.* London: National Children's Bureau.

Gascoigne, M.T. (Ed.) (2012). *Better communication – shaping speech, language and communication services for children and young people.* London: RCSLT.

Gersch, I.S. (2001). 'Listening to Children' In Wearmouth (Ed.) *Special Educational Provision in the Context of Inclusion: Policy and Practice in Schools.* London: David Fulton Publishers.

Gersch, I.S., Holgate, A. & Sigston, A. (1993). Valuing the child's perspective – A revised student report and other practical initiatives. *Educational Psychology in Practice, 9*, 36–45.

Harding, E. and Atkinson, C. (2009). How EPs record the voice of the child. *Educational Psychology in Practice, 25*(2), 125–137.

Howarth, I.C. (2013). *An exploration of the ways in which children with Communication Difficulties can be enabled to express views on their experience of meeting educational professionals: An action research project.* Unpublished doctoral thesis, University of East London.

Jelly, M., Fuller, A. & Byers, R. (2000). *Involving pupils in practice: Promoting partnerships with pupils with special education needs.* London: David Fulton.

Kemmis, S. & McTaggert, R. (1990). *The action research planner.* Waurn Ponds, Victoria: Deakin University Press.

Komulainen, S. (2007). The ambiguity of the child's 'voice' in social research. *Childhood, 14*(1), 11–28.

Lewis, A. (2002). Accessing, through research interviews, the views of children with difficulties in learning. *Support for Learning, 17*(3), 110–116.

Lubel, R. & Greaves, K. (2000). The development of an EPS information booklet for primary age pupils. *Educational Psychology in Practice, 16*(2), 243–248. doi: 10.1080/713666049

Mortimer, H. (2004). Hearing children's voices in the early years. *Support for Learning, 19*(4), 169–174.

Norwich, B. & Kelly, N. (2006). Evaluating children's participation in SEN procedures: Lessons for educational psychologists. *Educational Psychology in Practice, 22*(3), 255–271.

Rabiee, P., Sloper, P. & Beresford, B. (2005). Doing research with children and young people who do not use speech for communication. *Children and Society, 19*, 385–396.

Stafford, A., Laybourn, A., Hill, M. & Walker, M. (2003). 'Having a say': Children and young people talk about consultation. *Children and Society, 17*, 361–373.

Websites

http://actionresearch.net/ A collection of living educational theories based on action research, with action planning process examples and guides for researchers.

www.cognable.com/ The pioneering site of Simon Evans, a researcher and developer with particular interest in use of the internet, assistive technologies and new media by and for people with Intellectual Disabilities (ID).

http://involver.org.uk/ An award-winning social enterprise that improves school councils and student voice.

www.nya.org.uk/ The website of the National Youth Agency, which works in partnership across public, private and voluntary organisations to improve services for CYP.

www.participationworks.org.uk The website of Participation Works, a partnership of six national CYP agencies.

www.thecommunicationtrust.org.uk/media/2612/communication_difficulties_-_facts_and_stats.pdf Facts and statistics on the prevalence and impact of CD.

www.selfdeterminationtheory.org/ Presents a brief overview of SDT and resources on human needs, values, intrinsic motivation, development, motivation across cultures, individual differences and psychological wellbeing.

www.triangle.org.uk/what-we-do/consultation-with-children The website of Triangle, national experts in a range of work conducted directly with CYP, including enabling communication and consultation.

Chapter 10 The future: Where next for educational psychologists?

Julia Hardy & Charmian Hobbs

The social and cultural climate remains ambivalent about hearing the voices of children and young people. There is a context that is apparently supportive of asking for children and young people's views, but is often resistant to really hearing and acting on those views. Despite the general acknowledgement that children and young people should be actively involved in making decisions about their own lives, they remain in a position of disempowerment, both in general and within our institutions, including those providing education and care. This is the case for all children and young people, but even more so for those who are further marginalised within society because of their economic position, their gender, their ethnicity, their sexuality, their religion and/or their disability. It is within this context that educational psychologists (EPs) are working to bring about change for all children and young people and particularly for those who are experiencing difficulties in their lives.

This book has highlighted ways in which the position of children and young people has been challenged and can continue to be challenged by EPs through the narrative of EP advocacy and the use of qualitative methodologies that enable children and young people (CYP) to talk about their lived experience.

What do we need to do now?

There is much to draw on from the work of EPs as both practitioners and researchers in terms of empowering children and young people. The brief research and practitioner illustrations in earlier chapters demonstrate the richness of information gained through careful questioning and listening. However, if EPs are going to raise the status of children and young people and enable them to contribute genuinely and fully to decisions about their lives, then there needs to be further discussion about what we mean by participation. Participation is a multi-layered concept and a term used widely to describe forms of social engagement, from joining in with your friend's conversation to being a member of a local community group and much more. Within the work of EPs, participation refers to active involvement of children and young people – but what does, or would, this look like?

- Is it about individuals or groups?
- Is it about being there or having influence?
- Is it about sharing power?
- Is it about having access to information?
- Is it about developing skills or an entitlement?

These questions have been raised by earlier contributions in this book, for example in Roffey's (Chapter 7) discussion of the importance of adults and students working together as equals within the community.

As a way of exploring this further consider the work of EPs in relation to individual children and their families as part of our statutory role. There is now a strong emphasis on person-centred approaches that see the child or young person's perspective as key to planning. What is important to the child or young person is acknowledged and built into the agreed actions. However, does the presence of the child or young person result in real influence over outcomes? The professionals involved could be said to be accountable for their agreed input, but power remains their prerogative. Indeed when asked, many children and young people are unclear about the role of different professionals (Gimrax & Bell, 2004). The culture of most institutions does not routinely invite consultation with children and young people, so they are inexperienced in marshalling their thoughts and presenting their views. The child or young person is a member of a group called 'SEND', who are expected to have a different ability to make decisions about their lives. These are examples of the norms and assumptions that inform the way we are in the world. They are the 'taken for granted' understandings that construct how we see children and young people. If we want to work in partnership with children and young people we may need to further examine some of these routine conceptualisations, especially in relation to our understanding of participation (see Godley & Williams, Chapter 4, for further discussion on the construction of childhood). We need to think about how we, as EPs, make assumptions about our understandings and those of children and young people, so that we are reflective about the dangers of epistemic power (Sewell, 2016); we need also to be actively reflective about how we wield the power of our EP 'expertise'.

What models are we using to encourage participation?

The significance of the United Nations Convention on the Rights of the Child (Office of the United Nations High Commissioner on Human Rights, 1989) cannot be overstated. Indeed many authors in this volume see their research as exploring the impact of this Convention in a particular setting (see for example Hill et al., Chapter 5). The Convention recognises the child as a full human being with the ability to participate freely in society. Furthermore it is the first convention to state that children have a right to 'have a say' in processes affecting their lives. Article 12 states:

1. States Parties shall assure to the child who is capable of forming his or her own views the right to express those views freely in all matters affecting the child, the views of the child being given due weight in accordance with the age and maturity of the child.
2. For this purpose, the child shall in particular be provided the opportunity to be heard in any judicial and administrative proceedings affecting the child, either directly, or through a representative or an appropriate body, in a manner consistent with the procedural rules of national law.

This entitlement is summarised as 'the child's right to express an opinion and to have that opinion taken into account in any matter or procedure affecting the child' (UN, 1989, Article 12).

The UN Committee on the Rights of the Child has more recently reaffirmed this image of a child as active in the process of shaping their lives, learning and future, with particular reference to the young child:

> The Convention requires that children, including the very youngest children, be respected as persons in their own right. Young children should be recognized as active members of families, communities and societies, with their own concerns, interests and points of view. (United Nations Committee on the Rights of the Child, 2005, unpaged)

Soni's contribution (Chapter 8.8) demonstrates ways in which research can be undertaken with very young children.

This right to 'have a say' has led to a number of models of participation perhaps the best known being that of Hart (1992). The models can be loosely grouped into those that are hierarchical (Arnstein, 1969; Hart, 1992, 1997; Shier, 2001; Thoburn et al., 1995), those that are dimensional (Kirby et al., 2003; Lardner, 2001) and those that offer a more explicit 'rights' basis (Lundy, 2007).

Hierarchical models suggest a stepped approach to participation (Hart (1992) provides a pictorial representation of a ladder) whereby there is the suggestion that greater participation will be achieved the nearer you are to the top. So in Hart's model you could move from manipulation through tokenism; assigned but informed participation; consulted and informed participation; adult-initiated participation; shared decisions with children; child-initiated and directed participation; to child-initiated, shared decisions with adults as the highest level of participation. It has been argued that these models provide a rather static (Hobbs, 2005), possibly simplistic (Woodhead, 2010) view of participation which does not take into account the conditions that might promote or inhibit participation in a particular context, or that different degrees of power sharing may be appropriate in different contexts. Kirby et al. (2003) emphasise the *process* of enabling participation rather than the structures that may be present. They identified three different cultures of participation:

- Consultation-focused organisations: these consult children and young people to inform services, policy and product development.
- Participation-focused organisations: these involve young people in making decisions (as well as in consultations) within participation activities that are time-bound or context-specific. Often a sample rather than all relevant children and young people are involved.
- Child/youth-focused organisations: children and young people's participation is central to these organisations' practice and they establish a culture in which it is assumed that all children and young people will be listened to about all decisions that affect their lives.

However, the boundaries between these are blurred as organisations move between types and there may be differences between areas. The three types are non-hierarchical, as each can be appropriate within different organisations or settings. Lundy (2007) argues that since adults can find compelling reasons for not giving due weight to children's views any model of participation must be firmly located within the 'rights' framework. Her model proposes a new way of conceptualising Article 12 of United Nations Convention on the Rights of the Child, which is intended to focus decision makers on four elements of the provision:

- Space: children must be given the opportunity to express a view.
- Voice: children must be facilitated to express their views.
- Audience: the view must be listened to.
- Influence: the view must be acted on, as appropriate.

These elements are interrelated and have an explicit chronology. The first stage is the opportunity to express a view; however decision-making is not static so that once a child knows they can have influence then the process may begin again. The model also highlights that Article 12 cannot be understood on its own but only in the light of other articles, in particular those concerning nondiscrimination (2), best interests (3), the right to guidance (5), the right to seek, receive and impart information (13) and protection from abuse (19). It can be seen from consideration of just a few models that involving children and young people is complex, often frustrating and never straightforward! In considering these models, it is clear that to enable participation we have to think about both our individual actions, whether with a single child or a wider group, and about the culture of the context where we are working.

> It does not diminish adults' roles and responsibilities, but on the contrary increases the challenges to scaffold children's participation effectively and appropriately in respect of their situation and capacities. (Woodhead, 2010, p.xxi)

What information is available from research into the participation of children and young people?
There is evidence of participation activity across the UK, but it is highly variable across services and sectors (Children's Commissioner, 2015). Although there is a wealth of documentation and publications providing guidance on how to encourage and develop participation (for example from Participation Works (n.d.), Hear by Right (n.d.), there is limited evidence available on the quality of participation or on its impact. Participation is mostly centred on activities seen to have an obvious impact on children, e.g. leisure activities. The last published review of practice (Kirby et al., 2003) concluded that there was an increase in structural mechanisms to involve children and young people in decision-making and a shift in attitudes towards involving young people in decisions. Increasing children's and young people's participation in decisions about their own care and about service development is a policy priority. However children and young people remain ignorant of their rights:

> The value that the children and young people placed on knowing their rights demonstrates the potential for the NHS Constitution to empower children and young people to understand that they have rights when using the NHS. However the lack of knowledge and understanding regarding their rights when using a health service is an issue that needs to be addressed by both policy makers and professionals working with children and young people in the NHS. (NCB, 2015, p.50)

Although in general participation is increasing, disabled children are less likely to be involved than non-disabled children (Franklin & Sloper, 2009) and it is unclear to what extent children with complex needs or communication impairments are being included in participation activities. The UK-wide Children's Commissioner Report recommends in relation to Article 12 that:

> The State Party [the UK] and devolved governments should renew their commitment to implement Article 12 and ensure that they provide the resources and mechanisms to enable all children, including younger children and those whose voices are less likely to be heard, to have their experiences understood and their voices heard and so to participate in strategic and individual decision-making processes at the local and national levels. Children should be expressly told and be able to recognise how their views and experiences have influenced the decisions that are made about them. (Children's Commissioner, 2015, p.13)

The onus remains with adults:

> These papers have shown that children are not a homogenous group but that as researchers, policy makers and practitioners we need to find ways that engage children. Firstly, to encourage the development of inquiring minds and to lay a foundation for an active citizenship for when they are older. Secondly, to allow us adults to benefit from the insights, personal experiences and views that children have on our society. If we do not do this we impoverish our knowledge and potentially end up writing polices or delivering practices that remain adult-centric, do not meet the needs of children and ignore the rich potential of what our children have to teach us – if only we would listen! (McLaughlin, 2015, p.78)

What do qualitative methodologies offer to hearing the voice of children and young people?

For many years psychological research and practice has been dominated by experimental methodologies. The gold standard for producing robust evidence rested with results from randomised control trials, with other approaches liable to the criticism of lacking scientific rigour. It was argued that people and their behaviour can be studied in a similar way to that of any other object, through testing and observation. Gradually there has been an increasingly vocal critique of this positivist approach. Pointed questions have been asked about the focus on experimental settings rather than real-life tasks; the reliance on samples drawn from limited groups (often students); the choice of problems which often related to particular financing arrangements (for example pharmaceutical companies); and, most vociferously, the absence of any examination of the social, political or cultural context of the work. The result was a call for psychological research with people rather than about them that might give voice to participants and improve their position in the world. This change mirrors the change in our conceptualisation of children, who were previously often seen as objects to be moulded and shaped by positive and negative influences, to that of social actors with agency over their lives.

This type of research was about empowerment that recognised the researchers' role in constructing data, prioritised the participants' voice and accepted the coexistence of multiple meanings attributed to the same event. This new paradigm, or the 'turn to language' (Shaw and Frost, 2015), led to a turn to qualitative methods as these focused on the examination of meaning, rather than statistical examination of numerical data. Listening to, considering and exploring participants' own words allowed for their own lived experience to come to the fore in discussion. Furthermore, the lived experience of particular groups was not silenced by the absence of consideration of their social and cultural context; instead there began to be some recognition of the importance of acknowledging diversity and difference (see Billington & Williams, Chapter 1, for further discussion).

This move to qualitative methodologies and a focus on meaning is pertinent to listening to and hearing the voice of children and young people. It provides a way of listening to individual stories of particular life experiences within a societal group that lacks power and provides a space for this experience to be recognised. There remains a significant paucity of literature that aims to develop a more in-depth understanding of what children experience, how they experience and how they make sense of their experiences. The emphasis when conducting such research would be to afford agency to the individual child or group through researching something of great significance in their lives and as such this research could contribute to mainstream psychological and educational knowledge surrounding children. Furthermore the importance of researching children's experiences links with the children's rights perspective discussed above. It respects the entitlement of children to be considered as persons of value who have knowledge and views about their own lives.

Some of this paucity of research is carefully addressed in this book. This is the case particularly in the recognition that children and young people have a unique understanding of their own experience and that this can be accessed only by enabling them to talk about it. The children and young people's voices come from groups who are little heard (see for example Hayton (Chapter 8.4) on young people from a rural community, or Baker (Chapter 8.1) on young people who have been away from school for an extended period) or perhaps even unheard (see for example Weidberg (Chapter 8.10) on the children of prisoners, or Cox (Chapter 8.2) on separated refugee young people). Other examples are from children and young people whose voices may have been denied because of their complex needs (see Hill (Chapter 5) on young people in residential settings, or Harding (Chapter 8.3) about children with complex need) or because of their vulnerability (see Reichardt (Chapter 8.7) on young people who self-harm).

This is not to suggest that quantitative methodologies should be abandoned. There is room for such approaches to consider the broad areas impacting on children's life chances, for example in the difference between the educational outcomes of looked-after children and those not in the care system. Shaw and Frost (2015) present a cogent argument for 'dialectical pluralism' (Johnson & Stefurak, 2014), through incorporating stakeholders' and researchers' epistemological and social/political values to guide research.

> One way forward toward sustaining childhood research would be to set the by-now commonplace qualitative studies of children's own perspectives, voices, and agency alongside other work that explores the structural conditions that shape childhood as a generational space. Such an integration would help ensure that we do not lose

sight of the different impacts that societal forces such as the market, neoliberalism, the state, urbanisation, and so on have on childhood as a generational unit. (James, 2007, p.170).

What is suggested is that only by providing a space for children to express their own understanding of their situation will we have some access to the complex, often fluid knowledge children have of their lives.

What are the principles that inform the way we work with children and young people?

What we have argued, along with the other authors in this book, is that we need to further develop ways to actively engage children and young people in making decisions about their lives. Children and young people's participation cannot be understood in isolation from the social, cultural and political contexts in which it occurs. It is the case that there is a genuine concern that in encouraging participation, children's welfare may be put at risk. There is often an expressed tension concerning the fact that greater participation is at odds with the adult role of protecting children. However, it is often unfortunately the case that by not enabling children to develop their own capacity to act, adults fail to provide them with the resources they need to be successful and to be safe from harm.

Participation is a slippery construct. Within western society, it is usually associated with larger-scale policymaking; however, participation has a much wider meaning. It can be seen to be about making an active contribution within the family, school and community. If we take this latter meaning, then questions arise as to how this capacity to act and gain agency is present in everyday interactions for children and young people. We would suggest that a set of possible principles could be as follows:

- Our work is underpinned by the children's rights agenda.
- Participation is part of everyday life.
- We examine our construction of children and childhood, how this shapes the way we work and the professional practices we draw on.
- Our work is with children rather than about them.
- There is room for a plurality of research approaches but as much importance must be given to genuine agency as to structures to achieve this.
- There are dangers in a narrow view of the 'evidence base' which draws only on outcome or impact studies, and it is essential to draw on practice-based evidence that provides a rich picture of children's particular experience.
- Collaborations and political will are necessary to achieve change.

The current context

Today there appears little dispute about children and young people's right to participation.

The right to participate is well founded in philosophy, and increasingly in law, and children's agency is now generally accepted in social studies of childhood, and increasingly in social policy concerning children. (Percy-Smith and Thomas, 2010, p.364).

However, the reality for most children and young people does not match this aspiration. There remains ambivalence about the active engagement of children and young people in contributing to and managing their own lives. This is evident within our educational systems, where there is ever-increasing pressure to ensure high levels of achievement and little time to encourage the development of children and young people as active citizens. In England, this tension is coupled with the fragmentation of school systems, where institutions receive little national support to promote participation. Indeed the most recent DfE document on participation provides a rather mixed message, which applies only to local authorities and maintained schools in England.

The UNCRC has not been incorporated into national law, so there is no statutory duty to comply with it. However, the government has reiterated its commitment to pay 'due regard' to the convention when new policy is made and legislation proposed. Schools are strongly encouraged to pay due regard to the convention. (DfE, 2014, p.1)

This contrasts with support for participation in other parts of the United Kingdom. Education Scotland has developed a resource specifically to encourage the realisation of children's rights across everyday activities (Education Scotland, 2013). Similarly the Welsh Government has formally adopted the UNCRC, producing a supporting document about pupil participation and a website, 'Pupil Voice' (Welsh Government, 2010). Perhaps the strongest statement comes from the Northern Ireland Department of Education:

> The Department recognises the value of all forms of pupil participation and the important contribution these can make in supporting pupils as key stakeholders and decision-makers within their schools. The Department is committed therefore to encouraging all schools to find meaningful ways of giving children and young people a voice, listening to them, respecting and responding to their views and by doing so enabling children and young people to understand that their opinions count. The education system exists for children and young people; ensuring their participation in that system and listening to their experiences helps them make the most of their education.' (DENI, 2014, p.1)

The current context then is one of variable encouragement with decreasing resources to further develop children and young people's participation. Nevertheless there is an onus on adults to enable and support this participation. Children's and young people's views are not replicas of adults' views. They have something to say and, through being able to exercise their right to offer their own understanding of their experience and what would benefit them, they grow and learn how to be active citizens.

How does this impact on our work as educational psychologists?

We work in a universal service. All children and young people go to school and for increasing periods. We can influence the way in which educational institutions support children and young people's participation. We can offer ways to examine the social climate within schools so that participation is at the forefront of practice. Furthermore, we can provide insight into the lived experience of children and young people through using methods that enable voices to be heard. The contributions in this book provide examples of ways in which this might be achieved.

We can ask ourselves about our own practice. We leave you with some practical steps to promote participation.

- Challenge constructions of childhood that that get in the way of participation. Acknowledge the contribution that children can make directly to change in their own lives and to social change.
- Promote a wider understanding of participation that goes beyond 'having a say', and support children's right to expression so that they develop the ability to articulate their views and make decisions.
- Develop enabling environments which provide for diverse ways of participating.
- Consider the professional practices available to you. How do they position children and young people? Do they enhance or limit participation?
- Consider the expectations within your workplace. Are these expectations encouraging of children and young people's participation? Are these wide-ranging, from involvement in recruitment to influencing service policy and practice?
- Consider how can we work together to support more effective practice.
- Consider how children and young people are involved in these discussions.

References

Arnstein, S.R. (1969). A ladder of citizen participation. *Journal of the American Institute of Planners, 35*(4), 216–224.

Children's Commissioner (2015). *Report of the UK Children's Commissioners: UN Committee on the Rights of the Child examination of the fifth Periodic Report of the United Kingdom of Great Britain and Northern Ireland.* Retrieved 14 September 2015 from www. childrenscommissioner.gov.uk/sites/default/files/publications/UNCRC%20final_0.pdf

Department of Education, Northern Ireland (2014). *Pupil participation circular 2014/14.* Retrieved 29 September 2015 from www.deni.gov.uk/pupil_participation-2.pdf

Education Scotland (2013). *Recognising and realising children's rights.* Retrieved 29 September 2015 from www.educationscotland.gov.uk/resources/r/childrensrightsresource.asp?strReferringCh annel=educationscotland&strReferringPageID=tcm:4-615801-64&class=l1+d86716

Franklin, A. & Sloper, P. (2009). Supporting the participation of disabled children and young people in decision-making. *Children & Society, 23*(1), 3–15.

Grimax, N. & Bell, P. (2004). *CAMHS: Teeside investing in children. Interim report, June 2004.* Durham: Investing in Children and Tees and North East Yorkshire NHS Trust.

Hart, R.A. (1992). *Children's participation: From tokenism to citizenship.* Florence: UNICEF.

Hart, R.A. (1997). *Children's participation: The theory and practice of involving young citizens in community development and environmental care.* New York: Routledge.

Hear by Right (n.d.). *Hear by Right.* Retrieved 18 July 2016 from www.nya.org.uk/our-services/hear-right/

Hobbs, C. (2005). *Professional consultation with pupils through teaching about learning.* Unpublished doctoral thesis, Newcastle University.

James, A. (2007). Giving voice to children's voices: Practices and problems, pitfalls and potentials. *American Anthropologist, 109*(2), 261–272.

Johnson, R.B. & Stefurak, T (2014). Dialectical pluralism: A metaparadigm and process philosophy for 'dynamically combining' important differences. *Quantitative Methods in Psychology Bulletin, 17,* 63–69.

Kirby, P., Lanyon, C., Cronin, K., & Sinclair, R. (2003). *Research report: Building a culture of participation. Involving children and young people in policy, service planning, delivery and evaluation.* London: Department for Education and Skills.

Lundy, L. (2007) 'Voice is not enough': Conceptualising Article 12 of the United Nations Convention on the Rights of the Child. *British Education Research Journal, 33*(6), 927–942.

McLaughlin, H. (2015). Reflections on children's involvement: Future trajectories. In H. McLaughlin (Ed.) *Involving children and young people in policy, practice and research.* Retrieved 14 September 2015 from www.ncb.org.uk/media/1176052/participation_essays_final.pdf

National Children's Bureau and Council for Disabled Children (2015). *Children's and young people's views on the NHS constitution.* Retrieved 15 September 2015 from www.ncb.org.uk/media/1202359/engaging_themes.pdf

Participation Works (n.d.). *Participation Works.* Retrieved 18 July 2016 from www.participationworks.org.uk/

Sewell, A. (2016). Exploring the theoretical application of epistemological oppression to the psychological assessment of special educational needs in order to develop emerging concerns and practical implications for anti-oppressive practice. *DECP Debate, No. 159,* p.13.

Shaw, R. & Frost, N. (2015). Breaking out of the silo mentality. *The Psychologist, 28*(8), 638–641.

Office of the United Nations High Commissioner on Human Rights (1989). *United Nations Convention on the Rights of the Child.* Retrieved 14 September 2015 from www.ohchr.org/EN/ProfessionalInterest/Pages/CRC.aspx

United Nations Committee on the Rights of the Child (2005). *General comment no. 7: Implementing child rights in early childhood.* Office of the United Nations High Commissioner on Human Rights. Retrieved 14 September 2015 from www2.ohchr.org/english/bodies/crc/docs/AdvanceVersions/GeneralComment7Rev1.pdf

Welsh Government (2010). *Pupil participation: Increasing the effectiveness in your school community.* Retrieved 29 September 2015 from http://gov.wales/topics/educationandskills/schoolshome/wellbeing/pupilvoice/?lang=en

Woodhead, M. (2010). Foreword. In B. Percy-Smith & N. Thomas (Eds.) *A handbook of children and young people's participation* (pp.xix–xxiii). London: Routledge.